NATURE GUIDE TO THE

NEW ZEALAND
FOREST

NATURE GUIDE TO THE
NEW ZEALAND
FOREST

John Dawson • Rob Lucas

GODWIT

ACKNOWLEDGEMENTS

During the long gestation of this book we have been fortunate to have enjoyed the support and encouragement of many generous and very talented people. In particular we acknowledge Jane Connor, who developed the concept for this book, 'persuaded' us to take it on and managed to keep us focussed— for most of the time; Barry Sneddon, who read the botany text and provided helpful comments; George Gibbs, who provided photographs and assisted with the text of the insect section; Tony Whitaker, who provided photographs and assisted with the text on birds and lizards.

Most of the photographs of plants and fungi, as well as some insects, are by Rob Lucas. We are grateful for others provided by John Braggins, Yvonne Cave, Brian Chudleigh, Department of Conservation, Brett Robertson, Ian St George and Eric Scanlen.

Photographers Gerry Keating and Les Maiden of Victoria University produced the plates.

PHOTO CREDITS

Eric Anderson & Chris Ecroyd: p. 286; John Braggins: pp. 227 (top), 233 (bottom), 241 (top right);Yvonne Cave: pp. 98 (bottom), 100 (centre & bottom), 128, 139 (bottom), 140 (bottom left), 226 (2), 228 (top), 230 (centre & bottom), 231 (bottom), 232 (bottom); Brian Chudleigh: pp. 245 (bottom), 247(bottom), 248 (right), 249 (top left & right), 251 (top right), 255 (top), 257 (top), 263 (3), 264 (2), 265 (2), 267 (top), 268 (2), 269 (2), 270, 271 (2), 272 (2), 274 (3), 275, 276 (2), 293 (top & centre), 299 (top), 300 (top & bottom right); John Dawson: pp. 149 (bottom left), 199 (bottom), 200 (bottom left); Department of Conservation: pp. 262, 266 (2), 267 (bottom), 273, 289.

Forest Research Institute: p. 294 (centre); George Gibbs: pp. 287, 288, 290 (3), 291 (top & centre), 292 (2), 294, 295 (top & bottom), 297 (2), 298 (top), 299 (bottom); Gerry Keating: Plates 1–35; Brett Robertson: p. 295; Ian St George: p. 186 (centre); Eric Scanlen: pp. 186 (bottom), 219 (bottom); Tony Whitaker: pp. 277–285 (22).

A GODWIT BOOK
published by
Random House New Zealand
18 Poland Road, Glenfield, Auckland, New Zealand
www.randomhouse.co.nz

First published 2000. Reprinted 2003, 2004

ISBN 1 86962 055 0

Design and production: Jane Connor and Kate Greenaway

Front cover photographs (from top left): fantail (Brian Chudleigh),
kahikatea fruit, gill fungus *Hygrocybe*, kidney fern (Rob Lucas)
Back cover photograph: climbing ferns (Gerry Keating)
Opposite title page: tawa forest with tree fern *Cyathea smithii*, Whirinaki

Printed in China

CONTENTS

LIST OF PLATES

ABOUT THIS BOOK

Nature Guide to the New Zealand Forest is a guide to one of New Zealand's most interesting and varied habitats. It covers the wonderful diversity of life forms that exist in the forest—from imposing conifers to minute mosses and fungi, from birds that live in the treetops to ground-dwelling lizards and insects—and draws attention to the interactions and connections between them.

The book approaches the forest in a way you might approach it yourself. You might first look upwards, struck by the awesome size of the conifers and other large trees that make up the canopy, so these introduce the first and most extensive section, **Trees & Shrubs**. While the general progression is from the tallest trees down to the smallest shrubs, some groups are accorded separate treatment. A section of text and 3 plates are devoted to the podocarps and other conifers, as distinct from the flowering trees and shrubs. Likewise, the tree ferns, strictly ferns but treelike in stature, have their own section. Small-leaved shrubs, which include the quirky divaricates, are also grouped together.

Looking upwards at the forest canopy, you may notice the ropey stems of climbing vines, or epiphytes perched in trees. These upwardly mobile plants, along with the parasitic mistletoes, make up the second section, **Vines, Epiphytes & Mistletoes**. Included here is a fascinating array of plants that make their homes on other plants—for example, climbing ferns, epiphytic orchids, nest epiphytes and the beautiful but endangered mistletoes.

The Forest Floor brings us down to earth, where keen eyes will be able to spot an enormous variety of curious plants with intriguing stories—from grasses, ferns and orchids to mosses, as well as lichens and fungi. These distinctive groups constitute subsections within this habitat.

The **Birds** of the forest live at all levels. Some nest and find their food on the forest floor, while others are more likely to be seen in the treetops. They are grouped here according to their eating habits, from the honeyeaters that feed off the flowers in the canopy to the ground insectivores like the kiwi.

The fifth section, **Lizards, Frogs & Bats**, covers the well-camouflaged, less frequently seen forest lizards (including geckos, skinks and the remarkable tuatara), several native frogs, and New Zealand's only native land mammal, the bat.

Insects & Other Invertebrates looks at the smallest animals in the forest, many of which are barely visible, such as scale insects and leaf miners. Others, such as the moths and butterflies, or those masters of disguise, the stick insects, can be delicately beautiful, while the fearsome wetas have a magnificence of their own.

Each of these 6 sections is colour coded for easy reference. Throughout the book, boxes highlight interesting features or interactions, drawing attention to the complexities of the forest habitat.

One of the challenges in compiling a book that attempts a comprehensive coverage of such a wide range of life forms is making it easy for readers to go straight to the reference in the book that relates to what they are looking at in the forest. By organising the material in the book from the forest canopy down to the ground, we have narrowed the possibilities, particularly for plants. If you are looking at a plant growing independently (ie not a climber), more or less at eye level, it will be found under Trees & Shrubs, colour coded light brown; if you are looking at a plant on the ground, then it will be in the section on the forest floor, colour coded green.

In general, the trees and shrubs are arranged according to leaf characteristics, both in the text and also in the plates on pages 24-49. The attributes that are useful in distinguishing one species from another—for example the arrangement of leaves on a stem—are outlined on pages 22-23. The plates are intended as the first stop for identification. While it may not be possible to go straight to the relevant plate; it will only be a matter of flicking through a few pages—or the list of plates on page 7 will provide a shortcut. Page references alongside each leaf on the plates lead to the entry in the text, where the full description includes measurements of height, trunk diameter, and leaf length and width, along with other identifying characteristics. Family names have been given for plants as an indication of their wider relationships.

The section on the forest floor covers several recognisable plant groups, including grasses, ferns, mosses and also fungi and lichens. It has been assumed that readers will be familiar with these broad categories and that the contents pages will point to the relevant pages in the text. Not all forest floor species have been covered, particularly for groups like fungi and mosses. Included is a representative selection that will provide an introduction to plants that are fascinating and appealing but which may be difficult to identify without specialist knowledge. There are references to further reading in most of these sections.

When it comes to animals, it has again been assumed that readers have a basic knowledge of the common groups and will be able to find the relevant sections—for example, for lizards, or moths and butterflies—by looking on the contents pages.

Insects and other invertebrates constitute a huge group and it has been possible to cover only a small proportion of the forest species. Identification can be difficult without a microscope and specialist knowledge, so they are dealt with here under broad but easily recognisable groups such as stick insects, snails or beetles, and only a few representatives of each group are included.

INTRODUCTION: OUR UNIQUE FORESTS

Most New Zealanders would be surprised to learn that the 'bush' they've grown up with is unique. What on earth could be so special about this ubiquitous forest cloak of ours? Wherever you are in New Zealand it's not difficult to find the odd patch of bush, even if it's only an untamed area in a city park or a tattered remnant lost up a gully. Although our forests have sustained two centuries of calculated destruction, they are still a prominent element in our perception of the landscape and indeed our national identity.

There's no doubt that New Zealand's forests are unique. There are plenty of convincing statistics to support this: although our forests are located in temperate latitudes, they have an almost tropical feel; of our 2,500 native species of conifers, flowering plants and ferns, over 80% occur nowhere else in the world; our forests have evolved in complete isolation for many millions of years; they contain animals unique to New Zealand alone. In addition, they are free from danger. Where else in the world can you sit on a mossy bank or log, confident that you won't be attacked by soldier ants, venomous scorpions and spiders, snakes, leeches or hornets?

Statistics are all very well, but most people who spend time in the bush are attracted by less tangible things such as the unique spirit of the place. To them, our forests look, feel and smell special. They constitute a unique experience we cannot replicate elsewhere, no matter where we travel on the globe.

Consider the giant kauri forests of Northland. To confront a grove of kauri with their trunks rising for 20 metres or more, clean, unbranched, parallel sided, is to confront botanical grandeur. There is no way around such plants, literally or figuratively. They are immense, rising like columns, supporting leafy ceilings that tower above us and contain complex communities. These kauri forests, which include specimens well over 1000 years old, are enormous in stature with an impressive lineage dating back over 100 million years.

Throughout the North Island there are still a few places where we can enjoy the cathedral-like atmosphere of our stately podocarp conifer forests. Like their kauri cousins of the far north, these communities connect us back through time to the days of the dinosaurs. The rimu forests of Whirinaki in the Urewera country are one such magic spot. Here, rank upon rank of the tall slender rimu trunks rise far above the other forest vegetation. Walking alone in such places at dawn or evening, you may feel transported to another world. If you are particularly fortunate, your solitude may be interrupted by a cacophony of kaka parrots flocking in to argue and banter.

In all this majesty, it's easy to overlook the tawa, tall trees that make a solid leafy canopy beneath the podocarps, their slim yellow leaves providing a golden glow. The ancient tree ferns are another feature of these forests, their long arching fronds gracefully silhouetted against the canopy.

As we climb higher or travel southwards, our forests change again. Higher ground, steeper slopes with poorer soils, windier aspects—these are factors that create an environment suitable for beech forests. Unlike the sometimes oppressive jungle-like atmosphere of the conifer forests, airy beech forests offer park-like scenes where well-spaced large beech trees with huge branches carry tiny leaves that filter the sun, creating dappled patches of shade and light across the forest floor.

An enchanting scene—but there's more yet. Climb higher still and you enter the realm of the cloud forests, where mist, fog or rain rule for much of the year. Here the character of the forest changes dramatically. The trees (usually beeches or kamahi) become stunted, their gnarled misshapen limbs looming out of the ever-present mist that sits softly though the forest. Ground shrubs are rare. The forest floor, tree trunks and branches in this fairy-tale setting are swathed in lichens and mosses, and it's no wonder that these cloud forests are often referred to as goblin forests.

Fairy tales and goblins? Are we guilty of an excessive flight of imagination here? Well, perhaps, but the story of New Zealand's forest plants and animals is as strange and wonderful as a good fairy tale—and as old, too. It goes back over 100 million years ago to when New Zealand was part of the ancient continent now called Gondwana. New Zealand's separation from the continent about 80 million years ago marked the start of a long period of isolation from other landmasses. As our plants and animals evolved in isolation, many developed quirky adaptations and lifestyles that are unknown or rare in other parts of the world.

WHAT'S SO SPECIAL ABOUT OUR FOREST PLANTS AND ANIMALS?

• Our flowering plants are neat but not gaudy
Native forest plants are not noted for their flamboyant and colourful flowers. On the contrary, many of the significant flowering plants are wind-pollinated, with very small inconspicuous flowers that produce abundant pollen but no nectar. These include the beeches, coprosmas (page 97), grasses and sedges. Other New Zealand forest plants, including mahoe and tawa, have small yellowish green flowers that are pollinated by insects including flies, and pale or white flowers pollinated by moths.

• Divaricating shrubs are common
These unusual shrubs are remarkable for their densely interlaced twigs and very small leaves. The twigs are often profusely branched and spread apart at wide angles, giving them a zig-zag appearance. Although divaricates do occur elsewhere in the world, New Zealand has an unusually large number. There are more than 60 species in a number of unrelated families; several of these are the juvenile stage of small trees. Various explanations have been put forward for this phenomenon. Some believe that divaricating shrubs evolved as a protection against browsing moa; others suggest that they are hardy plants and developed in response to the colder climate of the Ice Age. (See page 151.)

• Many plants have striking juvenile forms
A significant number of native trees, shrubs and vines are remarkable for their juvenile forms that are strikingly different from the adults in leaf form and sometimes branching pattern. Lancewoods (see page 112) provide the most notable example of this. The intriguing juvenile form looks rather like a collapsed umbrella, with a single trunk and long narrow downward-pointing leaves that can be coarsely jagged. As the tree mature, it branches and the new leaves are shorter, wider and less coarsely toothed.

In some trees (for example, *Pennantia corymbosa*) the juvenile is a divaricating shrub, but 3 m above the ground there is a change to the adult form with much larger, more efficient and presumably more palatable leaves. The explanations for juvenile forms are similar to those proposed for divarication—that they are a defence against moa browsing or cold.

• Many species hybridise naturally
Plants resulting from a cross between 2 species of the same genus are unusually frequent among New Zealand natives. The most surprising are those involving small-leaved divaricating shrubs such as *Coprosma propinqua* and much larger-leaved karamu, *C. robusta* (see Plate 27).

• Leaves often have unusual colours
In some trees and shrubs pigments other than chlorophyll are so strongly developed that they mask the green of the chlorophyll. In New Zealand the notable example is the mountain horopito (*Pseudowintera colorata*, page 141), which has leaves blotched with red and yellow and sometimes no green at all. The shrubs appear to be in a permanent state of autumn coloration, which is most marked at colder altitudes.

Some young New Zealand native plants have distinctive brown leaves, for example seedling lancewoods (page 112), the divaricating juvenile of pokaka and some seedlings of the vine *Parsonsia heterophylla* (see Plate 28). Among conifers young kauri and some young kahikatea and matai have brown leaves. Yet again, one suggestion is that this coloration is a camouflage against browsing moa.

• We have only 2 native land mammals
Our only native land mammals are 2 species of bat (page 286). It has been suggested that in the absence of forest mammals, the flightless kiwi and extinct bush moa may have filled the niche of larger mammals and the relatively large and flightless weta, related to the cricket, the role of smaller mammals

Page 12: Giants of the forest—kauri grove.

Page 13: A dense grove of the nikau palm (above); trunks of miro, northern rata and kamahi in a conifer-broadleaf forest (below).

Page 14: Blankets of moss in a high-altitude silver beech 'goblin forest' (above); a very different lower-altitude hard beech forest (below).

Page 15: The cool moist environment of a kamahi cloud forest.

Page 16: Emergent conifers dominate the canopy of a Westland forest (above); the interior of a tawa forest (below)

such as mice. Even the short-tailed bat is able to scramble round on the forest floor to find food using its folded wings as a second pair of legs.

Since human settlement, a number of mammals have been introduced and many of these pose threats to native plants and animals (see page 19).

• **There are surprisingly few native birds**
New Zealand's forests have been referred to as 'silent forests' because of the noticeable lack of bird song. However, this has not always been the case. Since humans arrived in New Zealand about 1000 years ago, approximately 40 percent of the more than 60 species of forest birds have become extinct and some of the survivors have very restricted distributions. In some places where possums have been eliminated or greatly reduced there has been an encouraging increase in native birds.We won't be able to regain the pre-human bird diversity in our forests but they may at least become less silent.

• **We have many flightless birds**
Flightlessness is common among birds on isolated islands, and New Zealand has many notable examples such as the kiwi, moa, weka and kakapo. The lack of mammal predators may have meant these birds evolved to fill the niches normally occupied by ground-dwelling mammals.

Raukawa anomalus showing the twiggy interlacing branchlets and tiny flowers typical of many New Zealand divaricates.

• **We have giant carnivorous snails**
New Zealand has an abundance of native snails. One ancient group of snails have giant shells up to 10 cm in diameter, many exquisitely patterned in shades of brown and gold (see page 289). They are also unusual in being carnivorous, some even eating their relatives. The carnivorous snails are widespread, but another small group of vegetarian giant snails is restricted to the northern tip of the North Island.

• **Our frogs do not have a tadpole stage**
Our 3 small frog species are unusual in that they do not have a free-swimming tadpole stage. Neither do they croak like other frogs—the best they can manage is faint squeaks (see page 285).

• **Our native lizards do not lay eggs**
All but one of our many species of skinks and geckos have young that are born alive, unlike most lizards, which lay eggs (see page 279). This may have been an adaptation developed during the Ice Age when the eggs would have been vulnerable to the cold.

Juvenile (left) and adult forms of the toothed lancewood, *Pseudopanax ferox*.

TYPES OF FOREST

There are 2 main types of forest in New Zealand: conifer-broadleaf and beech. **Conifer-broadleaf forest**, the most complex type, favours warmer climates and features many vines and epiphytes. The forest canopy or roof is usually a continuous layer of broadleaf (flowering) trees (see page 72) broken at intervals by very tall emergent conifers (page 50).

In the northern North Island, conifer-broadleaf forests tend to be dominated by the giant kauri (page 53). Throughout the country, swamp forests feature another conifer, kahikatea (page 62), often in association with the broadleaf pukatea (page 62). However the most widespread conifer-broadleaf forest, found from Northland to Stewart Island, is that dominated by rimu (page 64), often in association with northern rata (page 94).

The main canopy of rimu-dominated forest in Northland, below the emergents, features taraire (page 139), which is replaced further south or at higher altitudes by tawa (page 101) or kamahi (page 86). There are many other species of trees, shrubs and forest floor plants and a wide range of vines and epiphytes. The number of species in this type of forest decreases as one goes from north to south.

Conifer-broadleaf forest is generally replaced by **beech forest** at higher altitudes. It has few or no vines or large epiphytes, although mistletoe parasites (page 194) can be conspicuous. The canopy is dominated the southern beeches (page 127) and forms a uniform layer without emergents. Beech forest is sometimes absent from places where we would expect to find it, for example Mt Taranaki and the central west coast of the South Island. An explanation for this is that it hasn't yet spread to its fullest extent after the last Ice Age glacial period.

THE FOREST AS A COMMUNITY

Our New Zealand forests are extremely complex communities of plants and animals. The branches of trees often support gardens of orchids and other perching plants (epiphytes). Vines scramble and creep their way up tree trunks in their quest to reach the canopy and sunlight. Parasitic plants tap directly into the living tissues of their trunks and roots for their energy source. Shade-tolerant small plants—including grasses and other flowering plants, ferns, mosses and liverworts, fungi and lichens—inhabit the forest floor, relishing the sanctuary of this cool, moist and sheltered environment.

The forest is also home to a wide range of animals, including birds, lizards, frogs, bats and many insects and other small animals. The forest supports them with food and shelter and many repay the favour by pollinating flowers and dispersing seeds. Most flowers secrete nectar to attract insects, birds and sometimes bats and lizards. When they visit flowers, these animals are dusted with pollen, which they then convey to other flowers, resulting in fertilisation, seed production and consequently the survival of the species.

Another important service animals provide for plants is in the dispersal of their seeds. In many cases these are embedded in fruits (berries) consisting of fleshy tissue that is sweet and nutritious. Animals digest the fleshy tissue, but the seeds have hard coats that are resistant to digestive juices and they are eventually excreted unharmed, sometimes far away from the parent plant.

All forest plants and animals compete incessantly among themselves for the right to survive. Plants compete with each other for light, space, soil nutrients and water. However, they must also ensure they don't lose excessive amounts of foliage to hungry plant-eating animals, so they have developed a range of off-putting strategies including spines, poisons and unpleasant tastes. For example, horopito and kawakawa have leaves that taste hot; tutu and karaka are poisonous.

Hungry animals are a threat to plants but also to other animals. Many birds and lizards eat insects and some birds eat lizards. Larger insects eat their smaller relatives.

Although they are the most conspicuous organisms, plants and animals are not the only inhabitants of the forest with an important role to play. The pale threads or filaments of the fungi are mostly invisible, although their seasonal fruiting bodies (for example, mushrooms and toadstools) are often eye catching. The most beneficial fungi

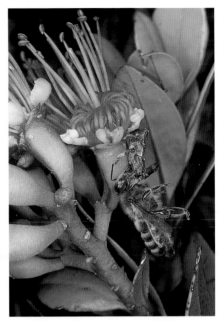

Laccaria toadstools jostling for space among mosses, a blechnum fern and the twiggy litter of a subalpine beech forest floor.

A spider in ambush beneath a rata flower drains life fluids from a hapless bee as its companion above continues to suck nectar.

and bacteria in the forests are those that break down the litter of dead and dying plant parts on the forest floor, thereby obtaining energy, and the simpler compounds that result can then be absorbed and recycled by the plants. Some plants have been able to make use of bacteria and fungi that invade them. Filaments of fungi penetrate the root tips of many trees. The fungi obtain sugar from the plant tissues and their filaments spreading far and wide through the soil are a source of water and mineral nutrients for the tree.

The fungi and bacteria are aided in their task by a myriad of tiny animals—insects and other invertebrates—including mites, insect larvae and caterpillars, beetles, spiders, worms and many others. Some of these, such as certain beetles and termites, bore into dead wood, and, aided by fungi, gradually turn it to powder. Others do likewise with leaves and other softer debris. The end result of this activity by fungi, bacteria and invertebrates is a fine dark humus that combines with mineral fragments resulting from weathering of the bedrock to form soil.

THREATS TO OUR NATIVE FOREST

Most of New Zealand was covered in forest for many thousands of years. After humans arrived, the forest cover was greatly reduced by felling and fire, and introduced mammals, birds and plants have altered long-established patterns in the forests. The kiore or Polynesian rat has been in New Zealand much longer than the other introduced mammals so was the first to interfere with the patterns and processes in our forests. The kuri or Polynesian dog, introduced by Maori, would also have killed native lizards and birds in pre-European times.

Introduced birds compete with native birds for berries and insects. Smaller mammals such as mice and rats eat fruits and seeds, lizards , frogs, insects, and the eggs and chicks of birds. Wild cats eat mice, rats and even possums, so they are of some benefit. However, they also eat adult birds and chicks. Stoats add insects and lizards to this menu.

The larger mammals—deer, goats, pigs and possums—are vegetarian or largely so. They have reduced the abundance of palatable plant species

THE POSSUM: NEW ZEALAND'S MOST DESTRUCTIVE FOREST PEST

From 1837 to 1924 Australian possums were released in New Zealand with the aim of establishing a fur trade, but it was not until the 1930s that it became clear that considerable damage was being done to native forests.

Possums are good climbers so can forage at all levels in the forest. They eat the foliage of a wide range of plants including kamahi, northern and southern rata (see page 95) and pohutukawa, five-finger, tree fuchsia, mahoe and wineberry, vines include the lawyers and supplejack, and the native mistletoes. The result is that many of the plants die and some species have been greatly reduced. Possums also eat a wide range of flowers, fruits and seeds and so compete with native birds, lizards and insects.

It is estimated that there are about 70 million possums in New Zealand. At one time trapping for skins was widespread, but the international campaign against the use of animal fur in clothing has largely ended this. Poison bait has been used either in bait stations or aerial drops, and individual trees have been protected by smooth metal bands around their trunks to prevent possums from reaching the crown.

and, in the cases of deer and goats, they may eat out seedlings on the forest floor, interfering with regeneration. Possums are our most destructive forest pest because unlike the other browsers, they can climb trees and completely defoliate them (see box).

Almost half our native birds have become extinct since human settlement (see page 261) as a result of the reduction of forest habitats, the depredations of introduced mammals and their exploitation by humans for food or as specimens.

Our famous reptile, the tuatara, once occurred on the mainland but is now restricted to offshore islands. A number of lizards and frogs have also become restricted or extinct.

Several plant species have disappeared and a larger number have become restricted or rare, such as the native mistletoes, regarded by the possum as a delicacy. Two endemic species on the Three Kings Islands were close to extinction when one plant of each was found, probably the result of human occupation and the depredations of goats. An introduced insect is thought to be responsible for the death of many cabbage trees (see page 74).

Larger stands of native forest have not been invaded by introduced plants to the extent that they have by introduced animals. The opposite is true, however, for disturbed forest remnants or pockets of regeneration. Here *Tradescantia* may cover the shady forest floor, old man's beard (*Clematis vitalba*) smother the canopy and, in warmer climes, wild ginger fill canopy gaps—and these are just a few of the alien species that invade forest fragments.

Trees &
Shrubs

Many of New Zealand's most attractive and remarkable trees and shrubs are easily identified by their brilliant or distinctive flowers or fruits. For example, most people would have no trouble pointing out a pohutukawa or a kowhai, a manuka or a hebe, or a karaka or a titoki. However, these more colourful features are not always obvious or are only present for part of the year. The most reliable way of identifying a tree or shrub is by its leaves. With one or two deciduous exceptions (eg tree fuchsia) these are present all year round.

Strictly speaking, leaves are either **simple** (not divided into leaflets) or **compound** (made up of a number of individual **leaflets**). Although simple leaves and leaflets look alike, the leaves can be distinguished by the presence of a **leaf bud** in the angle between the leaf stalk and the stem; a leaflet never has a bud here.

The arrangement of leaves on the stem can be either **opposite** (in pairs placed directly opposite each other) or **alternate** (attached separately along the stem, not in pairs). **Whorled** leaves are similar to opposite leaves but there are 3 or more attached to the stem. Leaflets can also be arranged in a **palmate** (hand-shaped) or a **pinnate** (feather-like with 2 rows of leaflets) fashion.

Leaves are considered **small** if they are less than 2 cm long. Some leaves are so small they are reduced to **scales** (as in some conifers). **Broad** leaves or leaflets are less than twice as long as they are wide; **narrow** leaves or leaflets are more than twice as long as they are wide.

Leaf margins also provide an important clue to identification. They can be **smooth** (without serrations or teeth), **toothed** (with teeth that can range from minute as in pate to heavily jagged as in *Pseudopanax ferox*) or **undulate** (wavy). They can also be **rolled** under.

Veins are another useful feature. They can be **parallel** as in the long narrow leaves of cabbage trees, **palmate** as in kawakawa or **pinnate** as in the majority of leaves. The main vein which runs along the centre of a leaf or leaflet is known as the **midrib** and the veins running off this are **secondary veins.**

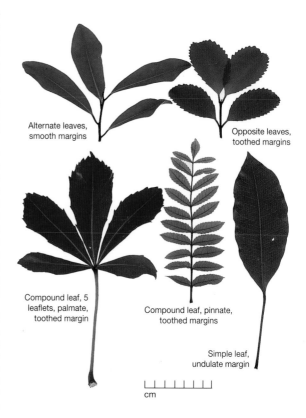

Alternate leaves, smooth margins

Opposite leaves, toothed margins

Compound leaf, 5 leaflets, palmate, toothed margin

Compound leaf, pinnate, toothed margins

Simple leaf, undulate margin

cm

Leaf shapes and margins.

In some species, such as ngaio, **oil glands** can be prominent on the undersides of the leaves.

Leaf hairs are very obvious in some groups of plants, such as the tree daisies, which have densely hairy undersides. Hairs can also be found on the margins, or in the angle where the leaf stalk joins the stem, as in *Alseuosmia*.

Domatia are small, frequently pouch-like cavities on the undersides of some leaves at the angles between the midrib and other veins. These are often visible as bumps on the upper surface. All coprosmas have domatia. In some species, for example red and silver beeches, the domatia are fringed with hairs.

The base of a **leaf stalk** where it is attached to the stem can be **sheathing** (an extreme example is the nikau palm) or sometimes **swollen** (as in kohekohe). In a few plants, eg raukawa (*Raukaua edgerlyi*), the leaf stalk is jointed, which indicates that it has been derived from a compound juvenile leaf.

Stipules, designed to protect the developing leaf buds, are like scales or small leaflets and are generally in pairs at the base of leaf stalks. In some plants with opposite leaves, eg coprosmas, the stipules alternate with the pairs of leaf bases.

The plates in the Trees and Shrubs section of the book show groups of species with similar leaf characteristics photographed together to give an indication of their relative size. For example, the five-fingers, all of which have palmate leaves arranged alternately on stems, occur together in Plates 4 and 5; the larger-leaved coprosmas, which are opposite and have smooth margins and domatia, are in Plate 11. The plates reflect the order of the entries in the main text, therefore the small-leaved coprosmas are shown separately in Plate 25 near the other small-leaved shrubs, and the conifers are grouped in Plates 1, 2 and 3.

It is not always possible to immediately identify a particular tree or shrub—local variation and juvenile forms can often confuse things. To give as many clues as possible, we have included juvenile forms, leaf undersides and sometimes variations in form in the plates. The text for each species offers a detailed description containing information on its distribution, height, bark, leaf dimensions, flowers and fruits. In some groups of related species, introductory boxes highlight the differences between them.

See page 72 for a description of flowers, fruits and seeds.

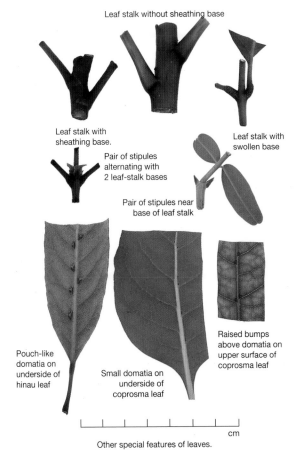

Leaf stalk without sheathing base

Leaf stalk with sheathing base.

Pair of stipules alternating with 2 leaf-stalk bases

Pair of stipules near base of leaf stalk

Leaf stalk with swollen base

Pouch-like domatia on underside of hinau leaf

Small domatia on underside of coprosma leaf

Raised bumps above domatia on upper surface of coprosma leaf

cm

Other special features of leaves.

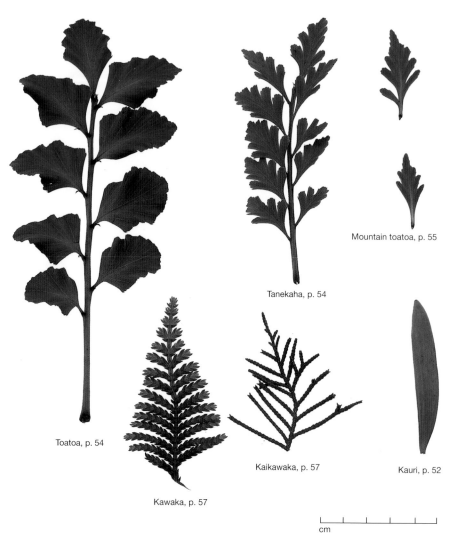

Mountain toatoa, p. 55

Tanekaha, p. 54

Toatoa, p. 54

Kaikawaka, p. 57

Kauri, p. 52

Kawaka, p. 57

cm

Plate 1. Conifers: celery pines, cedars and kauri.

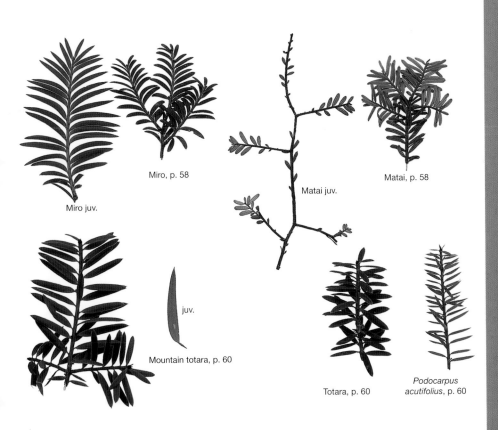

Miro, p. 58

Matai, p. 58

Miro juv.

Matai juv.

juv.

Mountain totara, p. 60

Totara, p. 60

Podocarpus acutifolius, p. 60

cm

Plate 2. Conifers: narrow-leaved podocarps.

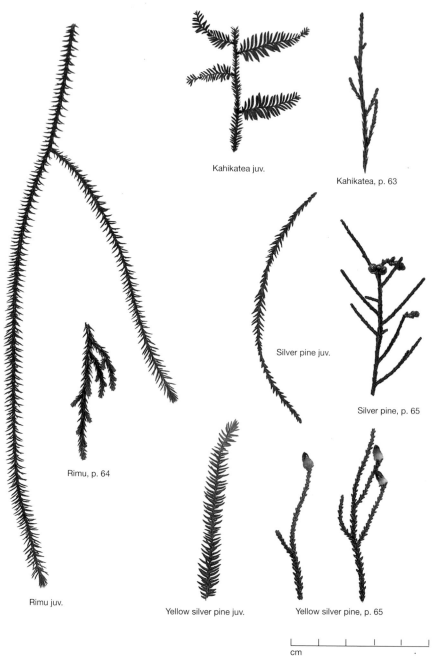

Kahikatea juv.

Kahikatea, p. 63

Silver pine juv.

Silver pine, p. 65

Rimu, p. 64

Rimu juv.

Yellow silver pine juv.

Yellow silver pine, p. 65

cm

Plate 3. Conifers: scale-leaved podocarps (gradual change from juvenile to adult).

Five-finger, p. 78

Pseudopanax laetus, p. 78

Mountain five-finger, p. 78

Houpara, p. 81

Pate, p. 78

cm

Plate 4. Leaves palmate, alternate on stems: five-fingers.

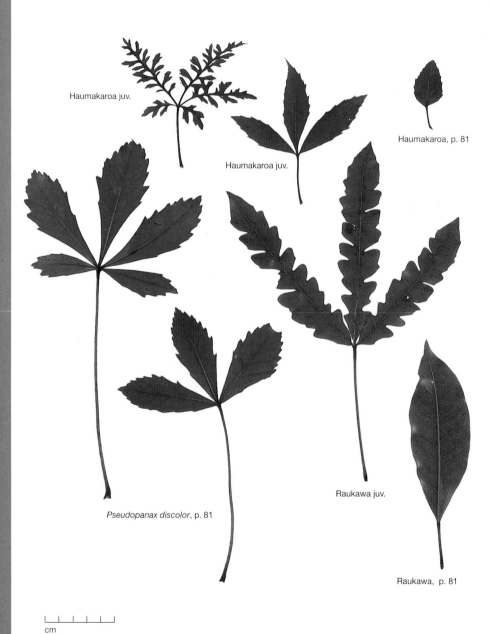

Haumakaroa juv.

Haumakaroa juv.

Haumakaroa, p. 81

Pseudopanax discolor, p. 81

Raukawa juv.

Raukawa, p. 81

cm

Plate 5. Leaves palmate, alternate on stems: five-fingers.

Titoki, p. 85

Kohekohe, p. 84

Puriri, p. 82

Wharangi, p. 83

cm

Plate 6. Leaves palmate, opposite on stems (wharangi, puriri);
leaves pinnate, alternate on stems (kohekohe, titoki).

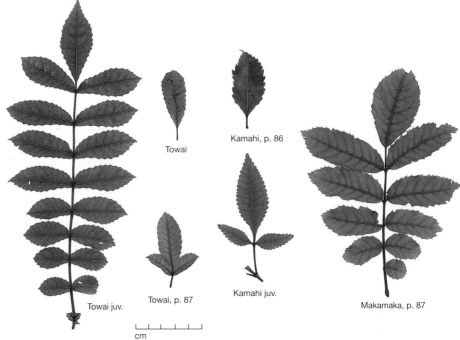

Towai

Kamahi, p. 86

Towai juv.

Towai, p. 87

Kamahi juv.

Makamaka, p. 87

cm

Plate 7. Leaves pinnate, opposite on stems: kamahi group.

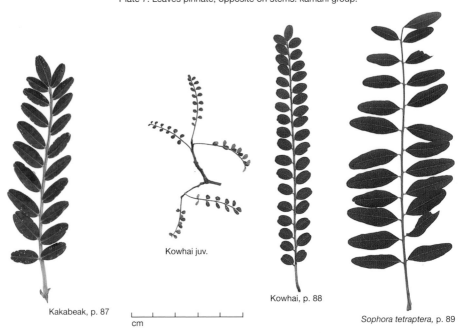

Kowhai juv.

Kakabeak, p. 87

Kowhai, p. 88

Sophora tetraptera, p. 89

cm

Plate 8. Leaves pinnate, alternate on stems: kowhai group.

Tutu, p. 90

Kawakawa, p. 91

Macropiper excelsum ssp. *peltatum*, p. 91

Whau, p. 90

cm

Plate 9. Palmately veined leaves.

Pohutukawa, p. 92

underside

Northern rata, p. 94

underside

Southern rata, p. 95

underside

Metrosideros parkinsonii, p. 92

underside

Metrosideros bartlettii, p. 94

underside

cm

Plate 10. Leaves smooth margined, opposite on stems: rata and pohutukawa.

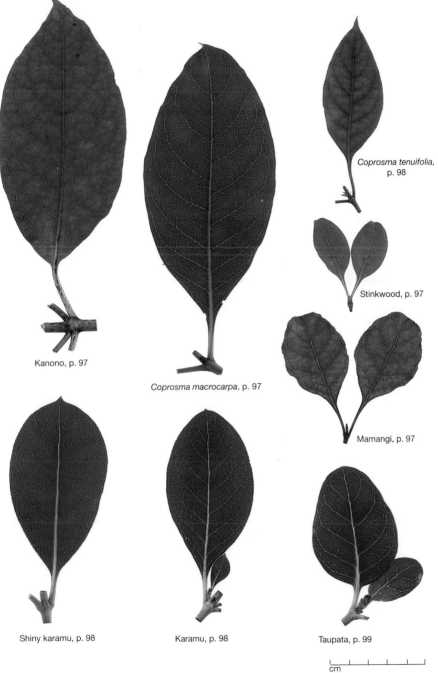

Coprosma tenuifolia, p. 98

Stinkwood, p. 97

Mamangi, p. 97

Kanono, p. 97

Coprosma macrocarpa, p. 97

Shiny karamu, p. 98

Karamu, p. 98

Taupata, p. 99

cm

Plate 11. Leaves smooth margined, opposite on stems: coprosmas.

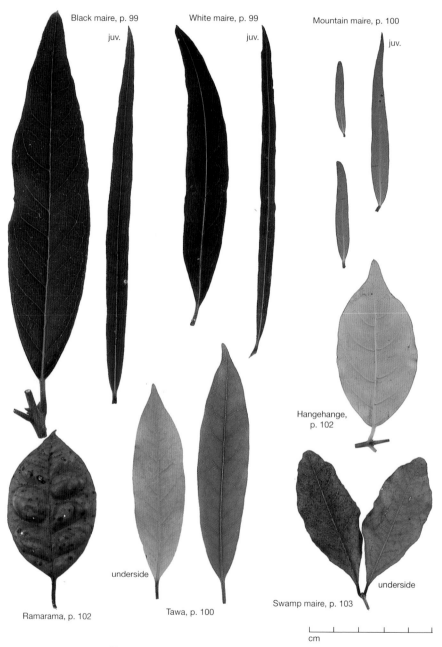

Black maire, p. 99

juv.

White maire, p. 99

juv.

Mountain maire, p. 100

juv.

Hangehange,
p. 102

underside

Ramarama, p. 102

Tawa, p. 100

Swamp maire, p. 103

underside

cm

Plate 12. Leaves smooth margined, opposite on stems.

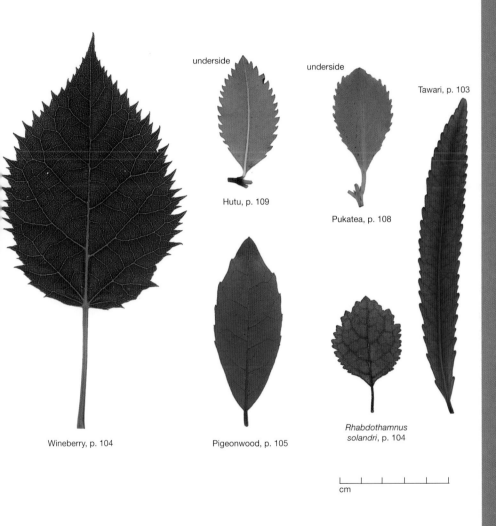

underside

underside

Tawari, p. 103

Hutu, p. 109

Pukatea, p. 108

Wineberry, p. 104

Pigeonwood, p. 105

Rhabdothamnus solandri, p. 104

cm

Plate 13. Leaves toothed, opposite on stems.

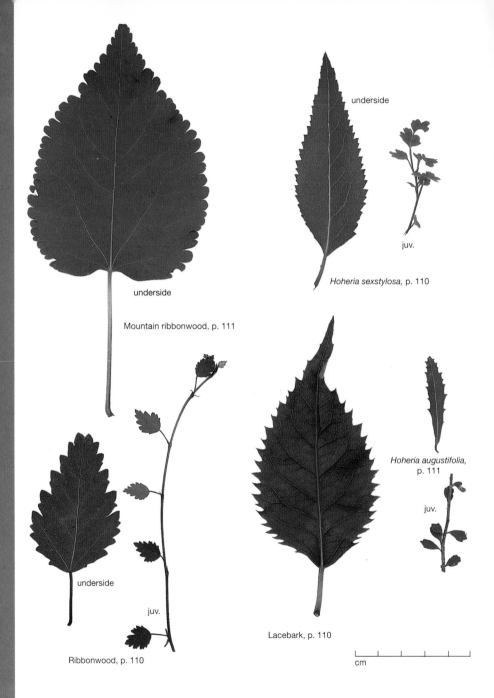

underside

Mountain ribbonwood, p. 111

underside

Hoheria sexstylosa, p. 110

juv.

underside

juv.

Ribbonwood, p. 110

Hoheria augustifolia,
p. 111

juv.

Lacebark, p. 110

cm

Plate 14. Leaves toothed, alternate on stems: lacebarks and ribbonwoods.

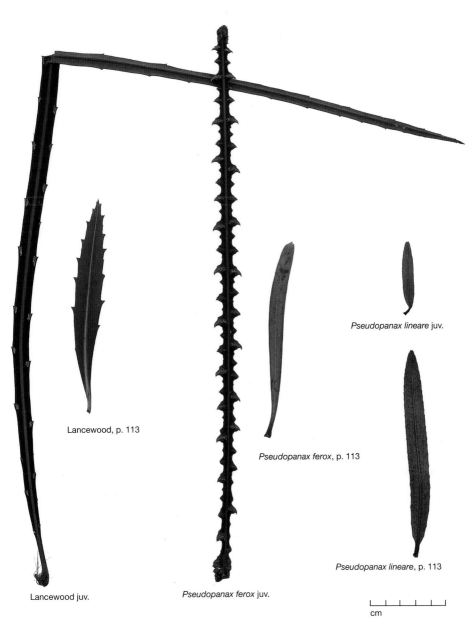

Pseudopanax lineare juv.

Lancewood, p. 113

Pseudopanax ferox, p. 113

Pseudopanax lineare, p. 113

Lancewood juv.

Pseudopanax ferox juv.

cm

Plate 15. Leaves toothed, alternate on stems: lancewoods.

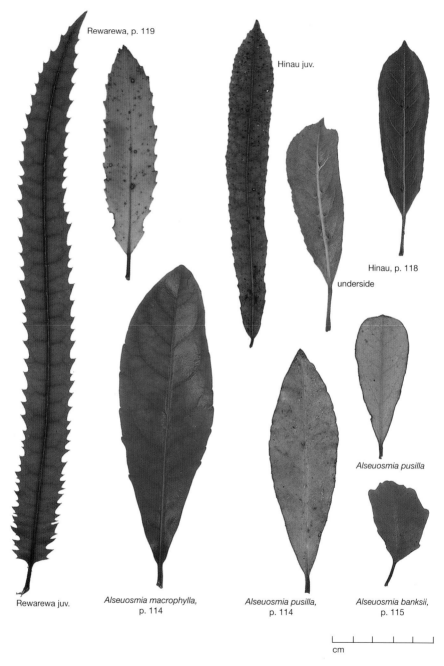

Rewarewa, p. 119

Hinau juv.

Hinau, p. 118

underside

Alseuosmia pusilla

Rewarewa juv.

Alseuosmia macrophylla,
p. 114

Alseuosmia pusilla,
p. 114

Alseuosmia banksii,
p. 115

cm

Plate 16. Leaves toothed, alternate on stems.

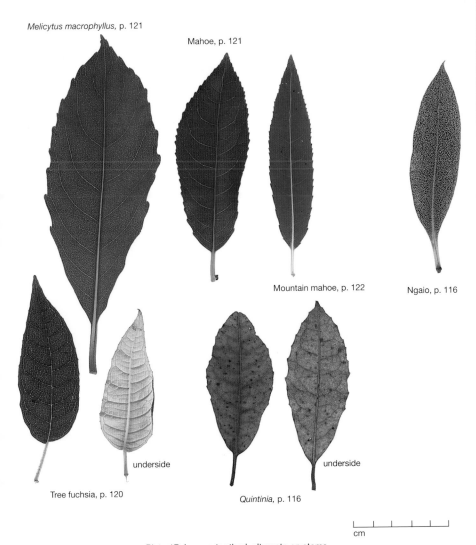

Melicytus macrophyllus, p. 121

Mahoe, p. 121

Mountain mahoe, p. 122

Ngaio, p. 116

Tree fuchsia, p. 120

underside

Quintinia, p. 116

underside

cm

Plate 17. Leaves toothed, alternate on stems.

Pokaka, p. 118

Pokaka juv.

Putaputaweta, p. 117

juv.

Pokaka

underside

juv.

Kaikomako, p. 120

juv.

Streblus banksii, p. 116

cm

Plate 18. Leaves toothed, alternate on stems.

underside

Silver beech, p. 126

underside

Red beech, p. 126

underside

Black beech, p. 126

underside

Hard beech, p. 126

underside

Mountain beech, p. 126

cm

Plate 19. Leaves toothed or smooth, alternate on stems: beeches.

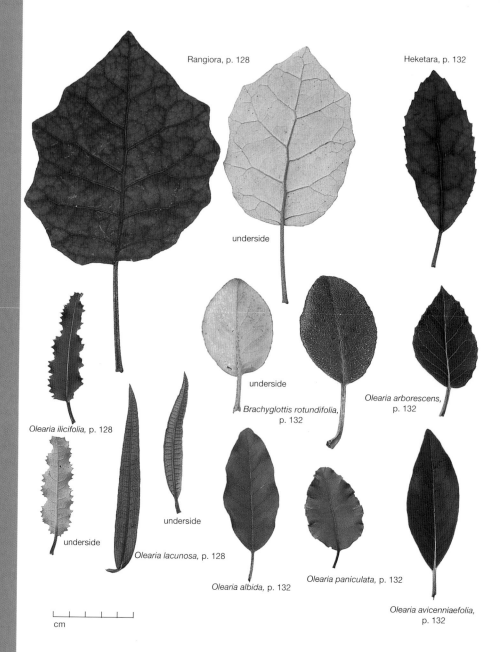

Rangiora, p. 128

Heketara, p. 132

underside

Olearia ilicifolia, p. 128

underside

Brachyglottis rotundifolia, p. 132

Olearia arborescens, p. 132

underside

Olearia lacunosa, p. 128

underside

Olearia albida, p. 132

Olearia paniculata, p. 132

Olearia avicenniaefolia, p. 132

cm

Plate 20. Leaves toothed or smooth, densely hairy below, alternate on stems: tree daisies.

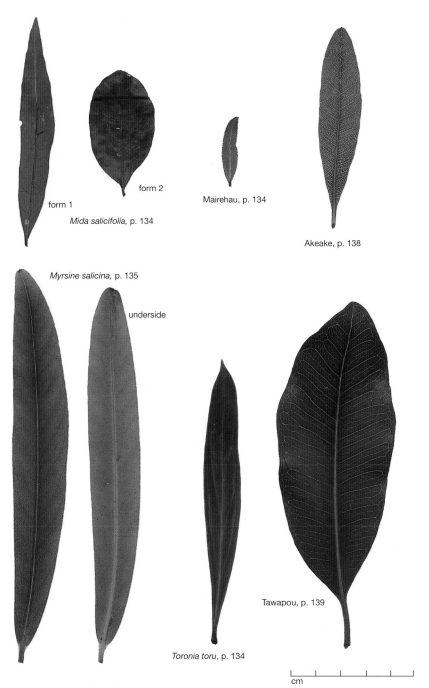

form 2

form 1

Mida salicifolia, p. 134

Mairehau, p. 134

Akeake, p. 138

Myrsine salicina, p. 135

underside

Tawapou, p. 139

Toronia toru, p. 134

cm

Plate 21. Leaves smooth margined, alternate on stems.

Mangeao, p. 144

Karaka, p. 146

Taraire, p. 139

underside

Mountain horopito, p. 141

Mapau, p. 140

Mangrove, p. 137

Horopito, p. 140

cm

Plate 22. Leaves smooth margined, alternate on stems.

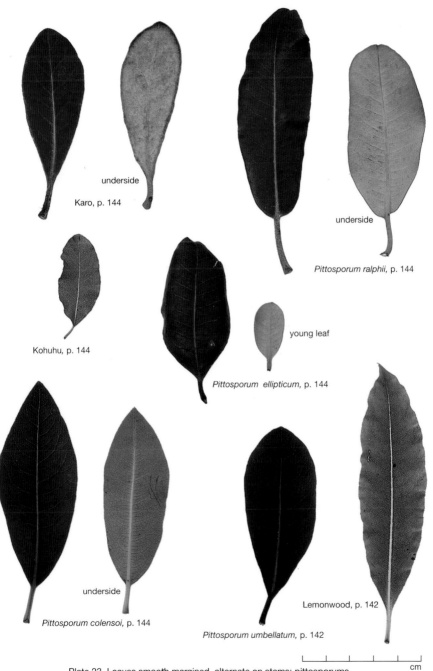

underside

Karo, p. 144

underside

Pittosporum ralphii, p. 144

Kohuhu, p. 144

young leaf

Pittosporum ellipticum, p. 144

underside

Pittosporum colensoi, p. 144

Lemonwood, p. 142

Pittosporum umbellatum, p. 142

cm

Plate 23. Leaves smooth margined, alternate on stems: pittosporums.

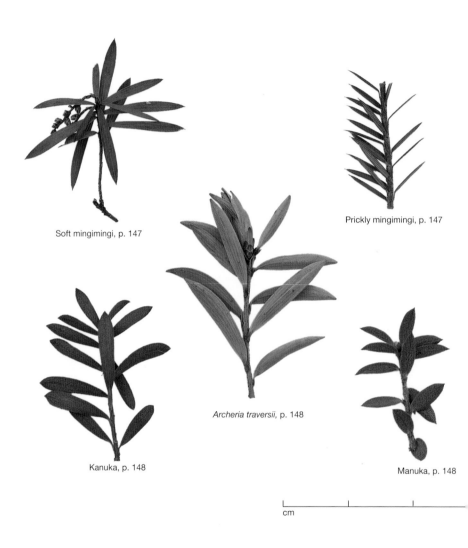

Soft mingimingi, p. 147

Prickly mingimingi, p. 147

Archeria traversii, p. 148

Kanuka, p. 148

Manuka, p. 148

cm

Plate 24. Leaves small and narrow, alternate on stems.

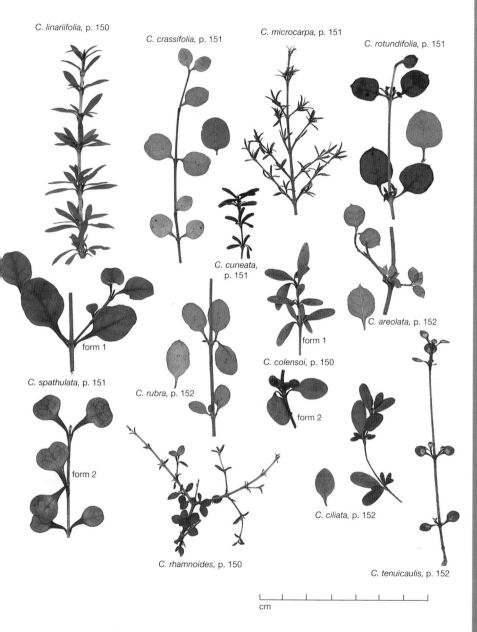

C. linariifolia, p. 150

C. crassifolia, p. 151

C. microcarpa, p. 151

C. rotundifolia, p. 151

C. cuneata, p. 151

form 1

C. areolata, p. 152

form 1

C. spathulata, p. 151

C. colensoi, p. 150

C. rubra, p. 152

form 2

form 2

C. ciliata, p. 152

C. rhamnoides, p. 150

C. tenuicaulis, p. 152

cm

Plate 25. Leaves small with domatia, opposite on stems: coprosmas.

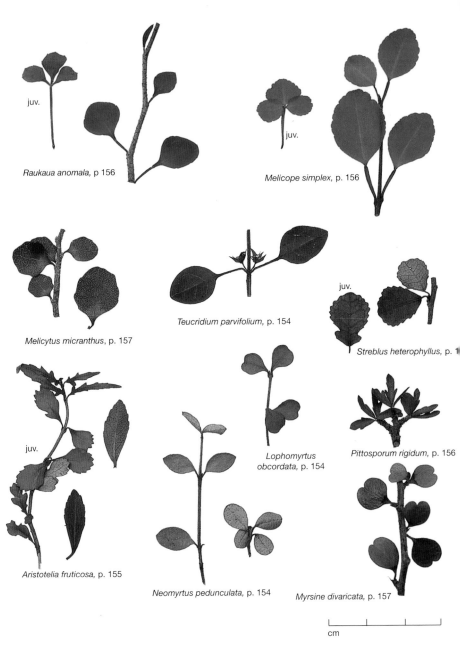

Raukaua anomala, p 156

Melicope simplex, p. 156

juv.

juv.

Melicytus micranthus, p. 157

Teucridium parvifolium, p. 154

juv.

Streblus heterophyllus, p. 1

juv.

Lophomyrtus obcordata, p. 154

Pittosporum rigidum, p. 156

Aristotelia fruticosa, p. 155

Neomyrtus pedunculata, p. 154

Myrsine divaricata, p. 157

cm

Plate 26. Leaves small, mostly broad.

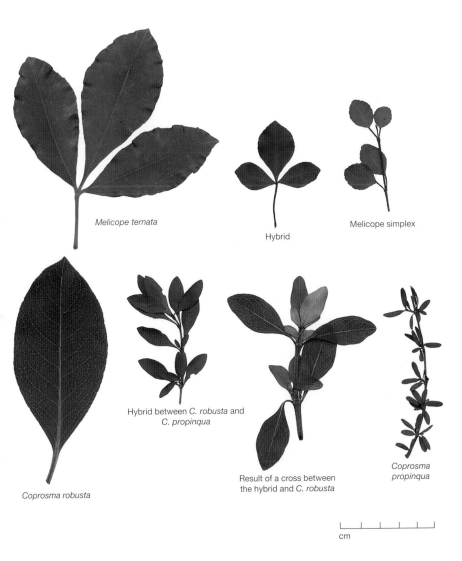

Melicope ternata

Hybrid

Melicope simplex

Hybrid between *C. robusta* and
C. propinqua

Result of a cross between
the hybrid and *C. robusta*

*Coprosma
propinqua*

Coprosma robusta

cm

Plate 27. Some natural hybrids.

A group of kauri towering over smaller trees and shrubs.

PODOCARPS & OTHER CONIFERS

Although flowering plants predominate in the canopies of our forests, conifers of towering stature are often the most conspicuous trees. Of our 20 native conifer species, 17 grow in forests and most of them are found throughout the country.

Both plant groups—flowering plants and conifers—reproduce by seeds. Flowers often have brightly coloured petals, nectar and perfume to attract pollinators such as insects and birds. The conifers, however, are wind pollinated and have no need of such blandishments. In most cases their seeds are formed in cones, whose dry and often woody scales are closely grouped on a central stem. The winged seeds form on the scales and eventually sift out between them. As well as these seed cones, conifers also have smaller pollen cones on the same or different trees.

With regard to seed cones, most New Zealand conifers are unusual. The kauri of the araucaria family has proper seed cones, as do kaikawaka and kawaka of the cypress family. The remaining 17 species, however, all belong to the mostly southern hemisphere podocarp family, and here the seed cones don't look like cones at all. Their scales are few and greatly reduced, so that the seeds are fully exposed from the earliest stage. Only 1–2 seeds enlarge to maturity and then they either develop a fleshy coat or are seated on fleshy often brightly coloured berry-like structures. The seeds are dispersed far and wide by birds, which swallow them and their attached 'berries'. By contrast, the winged seeds of conifers with dry cones are wind dispersed, generally for shorter distances.

Apart from the cone/flower contrast, conifers differ from flowering plants in mostly having very narrow to needle-like or scale leaves. They also produce resin that gives freshly cut wood or crushed foliage a smell of turpentine. Some conifers ooze resin from wounds in their trunks, abundantly so in the case of kauri. Hardened resin is sometimes known as amber but with the kauri it is known more prosaically as kauri gum.

A grove of kahikatea standing tall.

Close view of a metallic grey kauri trunk bearing unusual leafy outgrowths and oozing gum.

Remains of a kauri seed cone after the woody scales and the winged seeds between them have scattered.

Pollen cones of matai. These become yellow as they ripen and the pollen is carried away by the wind.

The fleshy seed cones of kahikatea typical of the podocarp family. The berry-like structure is attractive to birds.

Attractively spherical still-green kauri seed cones.

KAURI (Plate 1)

Agathis australis   Araucariaceae

The kauri is the giant of the native conifers and is numbered among the largest trees in the world. It can live for many centuries; some have been estimated to be 2000 years old. It grows in forests in the North Island from the Bay of Plenty region north. The largest surviving kauri is the much-photographed Tane Mahuta in Northland's Waipoua Forest.

The kauri grows up to 30–60 m tall with a trunk up to 3–7 m in diameter, tapering little with height. The bark is grey with a metallic sheen and separates in thick roundish flakes. Young trees up to a century or so old are narrowly conical with tiered branches from near the ground. As the trees mature the lower branches separate cleanly from the trunk leaving scars sealed by corky tissue. The upper branches grow out into massive deep and wide crowns with the foliage tufted at the branch tips.

The leaves of young trees are often a coppery colour, 5–10 cm long x 5–10 mm wide. The adult leaves are thick, oblong, 2–3.5 cm long x 1.5–2 cm wide.

Seed and pollen cones are on the same tree. Seed cones are more or less spherical, green, scaly, 5–7.5 cm in diameter. Pollen cones are finger-like, brown, 2–4 cm long x 1–2 cm wide. At maturity the seed cones disintegrate leaving only the peg-like cone axes behind (page 51).

Because of its straight-grained easily worked timber resistant to decay organisms, the kauri was extensively milled after European settlement. Trees were also bled for gum, which was once used for making varnishes and polishes. Gum was also dug out of the soil of the 'gumlands' where kauri forests grew in prehistoric times. The kauri trunks in the swamps gradually rotted away leaving the decay-resistant gum.

Other species of *Agathis* are found in Fiji, New Caledonia, northeast Australia and from New Guinea to the Philippines.

A narrowly conical kauri ricker or juvenile.

KAURI FORESTS

Although the far northern forests containing kauri come within the general conifer-broadleaf category, they are usually accorded separate status as 'kauri forests' because of the imposing size and dominant role of our largest tree.

In warmer times in the distant past kauri grew naturally throughout the country, however it is now largely restricted to the Northland and Coromandel Peninsulas. It is not present in all forests in this region but favours infertile sites such as on ridge crests and leached soils of upland plateaus. On the thin stony soils of ridge crests kauri may form a continuous canopy with rather spindly smaller conifers and broadleaved trees below them. On the plateaus, where the soils are deeper if still infertile, kauri are more scattered, although often massive.

Below them is a tier of smaller conifers—mostly rimu, miro and mountain totara—that in turn stand above broadleaved trees such as tawa, taraire and towai. Shrubs are fairly scattered and in places on the forest floor there are dense growths of kauri grass (*Astelia trinervia*), *Gahnia xanthocarpa* and the rampant vine kiekie. A wide range of vines and epiphytes is present.

The constantly flaking bark of the kauri makes it difficult for vines and epiphytes to gain and maintain a foothold on the trunk. However, the massive, inclined to horizontal branches of a mature kauri crown provide suitable and very long-term sites for epiphytes. Harrison-Smith, a forester based in Waipoua Forest during the 1930s, made a special study of kauri epiphytes. He climbed the trees using spiked boots and climbing hooks and spent many hours wandering about in their crowns. The descent was by 'bosun's chair' suspended from a rope. Among the usual range of epiphytes he found a young kauri and other conifers, although none of them would be able to grow to maturity in such a situation. (See also Epiphytes, page 181).

A kauri forest interior with kauri grass (*Astelia trinervia*) on the floor and spindly neinei (*Dracophyllum latifolium*) in the understorey.

Collospermum hastatum, a nest epiphyte commonly found in the crowns of kauri.

CELERY PINES

The species of *Phyllocladus* are unique among conifers in that what appear to be rather oddly shaped leaves are in fact flattened branchlets functioning as leaves. These are termed phylloclades (leaf stems). These phylloclades resemble leaflets of a compound leaf and have been compared in appearance with the leaves of celery, hence the common name.

CELERY PINE, TANEKAHA (Plate 1)
Phyllocladus trichomanoides Podocarpaceae

Tanekaha is mostly found on infertile lowland sites south to Taranaki and Hawkes Bay in the North Island and reappears on the northern fringes of the South Island.

It is a tree up to 20 m tall with a trunk up to 1 m in diameter. The bark is smooth and grey brown with many crustose lichens (see page 257). The main branches are attractively tiered after the fashion of a pagoda. The phylloclades are arranged in 2 rows on short slender branchlets grouped in radiating whorls at the tips of branches. The phylloclades are irregularly toothed and rhomboid to fan-shaped, 1.5–2 cm long x 1–1.5 cm wide.

Stalked pollen cones are formed in terminal clusters. When young they are dark purple and at maturity handsomely crimson. The smaller seed cones are more modest and form at the margins of the phylloclades. The scales of the seed cones are small and somewhat fleshy and each of them bears a seed enclosed by a white collar at the base.

Other species of *Phyllocladus* are found in Tasmania and from New Guinea to the Philippines.

TOATOA (Plate 1)
Phyllocladus toatoa

Toatoa grows from Northland to the central North Island, extending to higher altitudes than tanekaha.

It is a small tree up to 15 m tall with a trunk up to 60 cm in diameter. The bark is smooth and grey. The arrangement of branches and phylloclades is similar to tanekaha but the phylloclades are larger, thicker and fan-shaped to semi-circular, 2–4 cm long x 2–3 cm wide.

Left: Tanekaha with blue-purple seed cones attached to the phylloclades. Right: Tanekaha foliage with clusters of young yellow-green phylloclades bearing immature seed cones.

Toatoa with its thick rounded phylloclades and a cluster of yellow pollen cones.

Mountain toatoa with its small phylloclades and bright red pollen cones. Yellow pollen can be seen here and there.

Pollen and seed cones, on the same or different trees, are also similar to those of tanekaha but both are somewhat larger. Pollen cones are yellow.

MOUNTAIN TOATOA, MOUNTAIN CELERY PINE
Phyllocladus alpinus (Plate 1)

Mountain toatoa is the most wide ranging of our species, found from the top of the North Island to the bottom of the South Island. In subalpine forest it can attain a height of 9 m. It grows to a small tree on very infertile lowland sites in Westland. However, it is more often encountered as a grey-green shrub above the treeline than as a forest tree. The shrubs are able to spread laterally as a result of the lower branches forming roots where they touch the ground and by underground stems.

It is a shrub or small tree up to 9 m tall. The phylloclades are not arranged as in the other 2 species but are attached singly to ordinary twigs. They are mostly narrowly rhomboidal, about 2.5 cm long x 1 cm wide.

The pollen and seed cones are smaller than those of the other species. The former are red; the latter generally develop on the stalks of the phylloclades, and the seeds have a white collar.

A dense rounded shrub of mountain toatoa.

A group of kaikawaka with typical conical crowns.

A conical kaikawaka in a more sheltered site.

Left: A young kawaka. Right: The distinctive bark of kawaka separates from the trunk in long strips. Kaikawaka has similar bark.

THE NATIVE 'CEDARS'
Cupressaceae

These should really be called native cypresses as it is to that family that they belong, and indeed their foliage looks so like that of some of the northern hemisphere members of the family that they could be mistaken for introductions.

Both our species have very distinctive bark, which separates in long narrow strips that hang from the trunks like curtains. Their leaves are reduced to small closely overlapping scales arranged in exactly opposite pairs. Each pair is oriented at right angles to those above and below.

The crown of both species is attractively conical with nearly horizontal branches ending in densely rounded cushions of foliage.

In kaikawaka the adult twigs are not flattened and the scale leaves are all the same size. In kawaka the adult twigs are flattened and 2 rows of larger leaves alternate with 2 rows of smaller leaves.

The cedars are unique among our conifers in having small seed cones comprising a few thinly woody scales.

There are other species of *Libocedrus* in New Caledonia.

The attractively flattened and weeping foliage of kawaka.

Adult foliage of kaikawaka. The twigs with scale leaves are not flattened. The seed cones have thinly woody scales and most of the seeds have dispersed.

KAWAKA (Plate 1)
Libocedrus plumosa

Kawaka occurs in lowland forests in the northern North Island south to the Bay of Plenty region and reappears in the northwest corner of the South Island.

It is a tree up to 25 m tall with a trunk up to 1.2 m in diameter. The branchlets are distinctly flattened; in the juveniles they are up to 7 mm wide and in the adults up to 3 mm wide. There are 2 rows of lateral leaves and 2 median rows. In the adult the former are about 5 mm long and the latter 2.5 mm long.

Yellow pollen cones form at the tips of twigs and are 5–8 mm long. Brown seed cones on the same trees also form at twig tips. They are 1–1.5 cm long with 4 broad thinly woody scales.

KAIKAWAKA, PAHAUTEA
Libocedrus bidwillii (Plate 1)

This widespread and attractive tree is found mostly in higher altitude forests from a little north of Auckland southwards. It is absent from Stewart Island.

It is a tree up to 20 m tall with a trunk up to 1 m in diameter. The branchlets of the juveniles are rather flattened and about 3 mm wide, while those of the adults are more or less cylindrical and about 2 mm wide. The leaves are all the same size and about 2 mm long.

Pollen and seed cones are similar to those of kawaka but smaller.

MATAI (Plate 2)
Prumnopitys taxifolia
Podocarpaceae

Matai is found throughout the country except on Stewart Island, mainly on alluvial soils and volcanic ash in lowland forest.

The tree grows up to 25 m tall with a trunk up to 2 m in diameter. The distinctive bark separates in thick roundish flakes leaving a 'hammer-mark' pattern. Where a flake has recently fallen, the surface beneath is often bright red and gradually becomes brown.

The juvenile plants of matai are very distinctive. The twigs are freely branched at wide angles and are often drooping and untidily tangled. The leaves are often brownish and reduced to scales on some parts of the twigs. The longer leaves are 5–10mm long x 1–2 mm wide, pointed at the tip.

The adult leaves are green, distinctly whitish below, and tend to be flattened into 2 rows (but this is irregular), 1–1.5 cm long x 1–2 mm wide, rounded at the tip with a small point.

The yellow pollen cones are 1.2–1.5 cm long x 3–4 mm wide (see page 51). The seeds are similarly arranged. At maturity they are black, more or less spherical, 5–9 mm in diameter.

Despite being a 'softwood' (the forestry term for conifers), the wood of matai is very hard and resistant to decay and borer attack.

Species of *Prumnopitys* are also found in New Caledonia, southeast Asia and South America.

Matai with the straight leaves with whitish undersides and blue-black seeds.

Miro with curved leaves that are not whitish below and large red fleshy seeds.

MIRO (Plate 2)
Prumnopitys ferruginea

Miro is mostly found in hill-slope forests at lower altitudes throughout the country, including Stewart Island.

It grows up to 25 m tall with a trunk up to 1 m in diameter. The bark is similar to matai but the flakes are thinner and the hammer-mark pattern is not as marked nor as colourful.

Juvenile plants are very attractive with an almost fern-like appearance, dark green, tidily branched and densely leafy with the leaves flattened into 2 rows. Juvenile leaves are up to 3 cm long and pointed at the tip.

The adult leaves are also flattened into 2 rows, 1.5–2.5 cm long x 2–3 mm wide, blunt to pointed at the tip, pale green below.

The yellow pollen cones are 5–15 mm long x 3–4 mm wide. The seeds, single or in pairs, are on short branchlets, oblong at maturity, 1.5–2 cm long x 1 cm wide, bright red. These large fleshy seeds are very conspicuous and are a favourite food of the native pigeon.

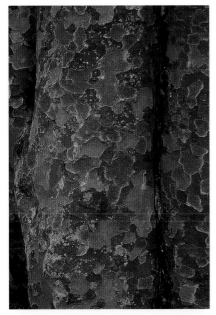

The 'hammer-marked' bark of matai; where bark flakes have recently fallen the scar is bright red.

Young matai are very different from the adult. The juveniles are untidily branched with brown foliage.

The young foliage of miro is little different from the adult. The leaves are longer and more pointed.

MATAI vs MIRO

Matai and miro both have flexible non-prickly leaves that are often flattened in 2 rows. Their seeds have fleshy coats, black in matai and red in miro. The 2 species can also be told apart by their leaves—those of matai have white undersides while those of miro are green. The leaf tips of matai are rounded, often with a small point right at the tip, while those of miro are mostly narrowed to a point.

A large matai.

TOTARA (Plate 2)

Podocarpus totara   Podocarpaceae

Totara is found throughout the country, mostly in lowland forest on fertile alluvial well-drained soils.

It is a tree up to 30 m tall with a trunk up to 2 m in diameter. The bark is thick and stringy, unlike that of the mountain totara, which is thin and papery. Juvenile leaves are about 2 cm long x 1–2 mm wide; adult leaves are 1.5–3 cm long x 3–4 mm wide, sharply pointed.

The yellow pollen cones, single or in clusters on short branchlets, are 1–1.5 cm long x 3–4 mm wide. The seed cones, on different trees, have a few scales, 1–2 of which form seeds. The lower scales enlarge and fuse into a smooth red berry.

The wood of totara is easily worked and resistant to decay, and was much used by the Maori, particularly for canoes.

Podocarpus is found throughout the southern hemisphere with extensions into east Asia and central America.

MOUNTAIN TOTARA, HALL'S TOTARA (Plate 2)

Podocarpus hallii

Mountain totara is found throughout the country and tends to replace totara at higher altitudes on infertile soils on slopes. It also grows on infertile soils on some lowland sites.

It grows up to 20 m tall with a trunk up to 1.5 m in diameter. It is distinguished from totara by its bark, which is thin and papery, separating in long strips. The juvenile leaves are 2.5–5 cm long x 4–5 mm wide and very sharply pointed. In other respects this species is very similar to totara.

Podocarpus acutifolius (Plate 2)

This is a small shrub, mostly less than 1 m high. Specimens have been recorded as attaining small tree dimensions but these may be hybrids with totara. The leaves are shorter and narrower than those of the other 2 species, 1.5–2.5 cm long x 0.75–3.5 mm wide, and are very prickly to the touch.

The reproductive features are similar to those of the other species.

This species is distributed through the northern half of the South Island, mostly as a small undershrub, particularly in higher-altitude beech forest. It also grows in mountain shrubbery. The shrubs can spread into thickets by the slender branches touching the ground and forming roots.

A thicket of low-growing *Podocarpus acutifolius*.

A remnant grove of totara on a river terrace.

Left: A mature totara. Right: Totara leaves and seed cones. The fleshy bases of the seeds change from green through yellow to red. The seeds are black when mature.

Totara bark (left) is thick and stringy. In contrast, the bark of mountain totara (right) is thin and papery.

KAHIKATEA SWAMP FOREST

Most trees of the widespread rimu-dominated type of conifer-broadleaf forest cannot tolerate waterlogged soils, so in forests on swamps we find a different set of species.

The tall kahikatea is the dominant tree throughout these swamp forests, in association with the tall broadleaf tree pukatea and the smaller swamp maire. The long-leaved vine kiekie can be abundant, as well as the swamp lawyer vine and several species of small-leaved shrubs. Groves of the tree fern wheki may also be encountered.

When you walk through such a forest, which is only easy to do when a boardwalk is provided, you could easily imagine yourself deep within a tropical swamp. Water glints among the roots of the trees that extend snake-like over the forest floor, while in better-lit places climbing kiekie totally obscures the tree trunks and the tree crowns are burdened with a heavy load of epiphytes.

The pukatea and swamp maire are very well equipped to live in wet places. They send up breathing roots (pneumatophores) above the surface of the swamp to take in air for their root systems.

There is often a well-marked zonation of vegetation around lakes in swamps. Nearest the water edge are small-leaved shrubs, native flax (*Phormium*) and scattered cabbage trees. Next comes a belt of kahikatea where the soil surface is a little higher and behind that, on rising ground, rimu-dominated forest.

With the accumulation of dead matter, the vegetation at the water's edge gradually encroaches on the lake and, in the fullness of time, can convert the lake to swamp. Further build-up can then raise the surface of the swamp to the point where it is well drained enough to support kahikatea swamp forest, followed by rimu-dominated forest.

Trunk bases of kahikatea with rounded buttresses growing in shallow water at the edge of a lagoon. At the other side of the lagoon is a dense stand of kahikatea with an undergrowth of small shrubs. On better-drained slopes above the lagoon there is a change to rimu-dominated forest.

KAHIKATEA, WHITE PINE (Plate 3)

Dacrycarpus dacrydioides   Podocarpaceae

Kahikatea is widespread in lowland, particularly swampy, forests throughout the country.

The tree reaches up to 50 m tall, sometimes more, with a trunk up to 1.5 m in diameter, often with rounded buttresses at the base. The bark is grey, in mature trees separating in rounded flakes. The young trees are conical; older trees have broad and deep crowns.

The leaves of the juveniles, 3–7 mm long x 0.5–1 mm wide, angle away from the twigs and are flattened into 2 rows. There is a gradual change to the adult scale leaves, 1–2 mm long, which are pressed to the twigs and drawn out into hair-like tips. The foliage is often grey green with twigs that are angled upwards.

The yellow pollen cones at the ends of twigs are up to 10 mm long. The seed cones, on different trees, are at the tips of short twigs. Only one seed matures and the few lower scales enlarge and fuse to form a smoothly rounded orange to red berry. The seed is black and shiny, 4–5 mm in diameter.

Other species of *Dacrycarpus* grow in New Caledonia, New Guinea and southeast Asia.

Kahikatea growing on their own, as here, and not crowded in groves have wide and deep crowns.

Left: In a good season kahikatea glow red with berries and are noisy with feasting birds. Right: In swampy sites much of the kahikatea root system extends snake-like over the surface of the swamp.

Juvenile rimu with characteristic weeping foliage at the base of a buttressed red beech.

RIMU (Plate 3)

Dacrydium cupressinum Podocarpaceae

Rimu is probably our commonest and most widespread conifer, being found throughout the country in lowland to lower mountain forests. It was once one of the important timber trees.

It is a tree up to 35 m tall, sometimes up to 60 m, with a trunk up to 1.5 m or more in diameter. The bark of mature trees separates in large flakes leaving a distinctive 'watermark' pattern. The juvenile stage provides one of the most attractive features of our forests with its cascade of delicately foliaged strongly weeping branches extending for sometimes several metres towards the ground. The juvenile leaves are 4–7mm long x 0.5–1 mm wide. The adult scale leaves, 2–3 mm long, are pointed but not hair-tipped. The foliage is brown green, and the twigs are moderately weeping even at the adult stage.

The pollen cones at the tips of twigs are 5–10 mm long. The seed cones, on different trees, have a few scales at the ends of upturned twig tips. Usually only one seed is formed. The seeds are black with a red fleshy collar at the base and often the sterile scales are also enlarged, fleshy and red.

The genus is also found from New Caledonia to southeast Asia.

Spreading crowns of mature rimu.

The bark of rimu is distinctly 'watermarked'.

SILVER PINE, MANOAO (Plate 3)

Manoao colensoi   Podocarpaceae

Silver pine grows in infertile high-rainfall often boggy sites at scattered localities in the North Island and more abundantly on the west coast of the South Island. It is absent from Fiordland and Stewart Island despite their wet climates. Silver pine has the ability to form new plants from spreading underground stems.

This small tree grows up to 15 m tall with a trunk up to 60 cm in diameter. The grey bark separates in large flakes. The juvenile stage has leaves 6–12 mm long. The fully adult yellowish green leaves are 1–2.5 mm long. They are not bulging so the twigs have a more or less smooth outline. The twigs are 1–1.5 mm in diameter.

The reddish green pollen cones at the tips of twigs are 3–5 mm long. The seed cones, on different trees, have several widely separated scales, only one of which forms a seed. The seeds are purple black with a yellow-green fleshy collar at the base.

There is a single species in the genus and it is restricted to New Zealand.

YELLOW SILVER PINE (Plate 3)

Lepidothamnus intermedius   Podocarpaceae

This small tree of infertile soils, wet climates and often boggy sites ranges throughout the country. It is not common in the North Island, but it is abundant on the west coast of the South Island and in Stewart Island, where it has a wide altitudinal range.

It grows up to 15 m tall with a trunk 30–60 cm in diameter. The grey-brown bark separates in small thick flakes. The juvenile stage has pointed leaves 9–15 mm long. The fully adult scale leaves are 1.5–3 mm long, rounded at the tip and bulging to give the twigs a bumpy outline. The twigs are 1–1.5 mm in diameter.

The reddish green pollen cones at the tips of twigs are 5–6 mm long. The seed cones, on different trees, have several scales, one of which forms a seed. The seeds are black with a yellow fleshy collar at the base. The sterile cone scales are also sometimes enlarged, fleshy and yellow.

The genus has only 3 species, 2 in New Zealand and one in southern Chile. The other New Zealand species, _L. laxifolius_ (pygmy pine), grows in alpine habitats.

Silver pine in cultivation.

Ripening seed cone of silver pine.

MONOAO

Halocarpus kirkii Podocarpaceae

Monoao occurs locally in lowland forest on the
Northland Peninsula.

It is a tree up to 25 m tall with a trunk up to 1 m in
diameter. The grey bark separates in flakes of
variable size.

The spreading juvenile leaves are 1.5–4 cm long
x 1–4 mm wide and pointed to rounded at the tip.
The adult scale leaves are about 2 mm long. The
twigs have a smooth outline and are 1–2 mm in
diameter.

The reddish green pollen cones are up to 10 mm
long and form at the twig tips. The seed cones have
several scales, 1–2 of which form seeds, which have
an orange fleshy collar at the base.

The genus is restricted to New Zealand.

PINK PINE

Halocarpus biforme

Pink pine, so-called because of the colour of its
wood, occurs in higher-altitude forest and shrubbery,
often on boggy sites, from the Coromandel
Peninsula to Stewart Island. It is also found in
lowland sites in the far south.

It is a shrub or small tree up to 10 m tall with a
trunk up to 60 cm in diameter. The grey bark
separates in small thick flakes. The spreading
juvenile leaves are 7–20 mm long x 1.5–3 mm wide
and are pointed at the tip. The adult scale leaves
are about 2 mm long and bulge to give the twigs a
bumpy outline. The twigs are 3–4 mm in diameter.

The reddish green pollen cones at the twig tips
are about 4 mm long. The seed cones, on different
plants, have several scales, 1–3 of which may form
seeds. The seeds have a yellow fleshy collar at the
base.

Shrubs of this species are able to spread by the
lower branches developing roots.

Unlike the species on page 26, monoao and pink
pine have flat juvenile leaves and an abrupt change
from juvenile to adult

Monoao: spreading juvenile and adult scale leaves .

Pink pine: juvenile and adult foliage.

TREE FERNS

Tree ferns are conspicuous in many New Zealand forests, playing an important role as pioneers where forest has been cleared, particularly on moist south-facing sites. They also establish in canopy gaps opened up by the collapse of old trees.

They are ancient plants that trace their ancestry back over 100 million years to the time of the dinosaurs. In New Zealand we have 2 genera of tree ferns: *Dicksonia* and *Cyathea*. Both have species throughout the tropics, mostly at higher altitudes, and in warmer temperate regions, particularly in the southern hemisphere.

The easiest way to distinguish a *Dicksonia* from a *Cyathea* is to examine their young fronds. Those of the former are clothed with hairs and those of the latter with scales.

Most species can be distinguished by obvious features of their trunks and fronds. In *Dicksonia squarrosa* (wheki) the old fronds drop away leaving slender outwardly angled stumps, whereas those of *D. fibrosa* (wheki ponga) hang down and persist as a thick skirt around the trunk.

Cyathea medullaris (mamaku) has black frond stalks and the fallen fronds leave a pattern of armour-like scars. *C. dealbata* (ponga or silver fern) has white undersides to the fronds. In *C. smithii* (katote) the stalks and midribs of the fronds persist in a skirt that looks like a bundle of sticks. The persistent frond stumps of *C. cunninghamii* (gully tree fern) are pressed closely against the trunks. *C. colensoi* has short prostrate trunks, covered by leaf litter, that sometimes turn up at the ends.

It has been suggested that the skirts of dead fronds in wheki-ponga and *C. smithii* serve the purpose of preventing the establishment of vines and epiphytes on the trunks . This is certainly the case in wheki-ponga but in tall old specimens the skirts don't reach the ground, and vines and epiphytes can be observed on the exposed parts of the trunks. (See Epiphytes & Vines on Tree Fern Trunks, pages 191–193.)

HOW TREE FERNS MAKE TRUNKS

Unlike conifers and most flowering trees, tree ferns are not able to form a woody trunk so they build their support in a different and somewhat clumsy way. The true stem of the tree fern is only a few centimetres in diameter at the centre of the trunk and it tapers downwards almost to a point at ground level. Such a flimsy stem could not hold up a large crown of fronds. As the plant grows and the fronds die, the closely packed bases of the dead fronds stay on the trunk and greatly add to the diameter of the true stem.

In addition, at the vulnerable base of the trunk there is an outgrowth of a multitude of densely interlaced wiry roots that form a solid mass to increase the trunk to 50 cm or more in diameter.

Although cumbersome, tree ferns have been successfully forming trunks in this way since before flowering trees evolved.

A typical tree fern scene in a shady moist forest site. The species is mamaku and the long-leaved climbing plant is kiekie.

A cut-through mamaku stump showing the true stem at the centre surrounded by a wide zone of interlaced wiry roots.

An impressive mamaku grove on a moist south-facing hill slope. Mamaku is often a pioneer on such sites.

Mamaku showing the black frond stalks and the hard scars of fallen fronds.

Left: A slender and elegant gully tree fern. Right: A close view of a gully tree fern trunk showing the distinctive embossed appearance of the persistent stumps of old fronds.

Left: Ponga with mature and young uncoiling fronds. The white undersides of the fronds can be seen here and there.
Right: Ponga trunks growing close together. The stout frond stumps are above, grading into the wiry root zone below.

A grove of the soft tree fern, katote, with the midribs of fallen fronds hanging down like a bundle of sticks.

MAMAKU

Cyathea medullaris   Cyatheaceae

Mamaku, *C. medullaris*, is our tallest and most handsome tree fern. It has jet-black stalks to its fronds and the trunks are covered by the rounded to hexagonal scars of fallen fronds.

It is a common species in lowland forest throughout the country, although it is mostly restricted to the west in the South Island.

It is a tree up to 20 m tall with a trunk up to 30 cm in diameter. The fronds have blades up to 6 m long x 2 m wide. In young plants the old dead fronds hang down untidily but in taller specimens they separate more readily.

This species also grows on Pacific Islands from Fiji to Pitcairn.

GULLY TREE FERN

Cyathea cunninghamii

The gully tree fern, *C. cunninghamii*, is sometimes difficult to distinguish from mamaku, but its trunk is more slender and when the old fronds drop off they leave short stumps that become closely pressed against the trunk. It is found throughout the North Island, particularly in moist places such as along streams in gullies. In the South Island it is scattered in coastal forests in the north and west. The species is also found in Australia.

It is a tree up to 20 m tall with a slender trunk about 10 cm in diameter covered with the closely appressed bases of fallen fronds. The fronds have black-brown stalks and blades up to 3 m long.

PONGA, SILVER FERN

Cyathea dealbata

Ponga or silver tree fern, *C. dealbata*, one of our national emblems, has distinctive white undersides to the fronds.

It is found throughout the North Island in lowland to lower mountain forest. In the South Island it is largely absent from the wetter west and south as, unlike the other tree ferns, it prefers better-drained sites.

It is a small tree up to 10 m tall with a trunk to about 20 cm in diameter, covered with the projecting bases of fallen fronds, which persist indefinitely. The fronds have silvery to pale brown stalks and the blades are up to 3 m long x 1 m wide.

SOFT TREE FERN, KATOTE

Cyathea smithii

C. smithii, soft tree fern or katote, is easily recognised by its hanging skirt of stick-like midribs of dead fronds whose other parts have dropped away. Found throughout the country mostly in mountain forests, it is also present in the Auckland Islands, which is the southernmost limit for tree ferns anywhere in the world.

It is a small tree up to 8 m tall or more with a trunk to about 30 cm in diameter. The stalks and midribs of the dead fronds persist as a skirt around the upper part of the trunk. The frond blades are very soft in texture and are up to 2 m long.

Cyathea colensoi

C. colensoi is not readily identified as its short trunk lies along the ground under leaf litter or is sometimes erect. Found in mountain to subalpine forest from the Bay of Plenty region southwards, this small tree fern often grows in higher-altitude forest with *C. smithii* and can be mistaken for young plants of this species.

This small tree fern has a trunk up to 1 m or more long and about 8 cm in diameter. The frond blades measure up to 1 m long x 60 cm wide and are softly hairy above. The frond stalks have distinctive straw-coloured scales.

WHEKI

Dicksonia squarrosa   Dicksoniaceae

Wheki is found throughout the country in lowland forests, where it often forms groves with a thick carpet of orange-brown fallen fronds on the ground beneath.

A small tree up to 6 m or more tall with a trunk up to 10 cm in diameter, wheki is alone among our tree ferns in sending out underground stems from its base that turn up to form additional trunks. The upper parts of the trunks are covered with the slender projecting bases of fallen fronds. The frond blades are up to 2.5 m long.

WHEKI-PONGA

Dicksonia fibrosa

In wheki-ponga, *D. fibrosa*, entire dead fronds persist on the trunk indefinitely to form extremely thick skirts and the entire trunk is surrounded by a thick layer of intertwined wiry roots, giving rise to the botanical name.

It is found from south of Auckland southwards in lowland forests mostly on alluvial soils.

It is a small tree up to 6 m tall with massive trunks up to 60 cm in diameter. The frond blades are up to 2 m long.

Cyathea colensoi, showing distinctive pale brown scales on the stalks.

A grove of wheki with the typical litter of orange-brown dead fronds on the forest floor.

Dicksonia lanata

This species is a small tree fern in which the trunk is either erect and up to 2 m tall, or prostrate and branching to form thickets. The trunk or prostrate stem is slender, up to 5 cm or more in diameter. The frond blades are 30–50 cm long and, in the erect form, the frond stalks are unusually long.

In the North Island the erect form of this fern is found in kauri forests in the north and the prostrate form in mountain forests from the Bay of Plenty southwards, although it is uncommon in the south. In the South Island the prostrate form grows in coastal and lowland forests in the north and west as far as central Westland.

A group of wheki-ponga with enormous skirts of dead fronds and stout trunks.

TREE FERNS & BIRDS NESTS

Many forest birds make use of tree ferns in building their nests. Wiry roots from their trunks are used as reinforcing in the body of the nest and frond scales from *Cyathea* tree ferns contribute to the soft lining of its bowl.

FLOWERING TREES & SHRUBS

Flowers of *Ixerba brexioides* showing the white petals, stamens each tipped with a pollen-producing anther, and the ovary and style in the centre of each flower, tipped with a stigma.

The flowering plants are the most recently evolved and most specialised of all the plant groups. They dominate most of the world's vegetation and, with about 300,000 species, vastly outnumber the conifers and ferns. Their wide range in growth form is remarkable, from tall trees at one extreme to such plants as the floating duckweed, only a few millimetres across, at the other. Lifestyles also vary widely from free-standing plants to vines, perching plants, parasites and a small, strange group that traps and digests insects.

Some of the success of the flowering plants derives from their close relationship with animals, particularly insects and birds, which are attracted to the bright colours and forms of the flowers, to their perfume, pleasant and unpleasant, and particularly to the nectar they contain. As they move from flower to flower they carry pollen with them and bring about fertilisation. A minority of flowering plants are wind pollinated. In New Zealand these include the native beeches, the coprosmas and grasses.

Birds particularly, but also mammals, are also involved in seed dispersal. Seeds in fleshy fruits pass through the digestive systems of animals and some dry seeds or fruits attach to them externally. Other flowering plants have wind-dispersed seeds.

Parts of the flower: the outermost parts are the usually green sepals that protect the flower at the bud stage. Then come the colourful petals signalling the presence of nectar to pollinators, followed by the stamens that produce the pollen. At the centre of the flower is the ovary, or sometimes ovaries, that contain the ovules. When fertilised, these develop into seeds. There is usually a stalk (style) at the top of the ovary with a sticky tip (stigma) to trap the pollen. The pollen grains send tubes down the stalk to fertilise the ovules.

The ovaries mature into fruits containing seeds. A common fruit is a capsule that splits open to release the seeds. Other fruits become fleshy, as in berries, or the seeds are partly or completely enclosed in a fleshy layer, brightly coloured red or yellow, known as an aril (see kohekohe, page 84, and titoki, page 85).

Seed capsule of *Pittosporum cornifolium* showing the black seeds embedded in a sticky yellow fluid.

NIKAU PALM
Rhopalostylis sapida   **Arecaceae**

The nikau is New Zealand's only palm and is the most cold-tolerant of these usually tropical plants. It can be common in coastal and warmer inland forests in the north of the North Island but becomes restricted to coastal forests further south. In the South Island it is abundant along northwestern coasts and reaches Banks Peninsula on the east. Its furthest southern occurrence is in the Chatham Islands.

The trunk is unbranched, up to 10 m tall with a diameter up to 25 cm, smooth and green, and ringed with horizontal leaf scars. The large sheathing leaf bases at the top of the trunk overlap to form a bulbous base to the crown of enormous leaves, each up to 3 m long by 1 m or more wide, made up of dozens of narrow pointed leaflets up to 1 m long.

The much-branched inflorescences grow out below the leaf bases and bear an abundance of small pink flowers during summer. The red berries, up to 10 mm long, often take about a year to ripen. Each contains a single large seed. The native pigeon and other birds feast on these berries and disperse the seeds.

There are 2 other species of *Rhopalostylis*, one on the Kermadecs and the other on Norfolk Island.

A grove of nikau palms showing trunks of mature specimens and an abundance of young plants.

Left: A nikau palm with an inflorescence of small pink flowers of the current season (above) and another (below) with ripe berries from the previous season. Right: Fronds of nikau palm.

CABBAGE TREE, TI KAUKA
Cordyline australis   Agavaceae

Found throughout in the lowlands at forest margins, scattered over open hillsides and often abundantly in and near swamps, the cabbage tree is a very distinctive feature of many New Zealand landscapes.

It grows up to 12 m or more tall with a trunk up to 1.5 m in diameter and a crown much branched by equal forkings. The bark is rough and fissured. The leaves are 30–100 cm long x 3–6 cm wide, tufted at the ends of the branches. In young plants the dead leaves may persist as skirts for some time.

The inflorescences, up to 1 m or more long, are openly branched and more or less erect. The fragrant white flowers are about 1 cm across and the purplish white berries about 4 mm in diameter. Flowering is from mid-spring to early summer with berries from mid-summer to mid-autumn.

C. kaspar is restricted to the Three Kings Islands. It is similar to *C. australis* but is much shorter with a wider crown. The genus *Cordyline* ranges from India to Queensland and the Pacific.

FOREST CABBAGE TREE
Cordyline banksii

This species is found throughout the North Island at lower altitudes and in the north and west of the South Island, mostly at forest margins; it is particularly abundant on banks and cliffs.

It is a shrub or small tree up to 4 m tall with slender often drooping stems 10–15 cm in diameter. There are usually a number of stems originating at ground level, each unbranched or little branched. The leaves are 1–2 m long x 4–8 cm wide, often drooping from the midpoint and strongly narrowed towards the base.

The inflorescences are unusually large, up to 2 m long, much and openly branched. The white flowers are very fragrant, about 1 cm across. The berries are about 4 mm in diameter, white or bluish. Flowering is from late spring to mid-summer with berries from late summer to mid-autumn.

DYING CABBAGE TREES

The widespread death of cabbage trees in New Zealand is most pronounced in Northland, where living trees are now almost rare. The culprit may be the Australian passion vine planthopper, a lacy winged bug that sucks sap and transfers a microscopic pathogen from tree to tree. The leaves of an infected cabbage tree turn yellow and gradually drop away to leave a stark skeleton.

A cabbage tree with many inflorescences.

Cordyline banksii with its unusually large inflorescences.

A handsome group of mountain cabbage trees.

A mountain cabbage tree inflorescence.

MOUNTAIN CABBAGE TREE
Cordyline indivisa

With its crowns of large broad pale green leaves, this species is a handsome component of higher-altitude forests. It is found in mountain forests from near Auckland southwards in the North Island and in the north and west of the South Island.

This small tree up to 8 m tall has a trunk 15–20 cm in diameter. Often the trunk is single and unbranched but sometimes there are groups of trunks originating at ground level. Leaves are 1–2 m long x 10–15 cm wide, whitish below. The old dead leaves often persist as a skirt below the crown.

The inflorescences, hanging down below the leaf crown, are massive and compact, up to 1.5 m long and little branched. The white to purplish flowers are densely crowded, about 1 cm across. The bluish berries are about 6 mm in diameter. Flowering is from early to mid-summer with berries from mid-summer through autumn.

Cordyline pumilio

C. pumilio is found in light lowland forest and shrubland south to the Bay of Plenty region.

This small shrub grows up to about 2 m tall with a stem about 15 mm in diameter. Often plants will flower before the stem develops above ground level. The leaves are 30–60 cm long x 1–2 cm wide.

The inflorescences are about 60 cm long and openly branched. The flowers are about 1 cm across, white to pinkish. The berries are 4–5 mm in diameter and bluish. Flowering is from early to mid-summer with berries from early to mid-autumn.

Cordyline pumilio, a diminutive cabbage 'tree' that eventually forms a short trunk.

The distinctive mountain neinei with its papery orange-brown bark and long narrow leaves.

MOUNTAIN NEINEI

Dracophyllum traversii   Epacridaceae

With its candelabra form, this is a distinctive and attractive species. It has 2 widely separated areas of distribution: the northern South Island in mountain to subalpine forest and shrubland; and in the northern North Island in lowland to mountain forest on Great Barrier Island, the Coromandel Peninsula and a little further south.

It is a tree up to 10 m or more tall with a trunk up to 60 cm in diameter. The reddish brown bark separates in long thin strips. The brownish green leaves with parallel veins typical of the genus are 30–60 cm long x 2.5–5 cm wide.

The inflorescences are terminal, erect and conical, 20–30 cm long. The flowers are small and pinkish. The seed capsules are 2–3 mm wide. Flowering and fruiting for this and the other species is mostly from November to May. The genus is also found in New Caledonia and Australia.

NEINEI

Dracophyllum latifolium

This species is found in upland forests south to Taranaki and the East Cape region.

Mountain neinei against a background of beech forest.

The slender-stemmed neinei in kauri forest.

It is a tree up to about 7 m tall with a brown trunk up to 30 cm in diameter. The bark is rough. The brownish green leaves are 25–60 cm long x 2.5–3.5 cm wide.

The inflorescences are terminal, slender, 15–30 cm long, drooping at the fruiting stage. The flowers are small and reddish. The seed capsules are 2–3 mm in diameter.

INANGA
Dracophyllum longifolium

The densely crowded long needle-like leaves of this species give it a very different appearance from its relatives with broad leaves. It has a very wide latitudinal range from East Cape in the North Island to the subantarctic islands. In the north it mostly grows at higher altitudes but descends to sea level in the far south. It can be found in shrubland, where it often forms dense thickets, at forest margins or sometimes within forest. The leaves become attractively red brown at the tips, particularly in colder habitats.

A shrub to small tree up to 12 m tall, it has a trunk up to 40 cm in diameter. The smaller specimens have no clearly defined trunk and many slender erect to spreading stems. The leaves are 10–25 cm long by 1–5 mm wide. The leaves of juveniles are often wider than those of adults.

The inflorescences are terminal on short lateral branchlets. The seed capsules are 3–5 mm in diameter.

Two other forest dracophyllums have restricted distributions: *D. townsonii* in the northwest and *D. fiordense* in the southwest South Island. **D. townsonii** is mostly found in beech forest from sea level to higher altitudes. It is a branching shrub to small tree with tufted long and quite broad leaves and drooping inflorescences arising below the leaves. **D. fiordense** is found in shrubland above the treeline and also in higher-altitude forest. It is a distinctive species with a usually unbranched trunk up to 3 m tall crowned by a mop-like cluster of downwardly curving broad leaves. The inflorescences arise on the trunk below the leaves.

Dracophyllum strictum

This species is found in lowland to mountain forests and shrubland from near Auckland southwards in the North Island and in the northwest of the South Island. A shrub up to 2 m tall, its leaves are 3.5–10 cm long x 7–12 mm wide.

The inflorescences are terminal, 5–10 cm long; the flowers are small and white. The capsules are about 2.5 mm in diameter.

Dracophyllum longifolium.

Dracophyllum strictum with clusters of small pink flowers.

THE FIVE-FINGERS
Araliaceae

Although this group is called the five-fingers, they have anything between 3 and 9 'fingers' or leaflets. Included are *Schefflera digitata*, 5 species of *Pseudopanax* and 2 of *Raukaua*. The leaves are palmately compound or reduced to simple leaves with jointed stalks, arranged alternately on the stem.

Pate stands apart with its numerous very small teeth on the leaflets. Of the other species, five-finger, mountain five-finger and *Pseudopanax laetus* have the base of the leaf stalk partly wrapping round the stem (sheathing), while in houpara, *Pseudopanax discolor*, raukawa and haumakaroa the leaf stalks are not sheathing.

The leaves of raukawa are very aromatic when crushed. Its adult leaves are simple and jointed. Houpara has thick leaflets with the teeth restricted to the outer half. *P. discolor* has yellow-green to bronze-green leaflets with undulate margins, while haumakaroa has green leaflets that are not undulate. One form of the latter has simple, jointed, adult leaves.

The differences show clearly on Plates 4 and 5.

PATE (Plate 4)
Schefflera digitata

Pate is widespread throughout the country in lowland to mountain forests. It grows in the forest understorey, in canopy gaps and other moist sheltered places.

A small tree up to 8 m tall, its leaves have stalks up to 25 cm long and bear 5–9 leaflets with stalks up to 3 cm long. The leaflets are thin in texture and up to 20 cm long x 8 cm wide with many small marginal teeth. Some young plants in the northern North Island have deeply lobed leaflets.

The inflorescences are much branched at the stem tips and bear many clusters of small greenish yellow flowers. The berries are rounded, white to purple and contain 5–10 seeds. Flowering is in late summer to early autumn with berries developing in the following few months.

Schefflera is a large genus in tropical regions. There is only one species in New Zealand but it has the distinction of being the first to be named and described following Cook's second voyage.

FIVE-FINGER (Plate 4)
Pseudopanax arboreus

Five-finger is a common species in lowland forests throughout the North Island and in the north and east of the South Island as far as Dunedin. It is most common in regenerating forest but can also be frequent as a tree fern epiphyte (see pages 191–192).

It is a small tree up to 8 m tall. The leaves have stalks up to 20 cm long and 5–7 leaflets with stalks up to 5 cm long. The leaflets are moderately thick in texture and up to 20 cm long x 7 cm wide with large teeth all along the margins.

The small brown-purple flowers are in hemispherical clusters at branch tips, opening during winter. The berries, ripening through spring and summer, are flattened, almost black, and contain 2 seeds each.

Species of *Pseudopanax* also occur in Chile; there is one in Tasmania and perhaps 3 in China.

MOUNTAIN FIVE-FINGER (Plate 4)
Pseudopanax colensoi

Mountain five-finger generally replaces five-finger in shorter, higher-altitude forests. It differs chiefly from five-finger in having no or very short leaflet stalks. It can be epiphytic on trees.

A shrub or small tree up to 5 m tall, its leaves have stalks up to 20 cm long and 3–5 leaflets without stalks or with stalks up to 1 cm long. The leaflets are thick in texture and up to 17 cm long x 7 cm wide with coarse teeth along the margins.

The small pale yellow flowers are in spherical clusters at branch tips and mostly open in the spring. The berries are flattened, almost black, and contain 2 seeds each. They ripen from spring through summer.

Three varieties of *P. colensoi* have been proposed. **Var. colensoi** generally has 5 leaflets and short leaflet stalks and has the same geographical range as five-finger. **Var. ternatum** has 3 leaflets with no stalks or very short stalks and occurs mostly at higher altitudes throughout the South Island; it is also found in lowland habitats in Westland. **Var. fiordense** has 5 leaflets with no stalks or very short stalks and is found in Fiordland; it is the only variety on Bluff Hill and on Stewart Island.

Pseudopanax laetus (Plate 4)

P. laetus is found from the Coromandel Peninsula to Taranaki in the North Island. It is mostly marginal to forest or in low forest on ridges.

A shrub or small tree up to 5 m tall, its leaves

Pate: the young berries in finger-like clusters.

Five-finger: the almost black berries in rounded clusters.

Foliage of the mountain five-finger.

The handsome foliage of *Pseudopanax laetus*.

Houpara.

Pseudopanax discolor.

Left: The very shiny leaves of raukawa. The upper leaves have the simple adult form; the 2 lower leaves with 3 and 2 leaflets are semi-juvenile. Right: A juvenile haumakaroa with very dissected compound leaves.

have stalks up to 20 cm long and 5–7 leaflets with stalks up to 3 cm long. The leaflets are thick in texture and up to 25 cm long x 13 cm wide with large teeth towards the tips or sometimes entirely smooth. The leaf stalks and the leaflet stalks and midribs are often attractively red purple.

The small brown-purple flowers are in spherical clusters at branch tips. The berries are flattened, purplish red and contain 2 seeds each. Flowering is mostly in the spring with fruits following during the summer. Because of its large compound leaves and purple-hued stalks and midribs, it is becoming popular as a cultivated plant.

HOUPARA (Plate 4)
Pseudopanax lessonii
Houpara occurs frequently in coastal forest and shrubbery in the northern North Island as far south as Gisborne.

It is a shrub or tree up to 6 m tall. The leaves have stalks up to 15 cm long and 3–5 leaflets up to 10 cm long x 5 cm wide, without stalks or with very short stalks. The leaflets are thick in texture with coarse teeth along the outer halves of the margins.

The small greenish yellow flowers are scattered singly or in clusters along the inflorescence branches. The dark purple berries are rounded and contain 5 seeds.

Flowering is during summer with berries forming during autumn.

Pseudopanax discolor (Plate 5)
This species is restricted to lowland forest and shrubland from Auckland northwards.

A shrub up to 5 m tall, its leaves have stalks up to 8 cm long and 3–5 leaflets up to 8 cm long x 2.5 cm wide, without stalks or with very short stalks. The leaflets have coarse teeth for their full length. The margins are sometimes undulate and the leaflets often have an additional reddish brown pigmentation that makes the shrubs appear bronze green at a distance.

The small pale yellow flowers are scattered singly or in groups along the inflorescence branches. The berries are rounded and contain 5 seeds.

Flowering is during summer with berries following during autumn.

RAUKAWA (Plate 5)
Raukaua edgerleyi
Raukaua was until recently included in *Pseudopanax*. The genus is restricted to New Zealand.

Raukawa is widespread throughout the country, including on Stewart Island. It is found mostly in moist lowland forests and quite often begins life as an epiphyte on tree fern trunks (see page 191).

The quite thin, very shiny and strongly aromatic leaves are the notable features of this species, as well as its very distinctive juvenile leaves.

It is a small tree up to 10 m tall. The juvenile leaves have stalks up to 8 cm long and 3–5 leaflets up to 15 cm long x 3.5 cm wide, without stalks or with very short stalks. The leaflets are thin in texture, deeply lobed in younger juveniles and coarsely toothed to smooth in older juveniles. Adult leaves are simple with stalks up to 5 cm long and blades up to 15 cm long x 5 cm wide with smooth margins. Both adult and juvenile leaves are very shiny above and strongly and pleasantly aromatic when crushed.

The small pale yellow flowers are in small clusters towards the ends of twigs. The berries are rounded and contain 3–4 seeds. Flowering then fruiting are from late spring to early autumn.

HAUMAKAROA (Plate 5)
Raukaua simplex
Haumakaroa is widespread in moist forests from Auckland southwards including the subantarctic Auckland Islands. In the north it is found mostly in mountain forests but descends to lower altitudes in the south.

The deeply lobed juvenile leaves of some forms of haumakaroa are very similar to those of raukawa although, unlike raukawa, they are not strongly scented when crushed.

A shrub to small tree up to 8 m tall, its juvenile leaves have stalks up to 10 cm long and 3–5 leaflets up to 15 cm long x 3.5 cm wide, without stalks or with very short stalks. The leaflets are thin in texture and in **var. simplex** are deeply lobed in younger juveniles and coarsely toothed in older juveniles. In **var. sinclairii** the leaves of both adult and younger plants have 3 leaflets that are similar to those of the older juveniles of var. *simplex*. Adult leaves of var. *simplex* are simple with stalks up to 8 cm long and blades up to 10 cm long x 4 cm wide with toothed margins.

The small greenish yellow flowers are in rounded clusters along the twigs. The berries are flattened and contain 2 seeds. Flowering and fruiting are from spring to early autumn.

A group of puriri trees with their wide and deep crowns merged into one.

Foliage and attractive tubular flowers of puriri.

An abundance of puriri berries—a feast for the birds.

PURIRI (Plate 6)

Vitex lucens   Verbenaceae

Puriri is a familiar and handsome tree of coastal and lowland forest in the northern North Island as far south as Taranaki.

A tree up to 20 m high with widely spreading branches, its trunk is up to 1.5 m in diameter with light-coloured smooth bark. The twigs are distinctly 4-angled. The opposite leaves are palmately compound and mostly have 5 leaflets, the 2 lowermost being much smaller than the other 3. The larger leaflets are 10–20 cm long x 5–10 cm wide with stalks 1 cm or more long. They are dark green and shiny with wavy untoothed margins and they sometimes bulge up between the secondary veins. Domatia are present in the angles between the secondary veins and midrib on the undersurface and sometimes at the junctions of other veins.

The bird-pollinated flowers are attractively red pink and 2.5–3.5 cm long. They are curved and tubular in the lower part then spread into asymmetrically arranged petals. The berries are more or less spherical, bright red and up to 2 cm in diameter. They are eaten and the seed is transported by the New Zealand pigeon (page 265) and other birds.

Flowering is mostly from early winter to mid-spring with the fruits ripening from late summer to mid-spring, although many puriri trees never seem to be without flowers or fruits, or sometimes both together.

The genus *Vitex* is also widespread in the tropics. A notable member of its family is the teak, with which it shares hard dark wood.

THE PURIRI MOTH

Our largest and perhaps most notable forest moth is the puriri moth, *Aenetus virescens*, which is restricted to the North Island. The commonest hosts for the caterpillar are puriri, the native beeches, putaputaweta and wineberry. The tiny larvae first feed on fungi growing on rotting logs then climbs a live tree when it is about 2 cm long. It then burrows into the trunk of the host tree for up to 15 cm and eats away a diamond-shaped area of bark and outer sapwood around the opening. The edges of the scar form a renewing callus that provides the food for the caterpillar for up to 5 years. The feeding area is covered by a silk and debris tent. The caterpillar can attain 10 cm in length and eventually metamorphoses into the adult state near the opening of the burrow. The adult is robust and attractively bright green in colour with a wingspan in the female up to 15 cm. Adults do not eat, and live for only about 2 days or even less if they are spotted by moreporks (native owls, see page 275).

A puriri moth.

WHARANGI (Plate 6)
Melicope ternata   **Rutaceae**

Wharangi can occur frequently in coastal and some lowland forests, especially at their margins, throughout the North Island and in the northeast corner of the South Island. Although having small dry fruits, wharangi belongs to the same family as the orange and other citrus fruits.

It is a shrub to small tree up to 6 m tall. The twigs are rounded and hairless. The opposite yellowish green leaves have stalks up to 5 cm long and 3 leaflets with short stalks. The leaflets are 7–10 cm long x 3–4 cm wide and have smooth margins. Wharangi leaves have a distinctive strong citrus smell when crushed.

The flowers, in clusters at branch tips, are small and yellowish green with 4 petals. The fruits are dry capsules each with 4 small pods forming a cross. Each pod releases one shiny black seed that can remain attached by a thread for some time. Flowering is in early spring and the capsules are formed from late spring to late summer.

The genus *Melicope* ranges from tropical Asia to New Zealand.

Yellow-green compound leaves of wharangi and small yellowish flowers.

Wharangi with distinctive seed capsules. The black seeds remain attached until eaten by birds.

A kohekohe trunk festooned with inflorescences. The ground below is strewn with fallen flowers.

Opening seed capsules of kohekohe, each with 3 large seeds enclosed by orange fleshy arils.

KOHEKOHE (Plate 6)
Dysoxylum spectabile Meliaceae

For a tree in temperate latitudes kohekohe is quite remarkable. It belongs to a tropical Asian genus and would not appear at all out of place in a tropical forest. The large leathery leaves are typical of many tropical trees, but the siting of the flowers and later capsules directly on the trunk is of greater significance as this is often considered to be an exclusively tropical phenomenon.

Kohekohe may be quite common in forests of warmer northern localities. In the north of the North Island it can be found from the coast to inland sites, where it is usually a subcanopy tree. In the southern North Island it becomes restricted to coastal forests and in exposed sites may dominate a low canopy. In the South Island it is only to be found in the Marlborough Sounds.

It grows up to 15 m tall with a trunk to 1 m in diameter. The bark is smooth and pale. The alternate leaves are large, up to about 40 cm long x 25 cm wide, and generally have 4 opposite pairs of leaflets and a terminal one. The leaflets are 7–15 cm long x 3–4 cm wide, bright green, shiny, hairless at maturity, mostly rounded at the tips and with smooth but often undulate margins (seedlings have leaflets with lobed margins). The base of the leaf stalk where it attaches to the stem is often swollen (this is known as a pulvinus). There are often similar swellings at the bases of the leaflet stalks. At first sight there may not appear to be any resting buds at the bases of the leaf stalks, but careful examination will reveal small tufts of hairs marking the sites of such buds.

The hanging inflorescences are produced on the trunks and branches, often in great abundance. The flowers are white and waxy, and open in May or June. The seed capsules develop slowly for about a year and come to look like hanging clusters of large green grapes. They become dry and brown eventually and split open to reveal 3 large seeds, each enclosed by a bright orange to red fleshy structure known as an aril. The larger native birds eat the arils, and the seeds are scattered in the process.

The genus *Dysoxylum* is widespread in tropical and subtropical forests, some species providing the wood known as mahogany.

TITOKI (Plate 6)
Alectryon excelsus
Sapindaceae

Titoki is frequent in coastal and lowland forests throughout the North Island, and to Banks Peninsula in the east of the South Island and central Westland in the west. It is most abundant on alluvial soils.

A small tree up to 10 m tall with a trunk to 60 cm diameter, its bark is fairly smooth and dark. The twigs are densely furry with brownish hairs, as is the case with the otherwise unprotected immature leaves. Many of the hairs persist, particularly on the undersides of the adult leaves. The alternate leaves are 10–40 cm long x 10–15 cm wide with 4–6 leaflets on each side, mostly attached alternately to the leaf stalk. There are swellings at the bases of both the leaf and leaflet stalks. The leaflets are dark green, 5–10 cm long x 2–5 cm wide. Their tips are pointed and in younger plants the margins are coarsely toothed and deeply lobed. In adult leaflets the teeth are restricted to the outer half or are sometimes lacking.

The much-branched inflorescences form at the tips of twigs. The flowers are very small and purplish. The capsules are furry and distinctive in shape. They are a little flattened with a flange like the crest of a classical helmet. When ripe the capsule splits, revealing a large shiny black seed partly enclosed by a convoluted bright red aril. Flowering is in the spring with the capsules developing gradually over the following year.

The genus is largely tropical, with species on the high islands in the Pacific as well as tropical Australia and New Guinea.

Capsules, red arils and black seeds of titoki.

The pinnately compound leaves of titoki.

KAMAHI (Plate 7)
Weinmannia racemosa
Cunoniaceae

Kamahi is one of the most widespread native trees in New Zealand, extending from near Auckland to Stewart Island, mostly in mountain forests except in the far south. It often begins as an epiphyte on a tree fern trunk (see page 193) and sometimes the still-living tree fern can be found among the several trunks of a mature kamahi.

It can become a tree up to 25 m tall, usually with several trunks, each up to 1 m or more in diameter. The bark is greyish and relatively smooth. The adult leaves are dark green, up to 7.5 cm long x 4 cm wide, pointed to rounded at the tip and with prominent marginal teeth. The leaf veins are often red, as are the rounded twigs. The red-toned juvenile leaf has one pair of opposite leaflets and a terminal leaflet; the adult leaf is reduced to the terminal leaflet with an often swollen joint at the base of the blade. The base of the leaf stalk is often swollen. Alternating with each pair of leaf stalks there

A forest with many kamahi in flower.

Finger-like inflorescences of kamahi with pinkish flowers.

Kamahi trunks with crustose lichens.

White-flowered inflorescences of towai.

is always a pair of much smaller, often toothed scales known as stipules. At an early stage when they are still adjacent to the stem apex, they enclose and protect the immature leaves.

The small white to pink flowers are in erect spike-like clusters. The capsules that form from the flowers are red brown and release small seeds with tufts of hairs at each end for air buoyancy. The flowers open in summer and the capsules mature in summer and autumn. When in flower kamahi crowns are pinkish in colour, changing to reddish as the capsules mature.

The genus *Weinmannia* is widespread in the southern hemisphere and the tropical mountains.

TOWAI (Plate 7)
Weinmannia silvicola

Kamahi's smaller relative, towai, overlaps with it just south of Auckland but continues alone through most of Northland. It occurs with makamaka in Northland — and is sometimes mistaken for it at the juvenile stage.

Towai is a small tree up to 15 m tall with a trunk up to 1 m in diameter. The bark is relatively smooth. The twigs and young leaves are densely hairy and the hairs tend to persist on the leaf undersides. The leaves are dark green, fairly thick and in the juveniles up to 20 cm long x 10 cm wide. The juveniles have up to 10 pairs of opposite leaflets, reducing to 1–2 pairs, or to simple jointed leaves, in the adult. The base of the leaf stalk is often a little swollen; the leaflets have no stalks. The largest leaflet is up to 6 cm long x 2.5 cm wide, pointed to rounded at the tip and with marginal teeth strongly curved towards the tip of the leaflet. The undersides of the juvenile leaflets are often strongly red coloured.

The inflorescences at branch tips are un-branched. The white flowers are 3–4 mm long and the capsules 4–5 mm long. Flowering is through spring to early summer with capsules ripening from late spring through summer.

MAKAMAKA (Plate 7)
Ackama rosifolia   **Cunoniaceae**

Makamaka is restricted to lowland forests in the northern half of Northland.

It is a small tree up to 12 m tall with a trunk up to 60 cm in diameter. The bark is greyish with corky projections. The twigs and young leaves are densely covered with brownish hairs that persist on the adult leaves, particularly on the undersides. The leaves are pale green, sometimes red below, fairly thin

Foliage and frothy inflorescences of makamaka.

and in the juveniles up to 25 cm long x 10 cm wide. The juveniles have up to 10 opposite pairs of leaflets reducing to 3–5 in the adult. The leaflets reduce in size towards the base. There is a swelling at the base of the leaf stalk and the short leaflet stalks are also often swollen. The largest leaflet is up to 7 cm long x 3 cm wide, pointed at the tip and with prominent narrow marginal teeth that angle away from the tip of the leaflet. Domatia are present in the angles between secondary veins and the midrib on the leaflet underside. These are discernible as bulges on the leaflet upper side.

The terminal inflorescences are much branched with many small cream flowers, each about 3 mm wide. The pale brown capsules are 3–4 mm long.

Ackama is a small genus with other species in Queensland and New Guinea.

KAKABEAK (Plate 8)
Clianthus puniceus   **Papilionaceae**

The common name of this shrub likens the flower to the beak of the native parrot kaka. Kakabeak grows in shrubbery and at forest margins. It originally occurred in small island and coastal sites from the Bay of Islands to Tolaga Bay on the East Coast as

The distinctively shaped flowers of kakabeak.

well as inland at Lake Waikaremoana. It is now extinct at a number of sites but is widely cultivated. A particularly robust form (**var. *maximus***) with flowers of a brighter shade of red is rare from East Cape southwards.

It is a softly woody shrub with spreading branches up to 2 m tall. The leaves are up to 15 cm long x 4–5 cm wide with up to 15 pairs of leaflets, each 1.5–2.5 cm long x about 5 mm wide. There is a pair of stipules at the base of the leaf stalk, each about 1 cm long.

The flowers are in hanging clusters. Each bird-pollinated flower is up to 8 cm long, scarlet, with the 2 lowermost petals forming a beak-like keel and the uppermost petal turned strongly upwards. The pods are plump and up to 8 cm long.

Clianthus is an Australian genus with one species in New Zealand.

KOWHAI (Plate 8)
Sophora microphylla   **Papilionaceae**
This species of kowhai grows throughout the country, mostly at lower altitudes at forest margins, often on river terraces or bordering lakes. The trees can also be scattered over hillside pastures. As it often grows near water, many seeds end up in rivers. They have hard yellow waxy coats and can be carried without harm to the sea, where they may be washed up onto beaches. However, they can go further than that and be carried by ocean currents for great distances. Some have been found on beaches on the Kermadec Islands where kowhai trees do not grow, but the species does grow in the Chathams, in Chile and on Gough Island in the South Atlantic. As an experiment, kowhai seeds were kept in a jar of sea water for 10 years and even after that time some seeds could still be germinated, so sea transport must have been the means of attaining the present distribution.

A tree to about 10 m tall with a trunk up to 60 cm

Hanging tubular flowers of kowhai and the curiously winged and constricted pods.

in diameter, its bark is smooth but becomes somewhat rough and fissured on old trees. There is a juvenile form of densely and untidily tangled twigs (Plate 8) that can persist for several decades. The leaves are up to 15 cm long with 20–40 pairs of lateral leaflets, each 5–7 mm long x 2–3 mm wide.

The flowers are large, bright yellow, tubular and hang downwards. They are produced in great abundance in the spring. They contain large quantities of nectar and are much visited by bellbirds and tuis, which act as pollinating agents. The unusual pods are formed in the months following and can persist on the trees for quite a long time. The pods are constricted into one-seeded compartments. The pods do not open but the seeds are sometimes extracted and eaten by native birds. Otherwise they eventually fall from the trees and the seeds are released after they decay.

The genus *Sophora* is found in temperate and subtropical regions of both hemispheres.

Sophora tetraptera (Plate 8)
This species grows in similar habitats to *S. microphylla* but is found only on the east of the North Island from East Cape to southern Hawkes Bay.

It is a tree up to about 12 m tall with a trunk up to 60 cm in diameter. The bark is similar to that of *S. microphylla*. There is no juvenile form. The leaves are up to 15 cm long with 10–20 pairs of leaflets, each 1.5–3.5 cm long x 5–8 mm wide — fewer and larger than *S. microphylla*.

The flowers and pods are very similar to those of *S. microphylla*.

Kowhai provides a golden display in spring.

Foliage of *Sophora tetraptera*.

TUTU (Plate 9)

Coriaria arborea   **Coriariaceae**

Tutu is found throughout the country in shrubby vegetation or marginal to lowland to montane forest. It is often a pioneer on new bare sites before a soil has developed. It is probably best known for being poisonous to stock but it is also poisonous to humans.

It is a much-branched rather untidy shrub or small tree up to 6 m in height. If there is a recognisable trunk it can be up to 30 cm in diameter. The bark is smooth, becoming rather rough with age. The leaves are opposite with short stalks, the blade 5–8 cm long x 4–5 cm wide with smooth margins.

The flowers are small in hanging spikes. The fruits are purple and berry-like. It flowers from spring to early autumn with the berries ripening through summer and autumn.

The genus *Coriaria* has an unusual distribution with species in southern Europe, eastern Asia and central and South America, as well as in New Zealand. The other species in New Zealand are smaller than tutu and grow in open places.

Tutu with hanging elongate clusters of black berries.

WHAU (Plate 9)

Entelea arborescens   **Tiliaceae**

Whau grows in shrubbery and low forest, along the coasts and inland southwards to the Bay of Plenty. It can be found here and there through the rest of the North Island near the sea and in the north of the South Island.

A shrub or small tree up to 6 m tall with a trunk up to 25 cm in diameter, its bark is smooth but with prominent corky spots. The leaves are large, soft and attractive; alternate with long stalks up to 20 cm long and softly hairy, very broad blades 10–15

Whau with flowers of the current season and spiky capsules from the previous season.

cm long x 10–15 cm wide or sometimes more. The leaf margins have many small teeth.

The attractive white flowers are about 2.5 cm across with many yellow stamens at their centres. The fruits are unusual — dry capsules covered with long but flexible spines. Flowering and fruiting are from early spring to mid-summer.

The wood of whau is very light, said to be as light as balsa, and was used by the Maori for fishing floats.

Whau is restricted to New Zealand and is the only species of its genus.

KAWAKAWA (Plate 9)

Macropiper excelsum   **Piperaceae**

Kawakawa is widespread as an undershrub in lowland forests of milder climates throughout the North Island and near the coast as far as Banks Peninsula and South Westland in the South Island.

It is a shrub or small tree up to 6 m tall. There is generally no well-defined trunk, but the stems are smooth and strongly jointed in a similar way to bamboo. The leaves are alternate, sometimes appearing to be opposite near twig tips. The stalks have strongly sheathing bases, and the blades are heart-shaped with smooth margins, 5–10 cm long x 6–12 cm wide.

Kawakawa leaves are usually riddled with holes, particularly late in the season. These are caused by the caterpillar of a native moth whose diet is restricted to kawakawa leaves. However, it poses no threat to the species.

The flowers are minute and crowded on an unbranched stalk. The small orange berries are equally crowded into vertical structures that look like small candles. Flowers and fruits can be found at most times of the year.

A distinctive and attractive variety of this species, **_M. excelsum_ ssp. _peltatum_**, grows on islands off the Northland Peninsula. It has larger darker green and much shinier leaves and the stems too are green. It is becoming popular as an ornamental as is a recently described species, **_M. melchior_**, from the Three Kings Islands.

Other species of _Macropiper_ are found on islands of the tropical south Pacific and in New Guinea. The kava plant of Fiji and the true pepper plant of Indonesia belong to the related genus _Piper_ and they share with kawakawa leaves that taste peppery.

Kawakawa with orange berries in candle-like clusters.

The shiny-leaved green-stemmed subspecies of kawakawa from northern offshore islands.

POHUTUKAWA (Plate 10)

Metrosideros excelsa   **Myrtaceae**

Pohutukawa is perhaps our most colourful and best-known tree, not only where it grows naturally along northern North Island coasts and around some Rotorua lakes, but also further south where it is cultivated. It is also known as the New Zealand Christmas tree as its wide crowns can turn completely red with flowers in December.

This is often a many-trunked tree up to 20 m tall and 52 m wide. The trunks can attain 2 m in diameter. The bark is rough and fissured. Aerial roots are readily produced on the trunks, growing down to the ground or hanging like straw brooms from the higher branches. The leaves, 5–10 cm long x 2.5–5 cm wide, have a dense covering of white hairs below.

The bright crimson stamens of the flowers are 3–4 cm long. The capsules are about 8 mm long.

As the flowers produce abundant nectar they are much visited by birds and insects. The thread-like seeds are released in the autumn following flowering.

Metrosideros is widespread in the Pacific.

Metrosideros parkinsonii (Plate 10)

This species is a straggling shrub or small tree up to 7 m tall. The branchlets are 4-angled. The leaves are 3.5–5 cm long x 1.5–2 cm wide.

The bright crimson flowers, about 3 cm long with many long stamens, are mostly on woody stems below the leaves. The capsules are 6–7 mm long. Flowering is from late spring to mid-summer with capsules following in the autumn.

It is found in coastal to mountain forests and shrubland in the northwest of the South Island with a widely separated occurrence on Great Barrier Island in the north of the North Island.

Pohutukawa growing in its typical rocky coastal habitat.

Flowers and woolly buds of pohutukawa.

Red-tipped aerial roots of pohutukawa.

Low pohutukawa forest on Rangitoto Island with a ground-cover of *Astelia banksii*.

NORTHERN RATA (Plate 10)
Metrosideros robusta

Northern rata can be common in lower-altitude forests throughout the North Island and in the north of the South Island. Where it grows near pohutukawa in the northern North Island hybrids between the species occur.

It is a tall tree, up to 25 m or more tall, which begins its life as an epiphyte (see page 160). Where it establishes terrestrially on open rocky sites it is a much smaller tree. The pseudotrunks, formed by the coalescing of descending roots after the supporting tree has died, may be 2 m or more in diameter. The bark is rough and flaky. The leaves are 2.5–5 cm long x 1.5–2 cm wide, hairless, rounded and a little notched at the tip with the fine vein network clearly visible below.

The flowers are red but smaller than those of pohutukawa, with stamens 1–1.5 cm long. The capsules are about 7 mm long x 3.5–5 mm wide. Flowers appear during the summer and seeds are released during the following autumn.

Another tree species, ***M. bartlettii*** (Plate 10), was not discovered until the 1970s. It is restricted to the North Cape peninsula. Like northern rata, it starts off as an epiphyte. Its bark is soft and pale, separating in thin flakes. The leaves are similar in size to those of the ratas but thinner, with pointed tips and evident veins below. The flowers are small and white.

A northern rata completely red with flowers.

Southern rata flowers and foliage.

Southern rata with red new growth.

POSSUM DAMAGE TO RATA

A tall northern rata in flower.

A skeleton of northern rata after possum attack.

The introduced possum has been described as 'New Zealand's Number One Forest Pest'.

It is particularly damaging to the northern and southern ratas. For an unknown reason particular trees are targeted and others left intact. The unfortunate trees are often completely defoliated and die.

An effective if somewhat unsightly method of protecting rata trees in small public reserves is to fix a smooth metal band around the tree trunks. The possums are unable to get a grip on the smooth surface so can't climb up to feed in the crowns.

SOUTHERN RATA (Plate 10)
Metrosideros umbellata

Southern rata tolerates cooler temperatures than northern rata. It is rare but widely scattered in the North Island and abundant in the west and south of the South Island and in Stewart Island. This is the New Zealand tree that reaches the highest latitude, forming a low coastal forest on the Auckland Islands at 51°S.

It is a tree up to 15 m or more tall with a trunk up to 1 m or more in diameter. As with northern rata, southern rata can sometimes be epiphytic but it is

more often terrestrial. The bark is rough and flaky. The leaves are 3–5 cm long x 1.5–2 cm wide, hairless, drawn out to a point at the tip. The veins are not evident below but there are prominent oil glands. Young leaves are bright red in colour.

The flowers are bright red and provide an impressive display in a good flowering year. The stamens are up to 2 cm long. The capsules are hard, 7–8 mm long x 6–8 mm wide. Flowers appear during summer but seeds are not released until about a year later.

COPROSMAS
Rubiaceae

With about 50 species in New Zealand, coprosmas are encountered in all types of vegetation from the coast to the mountain tops. The small flowers do not catch the eye but the berries, in a wide range of colours, certainly do. In a good season coprosma branches can be weighed down with berries that provide a feast for birds and, in some cases, lizards.

The first species to be collected by Cook's botanists had an unpleasant, rotten-cabbage smell when crushed or dried and must have been an unwelcome presence in their cramped cabins. They named the new genus *Coprosma* (*copros* means dung) and the species *foetidissima*. This could be translated as 'stinking dung plant'.

The coprosmas have opposite smooth-margined leaves with domatia, and opposite pairs of pointed stipules alternating with the pairs of leaf stalks.

The small wind-pollinated flowers, in lateral clusters or sometimes single, are male or female on different plants. They are very similar throughout the genus — pale yellow to yellowish green, sometimes streaked with purple or completely purple. Male flowers have long dangling stamens and the females diverging pairs of feathery stigmas that sift the air for pollen. Colourful berries follow the flowers and can be red, orange, yellow, blue or white depending on the species. Each berry contains 2 hard seeds.

Flower and berry times can be very variable, but generally flowering is between late winter and early summer and berries ripen from summer to autumn. In some species the berries take a year to ripen.

Kanono, *C. grandifolia,* has the largest leaves, as the specific name attests. They are more than 15 cm long. The blades of this species are thin and often mottled green and yellowish green.

In mamangi, *C. arborea,* and stinkwood, *C. foetidissima,* the leaf blade extends as narrow wings down the stalk. Stinkwood has an unpleasant smell when crushed. Mamangi does not offend in this respect.

In *C. tenuifolia* and *C. macrocarpa* the stipules become dry and papery. *C. macrocarpa* has dark green leaves while those of C. *tenuifolia* are mottled green and yellowish green.

Karamu, *C. robusta,* has shiny black tips to its stipules while those of shiny karamu, *C. lucida,* narrow to a small green point.

Taupata, *C. repens*, has extremely shiny leaves and its stipules bear rows of small black glands.

Most species of *Coprosma* are in New Zealand with a secondary centre in Hawaii. There are scattered species elsewhere in the Pacific, eastern Australia and, at higher altitudes, in New Guinea and Indonesia.

Small-leaved coprosmas are covered in Plate 25 and pages 150–153.

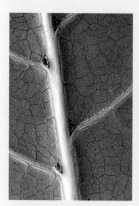  

Distinctive features of coprosmas: (left) domatia on the underside of a leaf, in this case *C. grandifolia*; (centre) papery stipules as in *C. tenuifolia* and *C. macrocarpa*; (right) black-tipped stipules as in *C. robusta*.

Kanono with berries.

KANONO (Plate 11)
Coprosma grandifolia

This species grows in moist sheltered places in lowland to lower mountain forests throughout the country.

A shrub or small tree up to 6 m tall, its leaves are thin, mottled, 15–20 cm long x 7–10 cm wide. The twigs often have purple flecks. The stipules have greyish translucent toothed glands occupying their outer halves.The berries are orange, 7–9 mm long.

MAMANGI (Plate 11)
Coprosma arborea

This species is found in lowland forests south to the Bay of Plenty.

It is a tree up to 10 m tall with a trunk up to 40 cm in diameter. The leaves of juvenile plants are 1.5–2.5 cm long x 1–1.7 cm wide. The leaves of adult plants are thin, 5–6 cm long x 3.5–4 cm wide with the blade extending as tapering wings down the stalk.

The berries are white, about 7 mm long.

STINKWOOD (Plate 11)
Coprosma foetidissima

This species is found mostly in higher-altitude forests from about Auckland southwards, including the Auckland Islands.

A shrub up to 3 m tall, its leaves are thin, dull green, 3–5 cm long x 1.4–2 cm wide with the blade

Stinkwood foliage and female flowers. The flowers have long stigmas to catch airborne pollen.

extending as tapering wings down the stalk.

The flowers are attached singly, not in groups.The berries are pale orange to orange, 7–10 mm long.

Coprosma macrocarpa (Plate 11)

C. macrocarpa occurs in coastal and lowland forest south to the vicinity of Auckland.

It is a shrub or small tree up to about 5 m tall. The leaves are dark green, 9–13 cm long x 4–8 cm wide. The stipules form a sheath around the stem and soon become dry and papery.

The berries are unusually large, orange red, 1–2.5 cm long.

Coprosma macrocarpa with large berries.

Karamu with berries.

Coprosma tenuifolia (Plate 11)

C. tenuifolia is found in lowland to mountain forest from south of Auckland to the central North Island.

It is a shrub or small tree up to about 5 m tall. The leaves are pale and often mottled, thin, 7–10 cm long x 3–4.5 cm wide. The stipules form a sheath around the stem and soon become dry and papery.

The berries are orange, 7–8 mm long.

KARAMU (Plate 11)
Coprosma robusta

Karamu is found in lowland forest or shrubland throughout the North Island and almost to the south of the South Island.

It is a shrub or small tree up to 6 m tall. The leaves are dark green, 5–13 cm long x 3–4 cm wide. The stipules have a single shiny black gland at their tips.

The berries are orange, 8–9 mm long.

SHINY KARAMU (Plate 11)
Coprosma lucida

This species occurs throughout the country in lowland to mountain forest and shrubland, sometimes as an epiphyte. It grows in drier habitats than karamu.

It is a shrub up to 3 m tall, its leaves are thick and shiny with the fine vein network clearly visible, 5–13

Shiny karamu with berries. In this case the berries take a year to ripen.

cm long x 3–4 cm wide, the tip often drawn out into a point. The stipules have small greenish tips.

The berries are orange red, 8–12 mm long.

TAUPATA (Plate 11)
Coprosma repens

This distinctive species is found in shrubbery and low coastal forest throughout the North Island and on the northern fringes of the South Island. It is notable for its very shiny leaves. In California, where it is cultivated and has become naturalised, it is known as the mirror or looking-glass plant.

A shrub or small tree up to 8 m tall, its leaves are thick, very shiny on both surfaces, 6–8 cm long x 4–5 cm wide, but about half that size in exposed coastal habitats. The stipules have a row of blackish glands.

The berries are orange, about 1 cm long.

BLACK MAIRE (Plate 12)
Nestegis cunninghamii   Oleaceae

Black maire is scattered as a canopy component through lowland forests in the North Island and the northern South Island.

It grows up to 20 m tall with a trunk up to 1.5 m in diameter. The bark is rough and fissured. Adult leaves are 7.5–15 cm long x 2–5 cm wide, opposite, the midribs sunken on their upper sides, the leaf stalk often dark coloured and swollen at the base.

The inflorescences of small inconspicuous flowers are densely hairy. The berries are 1–1.5 cm long and red. The greenish yellow flowers appear in late spring and the fruits in summer and autumn more than a year later.

The genus *Nestegis* is found in Australia and New Zealand and perhaps also in New Caledonia and Hawaii, but these species were formerly included in the same genus as the olive of the Mediterranean — *Olea*. The maires are sometimes known as New Zealand olives. Their wood is very hard and was used by the Maori to make a variety of implements.

WHITE MAIRE (Plate 12)
Nestegis lanceolata

White maire has a similar distribution to black maire but extends to higher altitudes. It differs from black maire in its smaller size, narrower leaves and hairless inflorescences.

It is a tree up to 15 m tall with a trunk up to 1 m in diameter. The bark is similar to that of black maire. The leaves are also similar but narrower, 5–12 cm long x 1–2 cm wide. The midrib, however, is not

Taupata with its thick very shiny leaves.

Juvenile maire with long narrow leaves.

sunken above but flush with the leaf surface.

The inflorescences are hairless or almost so. The berries are about 1 cm long and red. The greenish yellow flowers are found from late spring to mid-summer, and the berries mature in summer and autumn more than a year later.

MOUNTAIN MAIRE (Plate 12)
Nestegis montana

Mountain maire is found in lowland to lower mountain forests throughout the North Island and in the north of the South Island.

It is a tree up to 10 m or more tall with a trunk up to 60 cm in diameter. The bark is rough and furrowed. The leaves are dark green and very narrow, 3.5–9 cm long x 6–9 mm wide.

The flowers are very small and yellowish. The berries are red, 6–9 mm long. Flowering is from late spring to mid-summer. The berries mature through summer to early autumn.

COASTAL MAIRE
Nestegis apetala

N. apetala differs from its relatives in New Zealand in having juvenile leaves that are both longer and broader than the adult's. It is found on cliffs and in coastal forest and shrubland at Whangarei, the Bay of Islands and several islands off the east coast of Northland.

It is a shrub or small tree up to 6 m tall with spreading sometimes twisted branches. The leaves of juveniles are 7–15 cm long x 5–8 cm wide; those of adults are 3.5–7.5 cm long x 2.5–4 cm wide. The adult leaves are often undulate and very shiny.

The inflorescences are hairless. The berries are a bright red and about 1 cm long x 5 mm wide. Flowering is from mid-spring to early summer. The berries take about a year to ripen.

TAWA (Plate 12)
Beilschmiedia tawa   Lauraceae

Tawa is the dominant canopy tree in lowland forests through most of the North Island and the northeast of the South Island but is largely replaced in that role about Auckland and northwards by its relative taraire (page 139). There is also a smaller coastal relative in Northland that has been regarded as a broader-leaved form of tawa but was recently segregated as a third species — **Beilschmiedia tawaroa**. It is similar to tawa but has leaves up to 4 cm wide.

A small tree of white maire.

Foliage of *Nestegis cunninghamii*.

Shiny foliage of *Nestegis apetala*.

Tawa grows up to 30 m or more tall with a trunk up to 1.2 m in diameter. The bark is smooth. The smooth-margined mostly opposite leaves are narrow, pointed, willow-like, whitish below, 4–7.5 cm long x 10–15 mm wide.

The small inconspicuous flowers are followed by plum-like fruits, 2–3 cm long, dark purple to black in colour. The fruits are eaten and dispersed by the native pigeon. Tawa flowers through spring to early summer and the fruits form from mid-spring to late summer.

Adult tawa foliage and plum-like berries.

Young tawa with yellow willow-like leaves.

HANGEHANGE, NEW ZEALAND PRIVET (Plate 12)
Geniostoma rupestre var. *ligustrifolium*
Loganiaceae

Hangehange is an undershrub in many coastal and lowland forests throughout the North Island and in the north of the South Island.

A shrub up to 3 m tall, its opposite leaves are membranous, pale green below, sometimes whitish, 5–7 cm long x 2–3 cm wide. A pair of membranous, translucent stipules alternate with the bases of the leaf stalks.

Although small and greenish, the flowers are heavily perfumed. The fruits are dry capsules splitting into 2 valves. Flowering occurs through spring with the capsules maturing from late spring to early autumn.

The genus ranges from Madagascar to Malaya, New Guinea, Australia, New Caledonia and Polynesia.

RAMARAMA (Plate 12)

Lophomyrtus bullata　　　　　　Myrtaceae

Ramarama is found in coastal to lowland forests throughout the North Island and in the north of the South Island.

A shrub or small tree up to 5 m tall, its opposite leaves are shiny, strongly bulging upwards between the secondary veins, and become reddish in exposed sites, 1.5–3 cm long x 1–1.5 cm wide.

The flowers occur singly in leaf angles, white with many stamens, about 1.2 cm in diameter. The berries are 4–8 mm long, dark red to black. Flowering is from late spring through summer with berries from mid-summer to mid-autumn.

Ramarama hybridises with its smaller-leaved relative *L. obcordata* (page 154).

The genus is restricted to New Zealand.

Hangehange foliage and small greenish flowers.

Hangehange with distinctive 2-valved capsules.

The bubbly leaves of ramarama.

SWAMP MAIRE, MAIRE TAWAKE (Plate 12)

Syzygium maire   **Myrtaceae**

Swamp maire is found in lowland swamp and bog forest throughout the North Island and in the north of the South Island.

In waterlogged soils it sends up special roots that take in air for the submerged main root system to ensure it doesn't die from lack of oxygen. Breathing roots (pneumatophores) are also formed by pukatea (page 108) and mangrove (page 137).

This tree grows up to 10 m or more tall with a trunk up to 60 cm in diameter. The bark is smooth and pale. The opposite leaves are thin, 4–5 cm long x 1–1.5 cm wide.

The flowers are white, about 1.2 cm in diameter, with many stamens. The berries are 1–1.2 cm in diameter and bright red. Flowering and fruiting occur from mid-summer to mid-winter.

Syzygium is widespread with many hundreds of species. We have only this species in New Zealand.

Breathing roots of swamp maire standing above the swamp surface.

Colourful berries of swamp maire.

Starry flowers and coarsely toothed leaves of tawari.

TAWARI (Plate 13)
Ixerba brexioides
Escalloniaceae

Tawari is found in lowland and lower mountain forest south to Lake Waikaremoana. The massed white flowers are conspicuous in the forest canopy.

A tree up to 10 m or more tall, its trunk is up to 60 cm in diameter, smooth, becoming scaly when old. The leaves are mostly in whorls at the end of a season's growth, but leaves below these may be opposite or alternate. They are thick, dark green, 6–16 cm long x 1–4 cm wide and coarsely toothed.

The flowers are in groups at the centre of whorls of leaves. Each flower is 2–3.5 cm across with white petals. The capsules split open to reveal 5 shiny black seeds about 5 mm long, each partly enclosed by a fleshy red to orange aril. Flowering is from late spring to mid-summer with the capsules forming through summer to early autumn.

The genus has only one species and it is restricted to New Zealand.

Rhabdothamnus solandri
Gesneriaceae (Plate 13)

R. solandri is an undershrub in coastal and lowland forests throughout the North Island, although it is less common towards the south. It favours banks near streams, where its colourful gloxinia-like flowers catch the eye.

This much-branched shrub up to 2 m tall has leaves 1–3 cm long x 1–3 cm wide with stiff short surface hairs, making them sandpapery to the touch, and coarse marginal teeth.

The eye-catching flowers of *Rhabdothamnus solandri*.

The flowers are tubular, 2–2.5 cm long, yellow, orange to dark red. The capsule is 7–10 mm long containing many seeds. Flowering and fruiting occur through most of the year.

The family is widespread in the tropics and subtropics and includes a number of ornamentals such as *Gloxinia*. The genus has only one species, which is restricted to New Zealand.

WINEBERRY, MAKOMAKO (Plate 13)
Aristotelia serrata   **Elaeocarpaceae**

Wineberry is found throughout the country in lowland and mountain forests, often forming thickets in forest clearings where conditions are moist. It is semi-deciduous.

It is a tree up to 10 m tall with a trunk up to 30 cm

Left: Small but colourful flowers of wineberry. They start out pale in colour and gradually turn crimson.
Right: A wineberry tree with masses of small flowers before the new leaves appear in spring.

in diameter. The bark is smooth with corky stripes. The leaves are broad and thin, 5–12 cm long x 4–8 cm wide, with many narrow marginal teeth of varying lengths. At lower altitudes the stalks of the leaves are often red and the leaf undersides reddish.

The flowers are numerous and small but attractively coloured. When they first open they are white but change through pink to red. The berries are about 5 mm long, bright red to almost black. Flowering occurs through spring to early summer with berries from late spring to early summer.

Aristotelia is also present in South America and Australia.

Wineberry berries change through red to black when ripe.

PIGEONWOOD (Plate 13)
Hedycarya arborea   **Monimiaceae**

Pigeonwood is common in lowland and lower mountain forest throughout the country, except the eastern South Island south of Banks Peninsula.

A tree up to 12 m tall with a trunk up to 50 cm in diameter with smooth bark, its leaves are 5–12.5 cm long x 2–3 cm wide with small pointed teeth. The leaf stalk and midrib below are often reddish.

The flowers are greenish, very fragrant, 6–10 mm in diameter. The berries are bright orange, each attached to the tip of a stalk that is one of a radiating group resembling the spokes of a wheel. Flowering occurs through spring to early summer with berries forming from mid-spring through summer.

There is only one species of the genus in New Zealand; most of the others are in New Caledonia with a few elsewhere in Polynesia.

Fragrant male flowers of pigeonwood. Note the dark stems and reddish midribs of the leaves.

Bright orange berries of pigeonwood in groups attached to radiating stalks.

HEBES
Scrophulariaceae

Hebe is our largest genus with over 100 species. Most of these grow in open habitats but some are frequently encountered at forest margins in the lowlands and others, common in mountain shrublands, penetrate into more open forest near the treeline; a few grow on the forest floor.

The leaves are in opposite pairs, mostly smooth margined but sometimes toothed. The leaf buds are distinctive in being enclosed by a pair of immature leaves whose margins meet. When a bud becomes active the margins separate.

Horticulturally *Hebe* is our best-known genus in temperate gardens of the world. They are prized for the rounded form of many of the shrubs, the symmetry of the leaf arrangement and the colour of the foliage ranging from grey green to orange. The flowers are mostly white but a few are strongly coloured from mauve to magenta and they are much used in hybridising.

Hebe salicifolia with typical hanging inflorescences.

Hebe salicifolia

This is one of the willow-leaved species called koromiko. It is found in Stewart Island and throughout the South Island except the Marlborough Sounds. Its habitats are lowland to mid-altitude shrublands, streamsides and forest margins. *H. salicifolia* is also found at the southern tip of South America.

It is a shrub up to 5 m tall with pointed leaves 5–15 cm long x 1–2.5 cm wide, smooth margined or with a few small teeth. The margins of the pair of leaves enclosing the leaf bud separate near the base to form 2 openings known as sinuses.

The inflorescences are lateral and unbranched, their stems bearing many small white flowers with partly fused petals. The flowers are up to 8 mm wide. The capsules are up to 3.5 mm long. Flowering occurs in summer and autumn with capsules maturing through winter and spring.

There are 2 localised species in the North Island that are similar in appearance to *H. salicifolia*. **H. corriganii** differs in flower and capsule features. It grows in higher-altitude forest and shrubland on Mt Pirongia and the Kaimai Ranges to Mt Taranaki and the northern Ruahines. It is absent from Mt Ruapehu. **H. pubescens** is found in shrubland and open forest

on the Coromandel Peninsula. It is distinguished by its hairy twigs, leaf margins and flowers.

Hebe stricta

This species, very similar to *H. salicifolia,* with several varieties, is found throughout the North Island and in the Marlborough Sounds in the South Island. Habitats range from the coast to the treeline and sometimes beyond and include shrubland, cliffs and forest margins.

Two other species similar to *H. stricta* are localised in the North Island. **H. ligustrifolia** has leaves with orange midribs and ranges from North Cape to Whangarei in shrubland and at forest margins. **H. acutiflora** has orange-yellow midribs and grows near Kerikeri and in Puketi Forest nearby.

TREE HEBE
Hebe parviflora var. arborea

The several varieties of *H. parviflora* have shorter and narrower leaves than *H. salicifolia* and *H. stricta*. The var. *arborea,* as the name implies, becomes a small tree. It grows in lowland to mountain sites from near Whangarei in Northland to Marlborough in the South Island. It can be found in shrubland and at forest margins. On rocky hillside slopes the tree hebe sometimes grows *en masse* with its dense dome-like crowns providing an impressive sight.

It is a tall shrub to small tree up to 7.5 m tall, usually with several trunks. The leaves are 2.5–3.5 cm long x 4 mm wide with smooth margins.

The inflorescences are lateral and unbranched with small white flowers about 4 mm wide; the capsules are about 3 mm long. Flowering is mostly from late summer through autumn with the capsules maturing through autumn and winter.

Hebe canterburiensis

This species is found in tussock shrubland and higher-altitude beech forest in the southern North Island and the northern half of the South Island.

It is a spreading to erect shrub up to 1 m tall with leaves in 4 vertical rows but more or less flattened into one plane. The leaves are dark green and shiny above, smooth margined apart from short hairs, 7–17 mm long x 4–5 mm wide.

The flowers are in clusters, white, about 1 cm in diameter, with the petals fused into a spreading tube. The capsules are about 4 mm long. Flowering occurs during summer with the capsules maturing in late summer and autumn.

Flowering from late spring to mid-summer, **Hebe vernicosa** is very similar and also occurs in beech forest in Marlborough and eastern Nelson. It differs in not having hairs on the leaf margins and having longer flower clusters and smaller flowers.

Parahebe catarractae   Scrophulariaceae

Four subspecies of this small shrub are recognised but the overall distribution is Coromandel Peninsula and south of a line from Taranaki to East Cape in the North Island, and Marlborough, near Cape Farewell and Fiordland in the South Island. Its habitats are crevices in river banks and the flood zones of river cliffs from the lowlands to the treeline.

It is erect or prostrate, up to 50 cm tall. The leaves are opposite with toothed margins, varying greatly in size and shape from long and narrow to short and broad, mostly 7–40 mm long x 5–20 mm wide.

The inflorescences are lateral with attractive white, magenta or purple-striped saucer-shaped flowers 8–12 mm in diameter. The capsules are up to 4 mm x 4 mm. Flowering occurs from late spring to early autumn with capsules ripening through summer and autumn.

Hebe stricta.

Hebe canterburiensis.

Parahebe catarractae.

PUKATEA (Plate 13)
Laurelia novae-zelandiae
Atherospermataceae

This tree of wet places — swamp forests or along streams in better-drained places — is among the tallest of our flowering trees and can attain a height of 35 m. It is found at lower altitudes throughout the North Island, in the north of the South Island and down the west coast to Fiordland. The trunk is up to 2 m in diameter, often supported by thin plank buttresses spreading from its base. The bark is pale and smooth with corky spots. The twigs are green and 4-angled. The opposite dark green leaves, up to 8 cm long x 5 cm wide, are broadly rounded at the tip, attractively and evenly toothed, and very shiny above.

The male and female flowers are small and greenish. The green fruits are flask-shaped and at maturity release seeds that have parachutes of hairs for wind dispersal. Flowering is from mid-spring to early summer with fruits forming from spring to mid-summer.

Like a number of tropical trees growing in swampy places, pukatea, as well as having plank buttresses, also has breathing roots (pneumatophores), projecting above the swamp surface for

Foliage of pukatea.

PUKATEA vs HUTU

Pukatea and hutu foliage look very similar and people are often confused about which is which. Pukatea is completely green with 4-angled twigs. Hutu has dark purple twigs and black-tipped leaf teeth. The twigs have 2 pairs of ridges that extend into soft bristles.

Plank buttresses of a pukatea growing near a stream.

Breathing roots of pukatea.

Foliage of hutu.

as much as 1 m. These take in air for the waterlogged root system below.

There is another species of *Laurelia* in Chile.

HUTU (Plate 13)
Ascarina lucida   **Chloranthaceae**
This species occurs in lowland and lower mountain forest throughout the country, mostly locally, but it is common in the west of the South Island.

It is a shrub or small tree up to 6 m tall with a trunk up to 30 cm in diameter. The bark is smooth with corky spots. The opposite yellowish green leaves are 2–7 cm long x 1.5–3.5 cm wide, coarsely toothed.

The flowers are small and appear to consist of a single plump stamen. The berry is about 2.5 mm long and bluish. Flowering is through spring with berries from mid-spring to mid-summer.

Ascarina occurs from Polynesia to southeast Asia.

RIBBONWOODS & LACEBARKS
Malvaceae

Ribbonwoods and lacebarks are so named because their inner bark can be separated into thin lace-like layers. They can also be recognised by the star-shaped (stellate) hairs on their young and sometimes mature parts, which can be seen with a hand lens.

Ribbonwood leaves have persistent pairs of narrow stipules at the bases of their stalks while the hoherias do not, and it has abundant small greenish white flowers while those of the hoherias are 2–4 cm across and pure white.

Ribbonwood, often growing on frosty river flats, is regularly leafless in winter.

The small green flowers of ribbonwood are produced in great masses in spring.

The white flowers of lacebark are much larger than those of ribbonwood.

RIBBONWOOD (Plate 14)
Plagianthus regius

Found in lowland forest throughout the country, most abundantly on river terraces, this is one of the few species that are regularly leafless in winter.

It is a small tree up to 15 m tall with a trunk up to 1 m in diameter. The bark is rough. There is a distinct juvenile form with densely interlacing twigs and small leaves, 5–15 mm long x 3–10 mm wide. The alternate adult leaves are thin, 1–7.5 cm long x 5–50 mm wide and coarsely toothed. They turn pale yellow before they fall.

The flowers, in much-branched inflorescences, are 3–4 mm in diameter and greenish white. The yellowish fruits are small and dry, each containing a single seed. Flowering is from mid-spring to mid-summer and fruiting through summer to early autumn.

Ribbonwood hybridises with *P. divaricatus*, a small-leaved shrub of salt marshes.

Plagianthus is also found in Australia.

LACEBARK (Plate 14)
Hoheria populnea var. *populnea*

The lacebark is found in coastal and lowland forests in the North Island south to the Bay of Plenty.

It is a small tree up to 10 m or more tall with smooth bark. The young plants may be similar to the adults or interlacing and twiggy with leaves 1–3 cm long. The alternate adult leaves are 7–14 cm long x 4–6 cm wide and are coarsely toothed.

The flowers are about 2.5 cm in diameter and pure white with many stamens. The yellowish fruits are dry, strongly winged, with each containing a single seed. Flowering is in the autumn and fruiting from mid-autumn to mid-winter.

The genus is found only in New Zealand.

H. sexstylosa is now regarded by several botanists as a variety of *H. populnea* with a range mostly to the south of the latter. It is found in lowland and lower mountain forests from a little north of Auckland to the northwest South Island and Banks Peninsula.

There is always a twiggy interlaced juvenile with small leaves 1–1.5 cm long x 1–1.5 cm wide. The adult leaves are generally narrower than those of *H. populnea* var. *populnea*, 5–15 cm long x 2–5 cm wide, and the flowers and fruits are smaller. Flowering is in autumn; fruiting is from mid-autumn to early winter.

Hoheria angustifolia (Plate 14)

This smaller-leaved species is found in lowland and lower mountain forests from the middle of the North Island to the south of the South Island.

A small tree up to 10 m tall, it has a strongly marked juvenile phase with interlacing twigs and small leaves 4–8 mm long x 4–7 mm wide. The alternate adult leaves are 2–3 cm long x 5–10 mm wide with coarse pointed teeth.

The white flowers are less than 2 cm in diameter. The yellowish fruits are strongly winged. Flowering is from early summer to early autumn, fruiting from late summer to mid-autumn.

MOUNTAIN RIBBONWOOD (Plate 14)
Hoheria lyallii

This species occurs in mid-mountain to subalpine forest, often forming groves, throughout the South Island. There is also a widely separated occurrence on Mt Taranaki in the North Island. The relatively large pure white flowers are an attractive feature of this species. It stands apart from the other hoherias in being leafless in winter.

Eventually forming small trees up to 10 m tall, juvenile plants are not interlaced and twiggy but have smaller leaves than the adults, about 1–3 cm long x 1–3 cm wide. The alternate adult leaves are 5–14 cm long x 2–10 cm wide with mostly rounded teeth. They are densely to sparsely hairy, and turn yellow in the autumn.

The small-leaved *Hoheria angustifolia* with starry white flowers.

The flowers are 2–4 cm in diameter and pure white. The fruits are not winged or only slightly so. Flowering occurs through summer, fruiting from mid-summer to early autumn.

Mountain ribbonwood has the largest and most attractive flowers of the hoherias.

LANCEWOODS
Araliaceae

This is among the most remarkable of juvenile/adult contrasts in the New Zealand flora. The unbranched juvenile stage with its hanging tuft of long narrow leaves can persist for up to 20 years. There is then a change over to the much-branched adult state with many shorter, more or less erect leaves. What triggers the change is not known. Some suggest that it was a response to moa browsing, once the lancewood grew above moa reach the defences were not needed.

Lancewoods are conspicuous in forest regrowth and this has led to another suggestion: that the juvenile lancewood concentrates its efforts on attaining height to escape the shading of other species and only then changes to the adult state.

It is a curious fact that if sucker shoots develop at the base of the trunk of an adult lancewood, they have the juvenile form. Presumably the dormant buds that give rise to these shoots were formed when the tree was in its young phase and were 'programmed' to be juvenile.

The flowers of lancewoods are small and greenish yellow. Flowers and berries are in clusters at the tips of leafy twigs of the adults. The leaves are alternate.

Seedling lancewoods with mottled brown coloration making them difficult to see against the leaf litter.

A much-branched adult lancewood with short leaves (left) and a juvenile beginning to branch and change to the adult state (right).

LANCEWOOD (Plate 15)
Pseudopanax crassifolius

Lancewood is a commonly encountered species throughout the country in forest or regenerating forest mostly in the lowlands.

It is a small tree up to 15 m tall with a trunk up to 50 cm in diameter. The bark is smooth but with rope-like ridges in young trees. The very distinctive juveniles are unbranched with a cluster of strongly deflexed leaves at the top of a slender trunk. The juvenile leaves are remarkably long and narrow, up to 1 m long and only about 1 cm wide. The marginal teeth are sharply pointed and sometimes have attractive brown mottling on their upper sides. The adult stage is much branched and round headed with upwardly angled leaves. Adult leaves are green, much shorter and broader than the juveniles, 10–20 cm long x 2–3 cm wide, with teeth along the outer two-thirds or sometimes smooth margined.

The berries are purplish and 4–5 mm in diameter. Flowering and fruiting occur from mid-summer to mid-autumn.

Pseudopanax ferox (Plate 15)

This species is very similar to lancewood in its juvenile and adult habit, differing chiefly in the form of its juvenile leaves, which are more coarsely toothed, and in having larger berries. It is also similar in its range and habitats but is much more localised.

A shrub to small tree up to 5 m tall, its deflexed juvenile leaves are up to about 50 cm long x 7–15 mm wide with large jagged hooked lobes along the margins, interspersed with pointed teeth. The lobes often have attractive yellow mottling above. The adult leaves are similar to those of lancewood.

The berries are bluish grey and 8–9 mm in diameter. Flowering and fruiting occur from mid-summer to mid-autumn.

Pseudopanax linearis (Plate 15)

This species is very similar to lancewood but differs in its smaller stature and much less distinctive juvenile form. It is found in forest and shrubland near the treeline in the South Island, mostly along the western side.

It forms a shrub up to 3 m tall with a few spreading branches. The juvenile leaves are directed upwards, 15–25 cm long x 5–10 mm wide with small teeth; adult leaves are 5–10 cm long x 7–10 mm wide with teeth towards the ends.

Berries are purplish and about 4 mm in diameter. Flowers and fruits occur from mid- to late summer.

Pseudopanax ferox: juveniles (left) and young adult (right).

The tips of 3 juvenile leaves of *Pseudopanax ferox*.

Alseuosmias have tufts of reddish brown hairs in the angle between the leaf stalk and the stem.

Alseuosmia macrophylla (Plate 16)   Alseuosmiaceae

The alseuosmias are notable for the strong and pleasant perfume of the flowers. The name of the genus translates as 'perfume of the grove'.

A. macrophylla is an undershrub in forests south to Taranaki and Tongariro National Park in the North Island, reappearing again in the north of the South Island.

It is a much-branched shrub up to 2 m tall. The alternate leaves are dark green, 5–15 cm long x 2–6 cm wide. The margins have large but spaced teeth or lobes or are sometimes smooth.

The flowers are 3.5–4 cm long, tubular, crimson, with a strong and pleasant perfume. The berries are 8–10 mm long and crimson. Flowering is from late winter to early summer with berries from late spring to mid-autumn.

The genus is restricted to New Zealand.

Alseuosmia pusilla (Plate 16)

A. pusilla is an undershrub in forests from near Auckland to the middle of the South Island, mostly in the west.

It is a mostly unbranched shrub up to 50 cm tall. The alternate leaves are pale green and often blotched with red above, 5–8 cm long x 2–3.5 cm wide. The margins have a few small teeth or are sometimes smooth.

The flowers are 8–10 mm long, tubular, yellowish to reddish. The berries are 9–12 mm long, bright waxy red. Flowering is from late spring to early autumn with berries from mid-summer to autumn.

The foliage of this species looks very like that of mountain horopito (*Pseudowintera colorata,* page 141) and young plants are difficult to

Dark red tubular flowers of *Alseuosmia macrophylla.*

tell apart. However, leaves of *A. pusilla* are pale green below, not white, it often has small marginal teeth and the leaves are not peppery to the taste. Also the berries are elongate, not rounded, and look like bright red wax.

Alseuosmia banksii (Plate 16)

A. banksii is restricted to lowland forests in Northland.

It is a sparingly branched small shrub up to 1 m tall. The leaves are mostly 1.5–3 cm long x 1–3 cm wide but sometimes larger, often flecked with red and coarsely toothed or lobed at the margins.

The petals of the strongly perfumed flowers are fused into a yellow to red tube up to 12 mm long with spreading lobes. The berry is red and 4–7 mm in diameter. Flowering and fruiting times are uncertain as flowers have been found at most times of the year.

A. banksii seems to be a very variable species with leaves ranging in size from about 1 cm long and wide to several centimetres long. There is a form with bubbly leaves that look remarkably like those of the unrelated ramarama (page 102). The situation in Northland is further complicated by probable hybrids with *A. macrophylla*.

Alseuosmia pusilla with waxy red berries.

Left: Mountain horopito and *Alseuosmia pusilla* growing together and looking much alike. The turned-over white leaf is of the former. Right: The small-leaved *Alseuosmia banksii* with berries.

Quintinia serrata (Plate 17)   **Escalloniaceae**
Quintinia is found in lowland to mountain forests in the northern North Island as far south as Taranaki and in the northwest of the South Island.

It forms a small tree up to 12 m tall with a trunk up to 50 cm in diameter with smooth bark. The alternate leaves are 2–16 cm long x 1–5 cm wide, often with strongly undulate margins and rather widely spaced pointed teeth, which may be small or even absent on some leaves. The leaves are often attractively mottled with yellow, brown or red tints.

It has young parts that look as if they have been varnished and may be sticky to the touch when moist. They are covered with rounded scales which can be seen with a hand lens.

The yellowish flowers are small with the petals strongly bent back. The fruits are dry brown capsules that split open to release the seeds. Flowering is in mid- to late spring and fruiting from early to mid-summer.

Other species of *Quintinia* are found in Australia and New Guinea.

NGAIO (Plate 17)
Myoporum laetum   **Myoporaceae**
Ngaio is a very familiar salt-tolerant species found mostly in coastal, but also in lowland, forests throughout the country; it is uncommon in the far south. It is easily identified by the oil glands that are strikingly visible when a leaf is held to the light. These oil glands are poisonous.

It is a small tree up to 10 m tall with a trunk 30 cm or more in diameter with rough and furrowed bark. The alternate leaves are rather fleshy with prominent oil glands, 4–10 cm long x 2–3 cm wide, with small teeth along the outer halves.

The flowers are white spotted with purple and occur from mid-spring to mid-summer. The berries ripen through summer and autumn. Berries are red purple, 6–9 mm long.

The genus is mainly Australian with a few species in New Zealand and east Asia.

MILK TREE (Plate 18)
Streblus banksii   **Moraceae**
S. banksii derives its common name from the fact that it exudes milky juice when a twig is broken. It is also distinctive because when a leaf is held to the light the complete fine vein network can be clearly seen.

It is found in coastal and lowland forests throughout the North Island and in Marlborough

Sounds in the South Island.

It is a small tree up to 12 m tall with a trunk up to 60 cm in diameter. The bark is smooth with corky spots. The leaves of juvenile plants are 2–6 cm long x 1–3 cm wide and are often deeply lobed. The alternate adult leaves are 3.5–8.5 cm long x 2–3.5 cm wide with a prominent vein network and margins with many rounded teeth.

The greenish yellow flowers are very small in catkins and are wind pollinated. The berry is globose, red and about 6 mm in diameter. Flowering is from late winter to mid-spring with berries from late spring through summer.

Streblus is also found in Madagascar, south Asia, Indonesia and Australia.

PUTAPUTAWETA, MARBLE LEAF (Plate 18)

Carpodetus serratus   Escalloniaceae

Putaputaweta is found throughout the country in coastal to mountain forests.

A tree up to 10 m tall with a trunk up to 20 cm or more in diameter, its bark has many corky spots. The juvenile form has zig-zag branchlets, often attractively arranged in tiers on the main stem. The juvenile leaves are small, 1–3 cm long x 1–2 cm wide. The alternate adult leaves are 4–6 cm long x 2–3 cm wide, often mottled green and yellow green, with small but prominent pointed teeth. There are domatia on the undersides.

The flowers are 5–6 mm wide, star-like and pure white. The berries are black, more or less globose with a ridge around the middle, 4–6 mm in diameter. Flowering is from late spring to early autumn with ripe berries from mid-summer to mid-autumn.

There are several species of *Carpodetus* in New Guinea.

Opposite, above: Small flowers of *Quintinia serrata*.

Opposite, centre: Yellow-green wavy-margined foliage of *Quintinia serrata*.

Opposite, below: Ngaio with red-speckled flowers and leaves with prominent oil glands.

Left, above: Milk tree with berries. Note the corky spots on the twigs.

Left, centre: A young plant of putaputaweta showing the branches arranged in 2 tiers.

Left, below: Starry white flowers and foliage of putaputaweta. The mottled appearance of the leaves gave rise to the name marble leaf.

Hinau flowers with their distinctively incised petals.

HINAU (Plate 16)
Elaeocarpus dentatus   Elaeocarpaceae

Hinau grows as a canopy component in lowland forest throughout both islands.

It is a tree up to 20 m or more tall with a trunk up to 1 m in diameter. The bark is rather rough with narrow longitudinal fissures. The alternate leaves are 5–12 cm long x 2–3 cm wide, often with the 2 sides strongly rolled under. The teeth are blunt and sometimes very reduced, and the undersides have a satiny covering of hairs. At the angles of the secondary veins and midrib on the undersides there are prominent pouch-like domatia. The juvenile leaves can be up to 20 cm long by 1.5 cm wide, widest near the tip. They do not have domatia.

The flowers are white with petals with deep longitudinal incisions. The berry is purple black, 1.2–1.8 cm long x 9 mm wide. Flowering is from mid-spring through summer with fruits ripening from mid-summer to late autumn.

Elaeocarpus is widespread in the tropics.

POKAKA (Plate 18)
Elaeocarpus hookerianus

Pokaka is found throughout the country including Stewart Island, mostly at higher altitudes than hinau. It differs from hinau most notably in its juvenile form but also in its smaller stature and smaller parts generally.

It is a tree up to about 12 m tall with a trunk up to 1 m in diameter. Like hinau, the bark is rough with narrow longitudinal fissures. The alternate leaves are 3–11 cm long x 1–3 cm wide, more or less flat, hairless below and with rounded to pointed teeth. Domatia are infrequent. The juvenile of pokaka is remarkably different. It is densely twiggy with very small leaves of many different shapes, from round to elongate and variously toothed and incised. The leaves are generally of several shades of brown.

The flowers and fruits are similar to those of hinau but smaller. Flowering is from mid-spring to mid-summer with fruits ripening from late spring to autumn.

HINAU vs REWAREWA

The juveniles of hinau and rewarewa are 'look alikes' and often grow together. The juvenile leaves of rewarewa are stiff, coarsely toothed and even in width; those of hinau are flexible with large to small teeth and are widest towards the tip.

Pokaka flowers, similar to but smaller than hinau.

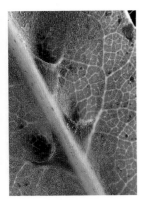

Left: Pouch-like domatia on the underside of a hinau leaf. Right: Abundant flowers among hinau foliage.

REWAREWA (Plate 16)
Knightia excelsa   **Proteaceae**

Rewarewa is found throughout the North Island and in the northeast tip of the South Island, mostly in lowland forests. It can be conspicuous with its columnar shape as an emergent in regenerating forests.

It forms a tree up to 30 m tall with a trunk up to 1 m or more in diameter. The bark is smooth. The alternate leaves are thick and stiff with coarse pointed teeth, 10–15 cm long x 2.5–4 cm wide. Juvenile leaves are up to 30 cm long x 1 cm wide and even in width.

The flowers are in dense clusters, each with 4 red furry petals that coil into tight spirals. The fruit is dry and somewhat woody and the seeds are winged for wind dispersal. Flowering is from spring to early summer but the seeds are not released until a year later. The flowers are visited by tuis and bellbirds for their nectar. *Knightia,* restricted to New Zealand, has one species.

Rewarewa with conspicuous red flowers.

The flowers have long styles and coiled-up petals.

KAIKOMAKO (Plate 18)

Pennantia corymbosa   Icacinaceae

Kaikomako is found throughout the country in lowland forest.

A tree up to 10 m tall with a trunk up to 50 cm in diameter, its bark is smooth. The juvenile stage has densely interlaced twigs and small leaves, 7–15 mm long x 5–10 mm wide, each with 3–5 rounded teeth around the outer half of the margin. The adult branches are stouter and not interlaced. The alternate adult leaves are 2–5 cm long x 2–4 cm wide with large rounded teeth.

The flowers are small, white and wind pollinated. The berries are black, 8–9 mm long. Flowering is from late spring through summer with berries from mid-summer through autumn.

Other species of *Pennantia* are found in eastern Australia and Norfolk Island.

A second New Zealand species, **Pennantia baylisiana**, was described in 1948 based on a single female tree on the Three Kings Islands. No other plants have been found. It looks quite unlike kaikomako with its large leathery smooth-margined leaves. However, in one case with a tree grown from a cutting, this species has hybridised with kaikomako, producing hybrids of intermediate form.

A small kaikomako with the twiggy juvenile state (below) and the larger-leaved adult state (above).

KOTUKUTUKU, TREE FUCHSIA (Plate 17)

Fuchsia excorticata   Onagraceae

The tree fuchsia is one of our few deciduous species and may be the world's tallest *Fuchsia*. Found throughout the country including the Auckland Islands, mostly in moist lowland and mid-mountain forests, it is often prominent in regenerating forests.

It forms a small tree up to about 12 m tall with a trunk up 60 cm or more in diameter. The bark is very distinctive, being orange brown and separating in narrow papery strips. The alternate leaves are thin, 3–10 cm long x 1.5–3 cm wide, often with minute widely spaced teeth along the margins. The undersides are whitish.

The flowers are 2–3 cm long, green and purple when young, changing to red after pollination. The flowers are mostly borne on the twigs among the

Left: Kaikomako showing adult leaves and male flowers. Right: A female kaikomako with some black seeds remaining. Occasional individuals have brightly coloured stalks as here.

Trunk of a tree fuchsia with bright brown peeling bark.

Tree fuchsia flowers arising from the trunk. The red flower is the oldest.

leaves, but also on larger branches and even the trunk. The berry is about 1 cm long, dark purple to black. Flowering is from late winter to early summer with the berries ripening through spring and summer. The berries are edible and known as konini.

The genus *Fuchsia* is strongly represented in South and Central America. The only species elsewhere are 3 in New Zealand and one in Tahiti.

Melicytus macrophyllus (Plate 17)   **Violaceae**
This species is found in lowland forest south to the Bay of Plenty.

A shrub to small tree up to 6 m tall, it has a trunk up to 40 cm in diameter. The bark is smooth with corky spots. The alternate leaves are thick, 7–15 cm long x 4–6 cm wide, with many marginal teeth.

The greenish flowers are 6–7 mm in diameter, in clusters, mostly on twigs among the leaves. The berries are white, sometimes flecked with purple, 5–7 mm long. Flowering is in spring with berries from spring to early summer.

MAHOE, WHITEYWOOD (Plate 17)
Melicytus ramiflorus   **Violaceae**
Mahoe is found throughout the country in lowland to lower mountain forest.

Melicytus macrophyllus.

Mahoe with small male flowers on woody twigs.

A female mahoe with intensely blue-purple berries.

It is a tree up to 10 m or more tall with a trunk up to 60 cm or more in diameter. The bark is smooth. The alternate leaves are 5–15 cm long x 3–5 cm wide, fairly thin with many small marginal teeth.

The yellowish flowers are 3–4 mm in diameter, in clusters, mostly on woody twigs below the leaves. They have a strong pleasant perfume. The striking berries are bright to dark violet blue, 4–5 mm long. Flowering is from late spring through summer with berries through summer and autumn.

In some places this species hybridises with the smaller-leaved *M. micranthus* (page 157).

MOUNTAIN MAHOE (Plate 17)
Melicytus lanceolatus
Mountain mahoe occurs in forests throughout the country, mostly at middle altitudes.

A shrub to small tree up to 5 m tall, sometimes more, its alternate leaves are 5–16 cm long x 5–30 mm wide, the margins having many small teeth thickened at the tips.

The flowers are purplish. Berries are dark purple, 4–6 mm long. Flowering is from early winter to early summer. The berries ripen from mid-winter to late summer.

The genus *Melicytus* also occurs in eastern Australia and the Norfolk, Tonga and Fiji Islands.

Narrow-leaved mountain mahoe.

THE NATIVE BEECHES
Nothofagaceae

The southern beeches (*Nothofagus* spp.) comprise 4 species, one with 2 varieties. They tend to dominate forests where conditions are too cold and/or infertile for many other native trees. Hard beech and black beech are known as the lowland beeches and they often occupy the thin soils of ridge crests in regions where lowland conifer-broadleaf forest predominates. The montane beeches — red, silver and mountain — grow at colder altitudes and latitudes.

Black and mountain beech have smooth-margined leaves less than 2 cm long, oblong in black beech and narrowing from the base in mountain. Silver beech has toothed almost round leaves less than 2 cm long. Red and hard beech have toothed leaves more than 2 cm long, with a few hair-fringed domatia below in the former but not in the latter.

Beech trunks are smooth when young but become rough and shaggy at maturity.

The leaves are alternate and the buds are scaly. The flowers are small and wind pollinated. The petals are pale yellow to green. In black and mountain beech the pollen-producing stamens are bright red, those of red beech are pale red and of silver and hard beech, yellowish brown.

The fruits are dry with 3–4 valves, and the seeds have narrow wings and can be carried by the wind for moderate distances. The native beeches flower abundantly throughout the country every few years, generally in unison.

The genus *Nothofagus* is also found in southern South America, Australia and at higher altitudes in New Caledonia and New Guinea. It is now considered to comprise its own family, Nothofagaceae, related to the Northern Hemisphere beeches and birches.

High-altitude silver beech forest with mosses and lichens on rocks and trunks and the small shrub *Podocarpus acutifolius* on the forest floor.

Hard beech forest with a large buttressed trunk and deep leaf litter on the floor.

Red male flowers of hard beech and leafy shoots sprouting from scaly buds.

A broad-crowned red beech.

Crowns of silver beech.

Black beech growing in the open.

Mountain beech with reddish new growth.

Mountain beech showing attractively layered foliage.

HARD BEECH (Plate 19)
Nothofagus truncata

Hard beech is found at low altitudes throughout the North Island and in the north of the South Island, with an isolated occurrence in south Westland.

It forms a tree up to 30 m tall with a trunk up to 2 m or more in diameter. The leaves are 2.5–3.5 cm long x 2 cm wide with 8–12 teeth along each side.

Flowering is from spring to summer with seed released in summer and autumn.

The wood of hard beech has a high silica content, making it hard and difficult to saw.

RED BEECH (Plate 19)
Nothofagus fusca

This species is found from about Auckland southwards, mostly in mountain forests although not reaching the treeline, descending to the lowlands in the far south of the South Island.

It is a tree up 30 m tall with a trunk up to 2 m or more in diameter, often strongly buttressed at the base. The leaves are 2–4 cm long x 1.5–2.5 cm wide with 6–8 teeth on the outer portion of each side. The notches between the teeth are strongly rounded. On the undersides, where the lower secondary veins meet the midrib, there are conspicuous domatia fringed with hairs.

Flowering occurs from spring to summer with seed released in summer and autumn.

The wood of red beech is dark red when fresh.

SILVER BEECH (Plate 19)
Nothofagus menziesii

Silver beech was probably so named because the bark is whitish, particularly in younger specimens. It is found from near Auckland southwards, mostly in mountain forests and reaching the treeline on some wetter mountains.

It is a tree up 30 m tall with a trunk up to 2 m in diameter. The leaves are small, thick and almost round, 6–15 mm long x 5–15 mm wide, with rounded teeth that are usually in pairs. There are a few hair-fringed domatia on the leaf undersides. This species alone has glandular hairs on the seed capsules.

Flowering is from late spring to mid-summer with seeds maturing from mid-summer to autumn.

Silver beech stands apart from the other species in 2 respects. The others hybridise in nature but silver beech is never involved and it is also the only species to host the strawberry fungus *Cyttaria*. Relatives of silver beech in Tasmania and South America also host species of *Cyttaria*.

STRAWBERRY FUNGUS

Cyttaria gunnii is a fungal parasite of silver beech. The round 'fruiting bodies' with their dimples appear in the spring and release their spores. Sometimes the water supply to a branch is blocked off by the parasite and the branch dies.

BLACK BEECH (Plate 19)
Nothofagus solandri **var.** *solandri*

The trunk of black beech is often black in colour, due mostly to the growth of a sooty mould (see page 246). Black beech ranges from south of Auckland, mostly in the lowlands, to the middle South Island.

It is a tree up to 25 m tall with a trunk up to 1 m or more in diameter. The leaves are small, oblong, smooth margined, whitish beneath, 10–15 mm long x 5–10 mm wide. Juvenile plants are densely twiggy with very small leaves, 5–7 mm long x 4–5 mm wide.

Flowering is from early spring to early summer and the seeds are released from late spring to autumn.

MOUNTAIN BEECH (Plate 19)
Nothofagus solandri **var.** *cliffortioides*

Mountain beech extends from south of Auckland, mostly in mountain forests, to the south of the South Island, where it descends to sea level. It often extends to the treeline, particularly on drier mountains.

It is a tree up to 15 m tall with a trunk up to 1 m in diameter. The leaves are small, ovate, smooth margined, whitish beneath, 10–15 mm long x 7–10 mm wide. Juvenile plants have smaller leaves, 4–7 mm long x 4–5 mm wide.

It flowers from late spring to mid-summer and releases seeds from late summer to autumn.

BEECH FOREST

Native beech forest contrasts strongly with conifer-broadleaf forests. It has fewer species with a canopy formed by one or more of the beeches. Particularly on drier sites with thin soils there may be few plants below the canopy and one can walk freely through the forest on a deep carpet of fallen beech leaves. There are no small subcanopy trees, but there are scattered small-leaved shrubs, mostly coprosmas and mingimingis, as well as beech saplings in canopy gaps.

On the forest floor, where it is not too deeply buried under leaf litter, there are often spreading cushions of the milk moss, *Leucobryum candidum* (page 239). Seasonally a range of orchids make an appearance along with often brightly coloured fungi. Specialised vines and epiphytes are rare or absent, although brightly coloured mistletoes sometimes provide splashes of red or yellow among the dark beech foliage.

Where the climate is wetter, at altitude or in the west, there are more subcanopy plants: small trees that are shared with conifer-broadleaf forest, such as kamahi, broadleaf and stinkwood; on the forest floor, tufts of astelias, and in the northern South Island, thickets of the small totara relative *Podocarpus acutifolius*. There is also an abundance of lichens, mosses, liverworts and small filmy ferns on exposed tree roots, rotting logs, rocks and the trunks and branches of the trees.

Conifer-broadleaf forest predominates in the North Island, while beech forest predominates in the South Island.

Along the axial ranges and adjacent central volcanoes in the North Island, conifer-broadleaf forest is replaced by beech forest at higher altitudes. The beech species are red, silver and mountain. Red beech is the largest of the three and grows on moist, more fertile sites. Silver and mountain beech can tolerate poorer soils and generally grow at higher altitudes than red beech. Mountain beech is also quite drought tolerant and is often the only species in drier eastern mountains of the South Island.

Beech forest is absent from some places where it might be expected, notably Mt Taranaki, the central west coast of the South Island and Stewart Island. The beeches with their dry seeds are considered to spread only slowly and, as fossil evidence shows that beech forest has only been expanding during the last few thousand years of the 14.000 or so years since the last glacial, perhaps it has yet to reach these places.

Left: Mountain beech draped with a lichen. Young plants of *Dracophyllum traversii* are in the foreground. Right: Cushions of pale milk moss growing in beech litter.

TREE DAISIES
Asteraceae

The 12 species in this group belong to the daisy family and are often referred to as 'tree daisies', a strange concept to those from the northern hemisphere where daisies are not woody. Their leaves are alternate and their white to rust-coloured undersides are due to a dense layer of hairs which can be seen with a magnifying glass. The trunks have bark that peels away in long thin strips and their buds do not have scales.

The tree daisies belong to the large and widespread family Asteraceae. In this family what are considered to be flowers are in fact groups of small flowers (florets) mimicking a single flower. If the centre of such a 'flower' is closely examined, the florets, each with 5 petals, can be seen. In most cases the outermost florets have the petals fused into a strap-like form that appears to be a single petal. The term flower is used here for this family in the popular sense. The seeds in most of the Asteraceae have parachutes of hairs for wind dispersal.

The handsome large-flowered *Olearia chathamica*, very similar to *O. oporina* of Foveaux Strait.

Olearia lacunosa (Plate 20)

This is a handsome species found from the Tararua Range in the southern North Island southwards, mostly in forests near the treeline.

A shrub to small tree up to 5 m tall, its leaves are particularly long and narrow, 6.5–16 cm long x 0. 8–2.5 cm wide. The margins have small teeth and are strongly rolled towards the undersides. The midrib and secondary veins are strongly raised below. The hairs on the underside are rusty in colour.

Flowers are about 1 cm wide with long white petals. Flowering is from late spring through summer with seeds maturing from mid- to late summer.

The genus *Olearia* has most of its species in Australia and New Zealand with a few in New Guinea.

Olearia ilicifolia (Plate 20)

This species is found from the central North Island southwards, often in forests near the treeline.

It is a shrub to small tree up to 5 m tall. The leaves are 5–10 cm long x 1–2 cm wide with undulate margins with prominent, almost spiny teeth, hence the name *ilicifolia*, which means 'holly-leaved'. The covering of hairs below is buff to light brown.

The flowers are about 1 cm wide with long white petals. Flowering occurs from late spring to mid-summer with the seeds dispersing through summer.

Olearia oporina

This handsome species is found in low coastal forest in Fiordland, along both sides of Foveaux Strait.

It is a shrub or small tree up to 6 m tall. The leaves are 7–15 cm long x 1–2 cm wide; the margins have many small but prominent blunt teeth. The covering of hairs below is white to buff.

Unlike the other species of *Olearia* considered here, this species has large flowers, 3–5 cm in diameter, with white petals and yellow to purple centres. Flowering occurs from spring to mid-summer with the seeds dispersing through the summer.

RANGIORA (Plate 20)
Brachyglottis repanda

With its distinctive large thin leaves with very white undersides, rangiora has the largest leaves of all the tree daisies. It is common and well known in lowland forests throughout the North Island and in the northern South Island.

A small tree of *Olearia lacunosa* with narrow leaves and pale brown papery bark.

Masses of small rangiora flowers.

Olearia ilicifolia with flowers and holly-like leaves.

Olearia arborescens with dark-centred flowers.

Heketara flowering in regenerating forest.

Heketara in flower.

Olearia paniculata with seed heads.

Olearia albida with only a few petals.

Brachyglottis rotundifolia with no petals.

Olearia cheesemanii.

It is a shrub to small tree up to 6 m tall. The leaves are large and broad, 5–25 cm long x 5–20 cm wide; the margins have a few large pointed to rounded teeth. The hairy covering below is smooth and white.

The flowers are small and without discernible petals. Flowering is from late winter to mid-spring with seeds dispersing from late spring through summer.

Brachyglottis species are also found in Australia.

HEKETARA (Plate 20)
Olearia rani
Heketara is found in lowland forest throughout the North Island and in the north of the South Island. Its leaves are similar to rangiora but smaller.

A shrub to small tree up to 7 m tall, its leaves are 5–15 cm long x 5–6 cm wide with many pointed teeth along the margins. The veins are strongly raised below and the hairy covering is whitish.

The flowers are about 1 cm wide with many long white petals. Flowering is from late winter to late spring with seeds dispersing through the summer.

Olearia arborescens (Plate 20)
This species is found in forest and shrubland, often near the treeline, from the central North Island southwards.

A shrub or small tree up to 4 m tall, its leaves are 2–6 cm long x 2–4 cm wide, the margins having a number of pointed teeth that are sometimes only slightly developed. The hairy covering below is smooth and buff coloured.

The flowers are about 1.5 cm wide with long white petals. Flowering is from mid-spring to mid-summer with the seeds dispersing through summer and into autumn.

AKIRAHO (Plate 20)
Olearia paniculata
Akiraho is a mostly coastal and lowland species that occurs at forest margins and in shrubland from a little south of Auckland to the central South Island.

It is a shrub to small tree up to 6 m tall. The leaves are 3–7.5 cm long x 2–4 cm wide, yellowish green. The margins are smooth and usually strongly undulate. The hairy covering below is white to buff.

The flowers are small without discernible petals. The flowering and fruiting times contrast with those of the other species with the exception of *O. albida*. Flowering is through autumn with the seeds dispersing from mid-autumn to mid-winter.

Olearia albida (Plate 20)
This species is found in coastal forest from the Bay of Plenty northwards.

It is a shrub to small tree up to 5 m tall. The leaves are 7–10 cm long x 2.5–3.5 cm wide, greyish green, often moderately undulate. The hairy covering below is white to buff.

The flowers are about 1 cm wide with a few long white petals. Flowering is from mid-summer through autumn with seeds dispersing from early autumn to early winter.

Brachylottis rotundifolia (Plate 20)
(syn. *B. eleagnifolia*)
This species occurs mostly in forest and shrubland near the treeline from south of Auckland to the south of the North Island. There is a broad-leaved form in coastal forest and shrubland in the southwest South Island and Stewart Island that was formerly known as *Senecio reinoldii*.

A shrub to small tree up to 6 m tall, its leaves are 4–10 cm long x 3–9 cm wide, leathery, smooth margined and not undulate. The hairy covering below is pale tan.

The flowers are up to 1 cm wide but are without petals. They occur through summer with the seeds forming soon afterwards.

AKEPIRO
Olearia furfuracea
This species grows in shrubland and along streamsides and forest margins from North Cape to Wanganui and Hawkes Bay.

It is a shrub to small tree up to 5 m tall. The broad leaves are 5–9 cm long x 3–6 cm wide, usually with toothed and undulate margins.

The small flowers have 2–5 white petals. Flowering is from mid-spring to mid-summer with seeds maturing through summer.

Olearia avicenniaefolia (Plate 20)
This species is widespread from the lowlands to the mountains throughout the South Island and in Stewart Island. It is mostly found in open habitats, including shrubland, but also along forest margins.

It is a shrub or small tree up to 6 m tall. The leaves are 5–10 cm long x 3–5 cm wide with smooth margins. The inflorescences have long, sometimes drooping stalks. The flowers are small with few or no petals. Flowering is from late spring through summer and the seeds disperse through summer into autumn.

Olearia avicenniaefolia.

Olearia cheesemanii

The shrubby *O. cheesemanii* usually grows on lowland rocky river banks in forest from the Coromandel Peninsula in the North Island to the Buller River in the northwest South Island. The abundant many-petalled flowers provide a showy sight.

A much-branched shrub up to about 2 m tall, its leaves are 5–9 cm long x 2–3 cm wide with smooth but often undulate margins.

The many-flowered inflorescences have long stalks. The flowers are about 1.5 cm in diameter with many white petals. Flowering is from late winter to mid-summer with ripe seeds through summer and autumn into early winter.

Olearia furfuracea.

TORU (Plate 21)

Toronia toru   **Proteaceae**

Toru is found in lowland to mountain forest and shrubland south to the Bay of Plenty.

A tree up to 10 m or more tall, its trunk is up to 20 cm or more in diameter. The bark is smooth with corky spots. The alternate leaves are long and narrow, 16–20 cm long x 8–15 mm wide. Young leaves and twigs have reddish brown hairs.

The flowers are fragrant, 1–1.8 cm in diameter with 4 yellow petals. The berries are 1.2–1.8 cm long, white to reddish. Flowering and fruiting occur from mid-spring through summer.

The genus has only this species, which is restricted to New Zealand.

Mida salicifolia (Plate 21)   **Santalaceae**

This species has 2 varieties, both of which can be found in lowland to lower mountain forest locally throughout the North Island, but they are more common in the north.

It is a tree up to 6 m tall with a trunk up to 20 cm in diameter. The bark is rough and fissured. This tree is parasitic on the roots of other trees, a distinctive but not readily observable feature. In **var. salicifolia** the alternate leaves are 5–10 cm long x 3–10 mm wide and in **var. myrtifolia** they are 5–8 cm long x 2–3 cm wide.

The flowers are small and greenish. The berries are 7–12 mm long and bright red. Flowering occurs through spring with berries from mid-spring to autumn.

Mida has an unusual distribution: one species in New Zealand and another in the Juan Fernandez Islands in the eastern Pacific near South America. Sandalwood, from which a perfume is obtained, belongs to this family.

MAIREHAU (Plate 21)

Phebalium nudum   **Rutaceae**

Mairehau occurs in forests through Northland to a little south of Auckland.

A much-branched shrub up to 3 m tall, its alternate aromatic leaves are 2.5–4.5 cm long x 5–10 mm wide, dotted with oil glands.

The flowers are 8–10 mm in diameter, white and fragrant. The capsule separates into several valves, each releasing a single black seed. Flowering is from mid-spring to early summer, fruiting from late spring to mid-summer.

The genus has only this species in New Zealand and a number of others in Australia.

Toru with long narrow leaves and orange-yellow flowers.

Broader-leaved form of *Mida salicifolia* with berries.

TORO (Plate 21)

Myrsine salicina   **Myrsinaceae**

Toro occurs in coastal to lower mountain forest throughout the North Island and in the northwest of the South Island.

It is a tree up to 8 m tall with a trunk up to 60 cm in diameter. The bark is a little rough. The alternate leaves are 7–18 cm long x 2–3 cm wide. The veins are obscure, but oil tubes are visible below as longitudinal streaks.

The flowers are small and pink, borne on the woody twigs mostly below the leaves. The berries are 8–9 mm long, red. Flowering is from late winter to early summer with berries from spring to autumn.

The genus is widespread in the tropics and subtropics.

KOROKIA

Corokia buddleioides   **Escalloniaceae**

Korokia is found in coastal and lowland forest and forest margins through Northland to Rotorua.

It is a much-branched shrub up to 3 m tall, with leaves alternate, smooth margined and densely covered with white hairs below, 5–15 cm long x 1–3 cm wide.

The inflorescences are terminal and lateral with starry bright yellow flowers about 1 cm in diameter. The berries are dark red to black, 6–7 mm long. Flowering is from mid-spring to early summer with the berries ripe through summer to mid-autumn.

The shrub *Phebalium nudum* in flower.

Corokia buddleioides with yellow starry flowers.

Toro with pale curled first leaves of new growth.

MANGROVE, MANAWA (Plate 22)

Avicennia marina   Avicenniaceae

Manawa is found in tidal creeks and estuaries south to Kawhia and the Bay of Plenty.

It is a shrub or small tree up to 8 m tall with a trunk up to 30 cm in diameter. The bark is grey and furrowed. The alternate leaves are thick and smooth margined, 5–10 cm long x 2–4 cm wide and densely hairy below. The roots are widely spreading in the mud of the sea floor and give rise to numerous erect peg-like pneumatophores (breathing roots) that take in air at low tide.

The flowers are 6–7 mm in diameter and yellowish. The capsule is about 2 cm in diameter. It flowers from late summer to mid-autumn and the capsules are mature about a year later. The capsules each contain a single seed, which germinates while still on the tree and is able to establish itself rapidly when it drops.

Avicennia is widespread in the tropics with *A. marina* occurring elsewhere in the Pacific.

MANGROVE FOREST

Some might say 'What mangrove forest?' as near Auckland and elsewhere the mangroves are mere shrubs, often quite widely spaced. But at more favourable sites at the heads of estuaries and along tidal creeks one can walk on boardwalks under a closed canopy of small mangrove trees up to 8 m in height.

In the tropics mangrove forests are generally taller than this and comprise a number of different species. We have just one species.

At low tide the breathing roots are submerged, often along with the trunks and lower branches of the trees.

The capsules developing from the small yellowish flowers each contain a single large seed, which begins to germinate while still on the tree. When the seedling falls into the sea it floats around for a while and if it is stranded in a suitably muddy spot it is quickly able to anchor itself with roots.

No other plants are associated with the mangrove, but there are a number of small animals including the juvenile stages of about 20 species of fish. Old breathing roots become encrusted with barnacles, oysters and flea mussels.

Shrubby mangroves near Auckland city.

Mangrove leaves have yellow stalks and midribs. The pale yellow capsules each contain a single seed.

Opposite: Interior view of a low mangrove forest at low tide. The mud is covered with breathing roots and mangrove seedlings.

AKEAKE (Plate 21)
Dodonaea viscosa
Sapindaceae

Akeake is found in coastal and lowland low forest and shrubland throughout the North Island and to the middle of the South Island.

It is a shrub or small tree up to 6 m tall with a trunk up to 30 cm in diameter. The bark separates in long thin strips. The leaves are 4–10 cm long x 1–3 cm wide.

The flowers are very small, greenish to reddish. The fruits are dry with 3 very wide wings so they are presumably wind dispersed. They are sometimes mistaken for flowers. Flowering occurs through spring to mid-summer, fruiting from late spring to early autumn.

The genus is mainly Australian with a few species widely spread through the tropics and sub-tropics. Our sole species is wide-spread in those regions.

Brachyglottis kirkii
var. *angustior*   Asteraceae

This is an undershrub in lowland to lower mountain forests through Northland to south of Auckland.

It is a shrub up to 3 m tall. The leaves are smooth margined or with a few teeth, rather fleshy, 5–12 cm long x 1–2 cm wide.

The flowers are up to 4 cm across and pure white. The seeds have parachutes of hairs. Flowering is in autumn and early winter with the seeds dispersing from late autumn.

Akeake with pale yellow seeds.

A bronze form with red seeds.

An akeake with fully ripe brown seeds.

Brachyglottis kirkii var. *angustior*.

TARAIRE (Plate 22)

Beilschmiedia tarairi   **Lauraceae**

Taraire ranges from a little south of Auckland northwards, where it can be an important component of the forest canopy. Taraire leaves contrast strongly with those of its relative tawa (pages 100–101), but the two are very similar in their flowers and fruits.

It is a tree up to 20 m tall with trunks up to 1 m in diameter. The bark is smooth. The new growth is densely covered with reddish brown hairs that persist on the prominent raised veins on the leaf undersides. The mostly alternate leaves are very thick, 5–7.5 cm long x 3–5 cm wide, sometimes wider, smooth margined, rounded at the tip and whitish below, with red-brown hairs on the larger veins. They sometimes bulge upwards between the secondary veins.

The flowers are small and yellow or green. The berries are purple and plum-like, 2.5–3.5 cm long. Flowering is from early spring to early summer with fruits ripening from late spring to late summer.

The parasitic orchid *Danhatchia australis* (page 219) grows in association with taraire in Northland.

The genus *Beilschmiedia* is widespread in the tropics and subtropics.

TAWAPOU (Plate 12)

Pouteria costata   **Sapotaceae**

(syn. *Planchonella costata*)

Tawapou is found in low coastal forest and

Tawapou with large red-orange berries.

shrubbery south to East Cape, mostly on eastern shores.

It is a tree up to 15 m tall with a trunk up to 1 m in diameter. The bark is rough. Broken twigs and leaves exude a milky juice. The leaves are 5–10 cm long x 2–5 cm wide and very shiny.

The flowers are very small and greenish. The berries are about 2.5 cm long, changing in colour from bright orange with red flecks to dark red. Flowering occurs in the summer with the berries taking 12–15 months to mature. Each berry contains several large shiny black seeds.

Pouteria is restricted to New Zealand with only one species.

Taraire showing rolled exposed leaves and plum-like berries.

MAPAU (Plate 22)

Myrsine australis   **Myrsinaceae**

Mapau is found throughout the country in lowland to mountain forest and shrubland.

It is a shrub or tree up to about 6 m tall with red branchlets. The bark is smooth with corky spots. The leaves are yellow green, 3–6 cm long x 1.5–2.5 cm wide with smooth undulate margins. Red oil glands are visible in the young leaves.

The flowers are very small, yellowish and are borne on woody twigs. The berries are 2–3 mm in diameter and black when mature. Flowering is from mid-summer to mid-autumn with berries ripening from mid-spring to early autumn in the following season.

HOROPITO, PEPPER TREE (Plate 22)

Pseudowintera axillaris   **Winteraceae**

Horopito is found as an undershrub in lowland to lower mountain forest throughout the North Island and in the northwest of the South Island. It is generally succeeded by its relative mountain horopito at higher altitudes.

A shrub or small tree up to 8 m tall with dark smooth bark, its leaves are dark green, very shiny, 6–10 cm long x 3–6 cm wide and peppery to the taste. The leaf stalks and twigs are dark purple to black.

The flowers are greenish white, about 1 cm across, and are borne on woody twigs. The berries are red, 5–6 mm in diameter. Flowering is through spring to early summer, fruiting from mid-spring to early winter.

Pseudowintera is restricted to New Zealand.

Reddish twigged mapau with maturing berries.

Left: Horopito with almost black stems and small orange berries. Right: Shiny foliage and black stems of a young horopito.

A colourful shrub of mountain horopito.

MOUNTAIN HOROPITO (Plate 22)
Pseudowintera colorata

This species is found throughout the country, except the far north, mostly as a forest undershrub at higher altitudes. It often persists in thickets after forest destruction. Because of its colourful leaves with their permanent autumn tints, this is among our most attractive shrubs.

It reaches up to 2 m tall, sometimes more. The leaves are 2–6 cm long x 1–3 cm wide, smooth margined, blotched with red and sometimes yellow above, the white undersides often tinged with purple. They taste peppery when chewed.

Introduced browsing mammals avoid eating the foliage of horopito because of its peppery taste. Some suggest that browsing moas would have behaved in the same way.

The flowers are about 1 cm wide and star-like. Berries are 3–5 mm in diameter, black. Flowering is through summer to early autumn with berries ripening from mid-summer to early winter.

Alseuosmia pusilla (page 114) is often mistaken for this species.

Mountain horopito foliage. In most of the leaves green chlorophyll is masked by red and yellow pigments.

THE PITTOSPORUMS
Pittosporaceae

In New Zealand there are more than 20 species of this widespread genus, notable for its sticky seeds and small but attractive flowers ranging in colour from dark purple or almost black to yellow and various shades of red and pink. About a third of the species are unusual in having very small leaves and densely interlacing twigs (see also page 156).

The pittosporums have alternate, smooth-margined leaves and scaly buds. The bark is generally smooth with raised corky spots. Damaged bark often exudes a sticky gum.

The flowers and capsules are distinctive. The 5 petals of the flowers curve backwards strongly and the capsules open to reveal black seeds immersed in a very sticky fluid. Birds eat the seeds but some become stuck to their beaks and feathers and are dispersed in this way.

Pittosporum eugenioides (tarata) has leaves that smell strongly of lemon when crushed and yellow flowers. *P. umbellatum* has yellowish hairs on its young twigs and pink flowers. *P. tenuifolium* (kohuhu) and *P. colensoi* both have dark purple to black flowers but the leaves of the former have undulate margins and are less than 2 cm wide while those of the latter have flat margins and are more than 2 cm wide. *P. crassifolium* (karo) and *P. ralphii* have densely hairy leaf undersides. The leaves of the former are mostly less than 7 cm long x 2.5 cm wide while those of the latter are mostly longer and wider.

Species of *Pittosporum* are widely distributed in the tropical to temperate zones, particularly in the southern hemisphere.

Scaly buds of tarata.

TARATA, LEMONWOOD (Plate 23)
Pittosporum eugenioides

Lemonwood is found in lowland to lower mountain forest throughout the country.

It is a tree up to 12 m tall with a trunk up to 60 cm in diameter. The yellowish green leaves are 5–10 cm long x 2.5–4 cm wide, strongly lemon scented when crushed. The margins are undulate.

The flowers, in terminal clusters, are about 1.5 cm in diameter, pale yellow. The capsules are 5–6 mm long and mostly 2-valved. Flowering is from mid-spring to early summer. The capsules mature about a year later.

Pittosporum umbellatum (Plate 23)

This species is found in eastern lowland forests south to Hawkes Bay.

A tree up to 7 m tall, its leaves are 5–10 cm long x 2–5 cm wide; the margins are not undulate. The young twigs have yellowish hairs.

The pink flowers, in terminal clusters, are about 2 cm in diameter. The capsules are about 1 cm long and 2-valved. Flowering is through spring to mid-summer. The capsules mature from late spring through summer and autumn.

Foliage and yellow flowers of lemonwood.

Left: *Pittosporum umbellatum* with broad leaves and terminal clusters of immature capsules. Right: *Pittosporum colensoi* with dark purple flowers similar to those of *P. tenuifolium*.

Left: Karo with woolly leaf undersides, red flowers and open capsules with sticky seeds from the previous season. Right: *Pittosporum ralphii* with dark red flowers and furry leaf undersides.

KOHUHU (Plate 23)
Pittosporum tenuifolium

Kohuhu is found throughout the country in coastal to lower mountain forests, except in the west of the South Island.

It is a tree up to 8 m tall with a trunk up to 30 cm in diameter. The pale green leaves are 2–4 cm long x 1–2 cm wide with undulate margins.

The flowers, attached singly along the twigs, are about 1.5 cm in diameter, dark purple to black. The capsules are about 1.2 cm long and 3-valved. Flowering is from mid- to late spring. The capsules mature from mid-summer to early autumn.

Pittosporum colensoi (Plate 23)

P. colensoi is found in lowland to lower mountain forests from the Bay of Plenty southwards including the west of the South Island. It is related to P. tenuifolium and tends to replace it at higher altitudes, and some botanists regard it as a variety of the former and not a distinct species.

A tree up to 10 m tall with a trunk up to 40 cm in diameter, its leaves are 4–10 cm long x 2–5 cm wide and not undulate.

The flowers, attached singly along the twigs, are about 1.5 cm in diameter, dark to very dark red. The capsules are about 1.2 cm long and 3-valved.

KARO (Plate 23)
Pittosporum crassifolium

Karo is found at forest margins near the sea from North Cape to Poverty Bay in the North Island and also in the Kermadecs. It often grows with pohutukawa and their leaves look somewhat similar, however karo has alternate leaves and pohutukawa has opposite leaves.

It is a shrub or small tree up to 9 m tall. The leaves are very thick, 5–7 cm long x 2–2.5 cm wide, not undulate, and have densely hairy white undersides.

The flowers, in terminal clusters, are dark red. The capsules are 2–3 cm long, opening with 3 valves. The seeds are very sticky. Flowering and fruiting occur from early spring to early summer.

Pittosporum ralphii (Plate 23)

P. ralphii is found at lowland forest margins from near Auckland to Hawkes Bay and has naturalised further south.

A shrub to small tree up to 4 m tall, its leaves are 7.5–12.5 cm long x 2.5–5.5 cm wide, sometimes slightly undulate, white with densely hairy undersides.

The flowers, in terminal clusters, are dark red. The capsules are about 1.5 cm long with 3 valves. Flowering is from early spring to early summer with the capsules developing during the summer.

Pittosporum ellipticum (Plate 23)

P. ellipticum grows in lowland to lower mountain forests through Northland to the Raukumara Range.

It is a small tree up to 8 m tall. The leaves are 5–10 cm long x 2.5–5 cm wide, not undulate. Young leaves and twigs are covered with golden brown hairs.

The flowers, in terminal clusters, are pink to red, about 1 cm in diameter. The capsules are about 2 cm long with 2–3 valves. Flowering is through spring into early summer. Capsules ripen from mid-summer through autumn.

MANGEAO (Plate 22)
Litsea calicaris   Lauraceae

Mangeao is found in lowland forest southwards to the Bay of Plenty.

It is a tree up to 12 m tall with a trunk up to 80 cm in diameter. The bark is smooth. The leaves are 5–12.5 cm long x 3–5 cm wide, sometimes whitish below, with reddish brown stalks and midribs.

The flowers are about 8 mm across, greenish yellow. The berries are 1.5–2 cm long, dark purple to black and seated in small green cups. Flowering occurs in early spring. The berries are ripe through spring, probably in the following season.

Litsea is a widespread tropical genus with this one species in New Zealand.

Foliage of mangeao. The leaves have prominent veins.

BROADLEAF (Plate 34)

Griselinia littoralis　　　　Griseliniaceae

Broadleaf is found throughout the country in lowland to subalpine forest and shrubland. In wet climates it may be an epiphyte with roots descending to the ground.

It forms a tree up to 10 m or more tall with a short twisted trunk. The bark is rough. The yellow-green leaves are almost fleshy, 5–12 cm long x 4–5 cm wide, sometimes with one side a little shorter than the other at the base.

The flowers are very small, greenish and are borne on the woody twigs. The berries are 6–7 mm long, dark purple to black. Flowering is from late spring to mid-summer with berries ripening from mid-summer through autumn to winter.

Broadleaf's relative **puka** (*Griselinia lucida*) usually grows as an epiphyte but can grow terrestrially in sunny rocky sites. It is similar in general appearance to broadleaf but has more handsome broader leaves that are very lop-sided at the base. Because of the striking appearance of the thick-textured broad distinctively shaped and very shiny adult leaves, as well as the bright yellow green of the young leaves, this native species is popular in cultivation. (See Plate 34 and pages 188–189.) There are several species of *Griselinia* in Chile.

PARAPARA, BIRD-CATCHING TREE

Pisonia brunoniana　　　　Nyctaginaceae

Parapara grows in coastal forest from the Three Kings along the northeast coast of the North Island to East Cape.

It is a shrub or small tree up to 6 m tall or sometimes more with a trunk up to 60 cm in diameter. The leaves are thin, 10–40 cm long x 5–15 cm wide.

The inflorescences at stem tips are much branched and bear small tubular greenish flowers. The fruits are elongate, about 3 cm long x 6 mm wide, with longitudinal ribs. Glands on the ribs cover the fruits with a sticky glue, which is most pronounced at the brown, fully ripe stage.

Insects are trapped by this glue. Small birds, such as fantails and silvereyes, attracted by the insects, can also be trapped. Larger birds are able to escape, carrying sticky fruits with them, so aiding in the dispersal of the species.

Parapara is also found in Australia, Norfolk Island, the Kermadec Islands and Hawaii.

Yellow-green broadleaf foliage with immature berries.

Handsome foliage of *Griselinia lucida*.

Sticky capsules of parapara. Note the feather.

Karaka with large orange berries.

KARAKA (Plate 22)

Corynocarpus laevigatus   **Corynocarpaceae**

Karaka are found in coastal and lowland forests throughout the North Island and to about half-way down the South Island. Trees are an impressive sight when weighed down with their large orange berries. The single large seeds in the berries are poisonous until cooked and were an important food for the Maori.

It is a tree up to about 15 m tall with a trunk up to 60 cm in diameter. The bark is smooth. The leaves are dark green, leathery, 10–15 cm long x 5–7 cm wide.

The flowers are small, 4–5 mm in diameter and greenish. The berries are large, bright orange, 2.5–4 cm long. Flowering is from late winter through spring, and berries ripen from mid-summer through autumn.

The genus is also found in eastern Australia, New Guinea, New Caledonia and Vanuatu.

A karaka grove on the Wairarapa coast.

SMALL-LEAVED SHRUBS

A shrub is defined as small leaved if all or most of its leaves are less than 2 cm long. The mingimingis, *Archeria*, kanuka and manuka all have small narrow leaves, narrow branching angles, and the twigs are not interlacing. Most of the other species have an unusual growth habit — the twigs branch at wide angles and are often densely interlaced. They are called **divaricating shrubs** (see page 151). Some trees with adult leaves longer than 2 cm have juvenile forms with small leaves (see plates 8, 14, 18).

Soft mingimingi with several green and 2 ripe berries.

SOFT MINGIMINGI (Plate 24)
Cyathodes fasciculata   Epacridaceae
This species is found in the North Island and the northern half of the South Island in shrubland, coastal and lowland light forest, particularly beech forest.

A shrub up to 5 m tall with dark brown to black bark, its leaves are dull green above, 1.2–2.5 cm long x 2–4 mm wide, pointed at the tips but not really prickly. In the far north juveniles may have leaves up to 6 cm long x 1 cm wide but there are usually smaller-leaved adults nearby. The leaves of this and the 2 following species have several parallel veins visible as striations below.

The small greenish white flowers are in hanging clusters. The berries are about 5 mm in diameter, red on most plants, white on others. Flowering is from late winter to early summer and berries can be found from early spring to early autumn.

PRICKLY MINGIMINGI (Plate 24)
Cyathodes juniperina
C. juniperina is found throughout the country, including Stewart Island, in lowland to higher mountain forest and shrubland. This species also grows in Tasmania and southeast Australia.

It is a shrub up to 4 m tall with dark brown to black bark. The leaves are brown green above, 6–15 mm long x 0.5–1 mm wide, sharply pointed at the tips. Plants in wet habitats can have leaves up to 2 cm long x 2 mm wide.

The small greenish white flowers are attached singly. The berries are mostly about 5 mm in diameter and are red, pink or white on different plants. Flowering is from late winter to early summer with berries especially abundant in autumn but present most of the year.

Prickly mingimingi with many red berries.

Archeria traversii (Plate 24)   **Epacridaceae**
A. traversii is found in lowland to mountain forest and shrubland in the South Island, mostly in the west, and in Stewart Island.

It is a shrub up to 4 m tall with orange-brown bark. The leaves are dark green and shiny above, 7–20 mm long x 1.5–4 mm wide, pointed to blunt at the tips.

The small red to reddish orange flowers are in terminal clusters. The capsules are 2–3 mm in diameter and release many tiny seeds. Flowering is from late spring into summer with capsules ripening in the autumn.

KANUKA (Plate 24)

Kunzea ericoides   **Myrtaceae**
Kanuka grows throughout the North and South Islands, except the far south, in coastal to mountain forest and shrubland, mostly in drier eastern localities on well-drained fertile ground. It can be an important pioneer following forest destruction by fire and initially forms a low dense forest, which is gradually replaced by larger-leaved, taller forest species.

It forms a shrub or small tree up to 15 m tall or more with pale bark peeling off in long strips. The leaves are sometimes in clusters, 4–12 mm long x 1–2 mm wide, pointed at the tip but not prickly, aromatic when crushed.

The white flowers are about 5 mm in diameter and generally in clusters. The stamens are longer than the petals.The soft capsules are 2–4 mm in diameter. Flowering is from late spring to mid-summer with the capsules releasing their seeds in autumn.

MANUKA (Plate 24)

Leptospermum scoparium   **Myrtaceae**
Manuka, widespread throughout the country, has leaves very similar to those of kanuka. The easiest way to tell the 2 species apart is to grasp the foliage. If it feels prickly it is manuka; if it feels soft it is kanuka. Manuka flowers and capsules are twice the size of those of kanuka, the stamens in the flowers are short and the capsules are hard and woody, not soft.

Manuka is mostly found in open habitats, where it sometimes mingles with kanuka. It tolerates less fertile soils than kanuka, however, and these may be dry to swampy.

It is a shrub up to 4 m tall with flaking bark. The leaves are 4–12 mm long x 1–4 mm wide, prickly at the tip, not aromatic when crushed.

The white flowers are lateral and single, 1 cm or more in diameter with the stamens shorter than the petals. The capsules are hard and woody, 1 cm or more in diameter. Flowers and capsules can be present from spring through to early winter in the following year.

Near North Cape there are populations of manuka with pink to reddish flowers that provide an attractive sight. A number of popular garden plants have been derived from these including some double-flowered forms.

Manuka twigs are often covered with sooty mould, an unsightly black fungus that feeds on the honey dew of scale insects (see page 246).

A kanuka grove with the leafless broom _Carmichaelia arborea_ in the undergrowth.

Kanuka trunks.

Small flowers of kanuka.

Larger-flowered manuka with small-flowered kanuka (right).

A young manuka heavy with flowers.

SMALL-LEAVED COPROSMAS
Rubiaceae

It is not too difficult to identify a plant as a *Coprosma*—the leaves are opposite, smooth-margined and have domatia and pointed stipules. However, particularly with the twiggy small-leaved forms, determining the species can be difficult.

Here we include only those species that are frequently encountered in forests, although many of them are also to be found in open habitats. The small-leaved species are still being investigated by botanists and some are yet to be named and described.

Almost all small-leaved coprosmas are divaricating (see box on page 151). As with the larger-leaved species, flowering is generally through spring into summer with berries following through autumn into winter.

Coprosma rhamnoides with black berries.

Coprosma rhamnoides (Plate 25)

C. rhamnoides can generally be recognised by its mixture of almost round leaves and very narrow leaves on the same plant.

It is found in coastal to lower mountain forests and shrubland throughout the country.

A shrub 1–2 m tall with spreading interlacing branchlets often downwardly curved at the ends, its leaves are 7–15 mm long x 2–14 mm wide, dull green and hairless.

The berries are spherical, 3–4 mm in diameter, bright red and looking like redcurrants, or dark red or almost black.

Coprosma linariifolia (Plate 25)

C. linariifolia is found in lowland to mountain forest and shrubland in the southern half of the North Island and throughout the South Island, particularly in the east.

It is a non-divaricating tall shrub to small tree up to 8 m tall with ascending branchlets that are not interlaced. The leaves are dark green, 1.5–3 cm long x 2–5 mm wide. The stipules are distinctive in being fused into a long tube above each pair of leaf bases.

The berries are oblong, about 6 mm long, white, sometimes flecked with blue black.

Coprosma linariifolia with pale blue berries.

Coprosma colensoi (Plate 25)

This is found throughout the country from the Coromandel Peninsula southwards in lowland to higher mountain forests and shrubland.

It is a spreading spindly shrub 2–3 m tall. The

Coprosma colensoi with dark red berries.

leaves are narrow on some plants, 1.5–2.5 cm long x 2–3 mm wide, broad on others, 9–15 mm long x 5–8 mm wide, hairless, with some leaves indented at the tip.

The berries are broad-oblong, 6–7 mm long, orange red through dark ruby red to almost black.

Coprosma cuneata (Plate 25)

C. cuneata is found in lowland to higher mountain forests and shrubland from south Westland to Southland in the South Island, and on Stewart Island and the Auckland and Campbell Islands.

A more or less erect shrub up to 1 m tall, its leaves are 5–16 mm long x 1–3 mm wide, hairless, widening towards the tip, which is indented.

The berries are red, spherical, 3–5 mm in diameter.

Coprosma pseudocuneata

C. pseudocuneata is found throughout the country in higher-altitude forest and alpine shrubland and grassland.

It is an erect shrub up to 3 m tall but usually less. The leaves are densely crowded, thick and curved back, 1.5–2 cm long x 2–6 mm wide.

The berries are bright red and 5-6 mm long.

Coprosma microcarpa (Plate 25)

This is found in the southern half of the North Island and mostly in the east of the South Island as far as south Canterbury, in lowland to mountain forests, mostly beech, and sometimes in shrubland.

It is a shrub up to 1 m tall, sometimes more, with the branchlets often arranged in flat leafy tiers. The leaves are 5–15 mm long x 1–3 mm wide, dark green, hairless, and with a pointed tip.

The berries are more or less spherical, white, 3–4 mm in diameter.

Coprosma spathulata (Plate 25)

C. spathulata is found in lowland forest from Northland to Gisborne.

It forms a shrub up to 2 m tall with more or less erect branchlets. The leaf blade is 1–2 cm long x 1–2 cm wide with a fringe of short marginal hairs. The leaf stalk is flattened and narrowly winged, as long as the blade or longer.

The berries are spherical to oblong, orange, red or almost black, 6–8 mm long.

Coprosma rotundifolia (Plate 25)

This species is widespread throughout the country in lowland to lower mountain forests and shrubland

DIVARICATING SHRUBS

A puzzling feature of the New Zealand flora is the widespread occurrence of an unusual type of shrub that has very small leaves and densely interlaced twigs. These are often profusely branched and spread apart at wide angles. They are generally termed 'divaricating shrubs' and include the juvenile stages of several small trees. There are more than 60 species that have this form.

There is much theorising and some argument about what led to the evolution of this distinctive growth habit in so many New Zealand plants. One suggestion is that the divaricates are hardy forms that evolved from less-hardy larger-leaved forest species during the geologically recent Ice Age. An opposing view is that they are browse-resistant, enabling them to survive the onslaught of the large, only recently extinct, herbivorous moa. For one thing the small leaves of the divaricates would not have provided a decent meal for such large birds and secondly the many growing points on the many twigs would have enabled quick recovery from any browsing that might have occurred.

Divaricating shrubs are found elsewhere in the world, particularly in deserts, but they are a particularly notable feature of New Zealand vegetation and they mostly grow in moist habitats.

on fertile soils.

It is a shrub to small tree up to 5 m tall with spreading branchlets, densely covered when young with shaggy hairs.

The leaves are light green, sometimes with purple blotches, hairy on both surfaces, 1.5–2.5 cm long x 1–2 cm wide.

The berries are often distinctively narrowed between the 2 seeds within, bright orange, 4–5 mm in diameter.

Coprosma crassifolia (Plate 25)

This is found in the North and South Islands, mostly in the east, in coastal to lower mountain forests and shrubland.

It is a shrub to small tree up to 4 m tall with stiff widely spreading branchlets. The leaves have a fringe of marginal hairs when young, dark green above, white to greyish white below, 10–15 mm long x 5–10 mm wide.

The berries are spherical, white or pale yellow, 5–6 mm in diameter.

Coprosma ciliata (Plate 25)

C. ciliata is found on the Tararua Range in the south of the North Island, throughout the South Island except some eastern localities, and on Stewart, Auckland, Campbell and Antipodes Islands. It occurs mostly in mountain to subalpine forest and shrubland.

It is a shrub up to 3 m tall with spreading branchlets. The leaves are pale green with a conspicuous fringe of marginal hairs when young or shaded, 1–2 cm long x 5–10 mm wide.

The berries are spherical, white or pale yellow to bright orange or red, 6–7 mm in diameter.

Coprosma areolata (Plate 25)

C. areolata is found throughout the country in lowland to mountain forest and shrubland.

A shrub or small tree up to 5 m tall, mostly with ascending branchlets, its leaves are yellow green to brown green with a conspicuous dark-coloured vein network. They are 9–10 mm long x 7–10 mm wide with scattered hairs closely pressed to the lower surface. The leaf blades are drawn out to a point at the tip.

The berries are spherical, dark purple to black, 4–5 mm in diameter.

Coprosma tenuicaulis (Plate 25)

This is found throughout the North Island and in the northwest of the South Island in lowland swamp forest and shrubland.

It is a shrub up to 3 m tall with spreading branchlets. The leaves are 8–13 mm long x 8–10 mm wide and hairless. They have a conspicuous dark-coloured vein network and often yellow spots on the upper side above the domatia.

The berries are spherical, black, 3–4 mm in diameter.

Coprosma rubra (Plate 25)

This species occurs throughout the North and South Islands in lowland to lower mountain forest, mostly on fertile alluvial and volcanic soils.

It is a shrub up to 4 m tall with spreading reddish to orange-brown branchlets. The leaves, 1–2 cm long x 1–1.5 cm wide, have short hairs along the upperside mid- and secondary veins, and the margins are often coloured pink or red.

The berries are oblong, white, 4–6 mm long.

Foliage of *Coprosma pseudocuneata*.

Coprosma microcarpa with the small leaves on flattened branches.

A small tree of *Coprosma rotundifolia*.

Coprosma rotundifolia foliage showing the typical purple blotching of some leaves.

Coprosma crassifolia with a few leaves showing white undersides.

Coprosma areolata growing in forest shade.

Coprosma tenuicaulis. The leaves have dark veins and yellow spots above the domatia.

Neomyrtus pedunculata with whitish green leaves and translucent orange berries hanging on long stalks.

The heart-shaped leaves and white flowers with prominent stamens of *Lophomyrtus obcordata*.

Neomyrtus pedunculata (Plate 26)
Myrtaceae

N. pedunculata is found throughout the country, mostly in lowland to mountain forests, sometimes in shrubland.

It is a shrub or sometimes a small slender-trunked subcanopy tree up to 6 m tall. The twigs are 4-angled, hairless and not strongly interlaced. The opposite leaves are whitish, sometimes almost silvery green, 6–20 mm long x 4–15 mm wide, smooth margined.

The flowers are attached singly on long stalks, white, 6–7 mm in diameter with many stamens. The berries are about 6 mm long, hanging from the twigs, mostly bright yellow orange but sometimes yellow or red. Flowering occurs mostly in mid- to late summer with berries ripening through autumn and into winter.

Neomyrtus has only one species, restricted to New Zealand.

Lophomyrtus obcordata (Plate 26)
Myrtaceae

This is another species with rounded twigs. It is found in the North and South Islands in coastal and lowland forest and shrubland.

It forms a shrub to small tree up to 8 m tall with ascending rounded twigs that are not strongly interlaced. The opposite leaves are heart-shaped, notched at the tip, 5–10 mm x 5–10 mm, smooth margined.

The flowers are attached singly on long stalks, white, about 6 mm in diameter with many slender stamens. The berries are 5–6 mm in diameter, bright to dark red. Flowering occurs through summer to early autumn with berries ripening from mid-summer through autumn.

Rohutu hybridises with its larger-leaved relative ramarama, *L. bullata* (page 102).

Teucridium parvifolium (Plate 26)
Verbenaceae

T. parvifolium is found mostly on the drier eastern sides of the North and South Islands, often on river terraces at forest margins or in shrubland.

An often straggly shrub up to 1.5 m tall, its twigs are 4-angled, hairy when young and not strongly interlaced. The leaves are opposite. The leaf stalks are about as long as the blade. The blade is dull green to brown green, 4–12 mm long x 4–8 mm wide, smooth margined.

The flowers, attached singly or in small groups,

are small and white with the petals joined into a spreading tube. The fruit is a dry cup containing 4 seeds. Flowering is from late spring to mid-summer with seeds forming in summer to early autumn.

The genus has only one species, restricted to New Zealand.

Aristotelia fruticosa (Plate 26)
Elaeocarpaceae

A. fruticosa is found throughout the country mostly in mountain forest and shrubland.

It is a much-branched shrub up to 2 m tall with spreading interlaced twigs, The leaves of adults are 5–10 mm long x 4–5 mm wide, shiny above with a conspicuous vein network. The opposite leaves are .smooth margined on some plants and toothed on others. The leaves of young plants have remarkably variable leaves, from long and narrow to short, broad and deeply toothed or lobed.

The very small pendent flowers are attached singly or in groups and have toothed pink petals. The berry is 3–4 mm in diameter, white, pink, red or black. Flowering is from mid-spring to early summer with berries through summer and autumn.

A. fruticosa hybridises with its much larger-leaved relative wineberry, *A. serrata* (page 104).

A much-branched shrub of *Teucridium parvifolium*.

Adult foliage of *Aristotelia fruticosa*.

Leaves and flowers of *Teucridium parvifolium*.

Raukaua anomala (Plate 26)
(syn. *Pseudopanax anomalus*) Araliaceae

This species is so different from its *Pseudopanax* relatives that its species name, *anomala*, is very appropriate. *R. anomala* can be encountered throughout the country in lowland to mountain forests and is also abundant in some shrub vegetation on exposed sites.

It is a bushy shrub up to 3 m tall with stout zig-zagging densely interlaced twigs covered with black bristly hairs when young. The stalks of the alternate leaves are flattened and narrowly winged with a joint near the blade; the blade is 1–2 cm long x 1–1.5 cm wide with 5–10 small teeth, often with short bristles at their tips. The leaves of the seedlings have 3 small leaflets.

The flowers are small and greenish in small clusters. The berries are white to purple, flattened and contain 2 seeds each. Flowering and fruiting appear to be irregular.

The nearest relative of *R. anomala* is probably the much larger-leaved *R. simplex* (page 81). Natural hybrids occur where they meet.

Raukaua anomala.

Melicope simplex (Plate 26) Rutaceae

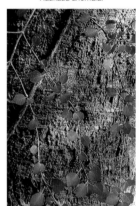

M. simplex is found in coastal and lowland forest and shrubland throughout the North Island and mostly in the east of the South Island. It hybridises in nature with the much larger-leaved *M. ternata* (page 83).

It forms a shrub up to 5 m tall with slender laxly interlaced hairless twigs. The leaves can be opposite and alternate on the same plant. The leaf stalks are flattened and narrowly winged with a joint near the blade; the blades are mostly 1–1.5 cm long x 1–1.5 cm wide with 20 or more small rounded teeth. The leaves contain oil glands, making them pleasantly aromatic when crushed. The seedling leaves have 3 small leaflets.

The flowers, in small groups, are small and greenish white. The capsules have 4 spreading compartments each releasing a single shiny black seed. Flowering occurs in spring with capsules maturing through summer into autumn.

Melicope simplex.

Pittosporum divaricatum Pittosporaceae

This species is found in lowland to mountain forest and shrubland from the volcanic plateau southwards in the North Island and mostly in the east of the South Island. It is often found in beech forest.

It is a shrub up to 2 m tall with slender interlaced twigs. The leaves of the juveniles are mostly narrow and variously toothed to elaborately lobed. The pale green alternate adult leaves are shorter on average; some are smooth margined and others toothed or lobed.

The flowers and capsules are up to 1 cm in diameter. They are formed from spring to mid-summer.

Pittosporum rigidum (Plate 26)

P. rigidum is found in higher-altitude forest and shrubland on the axial ranges of the North Island and mostly in the west of the South Island.

It is a shrub up to 3 m tall but usually much less with short stiff twigs that are not strongly divaricating. The leaves of the juveniles are lobed or toothed. The brown-green leaves of the adults are mostly

Pittosporum divaricatum.

smooth margined but there are usually some toothed leaves as well.

The flowers and capsules are up to 1 cm in diameter. Flowering is from mid-spring to early summer with capsules forming from late summer into autumn.

Myrsine divaricata (Plate 26) — Myrsinaceae

This is a widespread and in places common species in lowland to higher mountain forest and shrubland throughout the country and also on the Auckland and Campbell Islands.

It is a shrub or small tree up to 4 m tall with weeping interlaced branchlets. The alternate leaves are often heart-shaped, smooth margined and notched at their tips, 5–15 mm long x 5–10 mm wide, often dark-stained where the stalk meets the blade. When a leaf is held to the light oil glands can be discerned.

The flowers are very small and pale yellow to reddish. The berries are 4–5 mm in diameter and bright purple or mauve. Flowering is from late winter through spring with berries ripening from late summer to early winter.

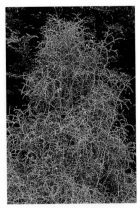

Myrsine divaricata.

SMALL-LEAVED MILK TREE, TUREPO (Plate 26)
Streblus heterophyllus — Moraceae

The small-leaved milk tree exudes milky juice when a twig is broken or the bark is cut. It is widespread in the North and South Islands in lowland forest.

It forms a small tree up to 12 m tall. Juvenile plants have zig-zagging interlaced branchlets and leaves 1–2 cm long x 1 cm wide with many small teeth. The juvenile leaves are deeply lobed, often resulting in a distinctive fiddle shape. The alternate adult leaves are 0.8–2.5 cm long x 5–12 mm wide with many small teeth but only occasional lobes.

The very small flowers are massed into drooping spikes. The berries are 4–5 mm in diameter and bright red. Flowering occurs from mid-spring through summer with berries ripening from late spring to autumn.

Berries of *Myrsine divaricata*.

Melicytus micranthus (Plate 26) — Violaceae

M. micranthus is found throughout the North and South Islands in lowland forest and shrubland, mostly on drier sites and alluvial ground. In some places this species hybridises with the much larger-leaved mahoe (page 122).

A shrub up to 2 m tall with interlacing branchlets, its alternate leaves are 1–2.5 cm long x 1–2 cm wide, sometimes smaller, with up to 10 or more small rounded teeth and sometimes a notch at the tip. There is often a pale patch at the base of the blade and the vein network is conspicuous. Small corky spots are prominent on the twigs.

The pale yellow to dark purple flowers are only about 2 mm in diameter. The berries are dark purple and 3–4 mm in diameter. Flowering is from mid-spring to mid-autumn with berries ripening from late spring to late autumn.

Helichrysum lanceolatum
(syn. *H. glomeratum*) — Asteraceae

This spindly shrub is found throughout the country in coastal and lowland shrubland and frequently at forest margins and in open forest.

Juvenile foliage of turepo.

It grows up to 3 m tall, but usually less, with slender spreading stems. The alternate smooth-margined mostly rounded leaves are 1–2.5 cm long x 1–2 cm wide and are densely covered with white hairs below.

The fragrant inconspicuous flowers are densely crowded in small heads. The seeds have parachutes of hairs for wind dispersal. Flowering is from late spring through summer with the seeds dispersing soon afterwards.

BUSH SNOWBERRY
Gaultheria antipoda   **Ericaceae**
This is found in the North, South and Stewart Islands in shrubland, at forest margins and in open forest from the lowlands to the mountains.

A shrub up to 2 m tall with the branchlets covered with bristly dark hairs, its small alternate leaves, mostly 7–10 mm long x 6–10 mm wide, are thick and toothed with prominent vein networks.

The small white bell-like flowers are single in leaf angles. The capsules are about 6 mm in diameter and are enclosed by the red or white enlarged and fleshy sepals of the flower. Flowering occurs from late spring through summer with capsules maturing from summer into autumn.

Helichrysum lanceolatum showing the white undersides of leaves.

Gaultheria antipoda. The fleshy berries are formed by the persistent sepals of the flower.

Opposite: A multi-stranded cable formed by supplejack (*Ripogonum scandens*) stems twining round each other. On the right are foliage and brightly coloured flowers of the climbing rata, *Metrosideros fulgens*. Flower colour of different vines of this species ranges from dark red to pale orange.

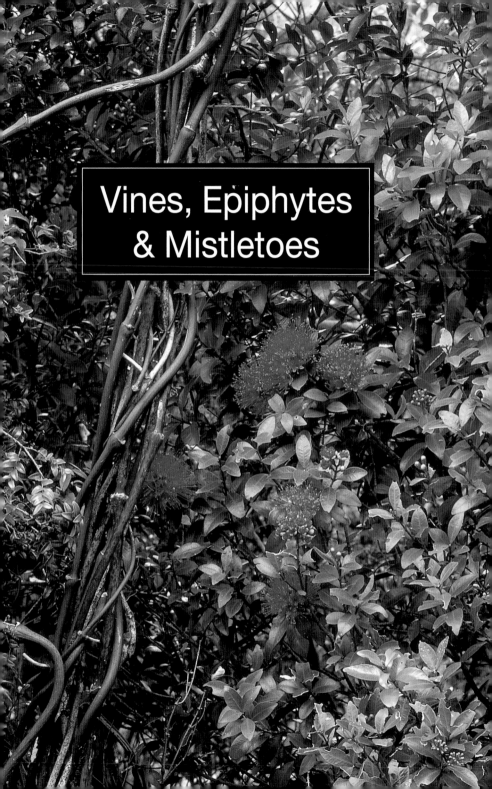

Vines, Epiphytes
& Mistletoes

VINES, EPIPHYTES & MISTLETOES

The previous section covered forest trees and shrubs, which stand independently on their own root systems, with their foliage held to the light by trunks and branches in the case of the trees, or by more slender stems in the case of the shrubs. This section includes a range of specialised forest plants that do not stand independently but take advantage of those that do.

VINES

The seeds of vines or, in the case of climbing ferns, spores, germinate on the ground and their weak slender stems climb the trunks of trees to attain the level of light required for their vigorous growth and reproduction. The means of climbing are very diverse. In some cases the stems twine around their support, as in the supplejack; or sensitive tendrils are formed that do the same, as in the native passion vine; or there are special attaching roots, as in the climbing ratas; or clinging hooks, as in the lawyer vines.

Some vines have slender non-woody stems, for example ferns, but others, such as the ratas, are woody and can become massive and cable-like. Some of the slender non-woody vines climb by attaching roots and finally lose their connection to the ground when the lower stem dies. They then live as epiphytes and depend on what water and nutrients they can absorb through their roots.

EPIPHYTES

The seeds of epiphytes or 'perching plants' germinate up in the branches or sometimes on the trunks of trees. Unlike vines, which at least expend sufficient energy to form slender stems, epiphytes don't even do that to secure their 'place in the sun'. But there can be a price to pay. Vines are usually connected to the ground to obtain water and mineral nutrients, but most epiphytes never have a ground connection, and those that do, achieve it only in the later stages of their lives. When the sun is shining, with summery temperatures and drying breezes, thirsty epiphytes could be deprived of sufficient moisture for their needs. They have overcome this problem in a variety of ways. Some store water from rainfall in fleshy leaves; some in tubes formed by overlapping leaves. In the case of the orchids, water is absorbed by layers of empty cells enclosing the roots. In large shrub epiphytes, some of which eventually become trees, long roots are sent down to the ground.

Some epiphytes are small and soft tissued, and include ferns, orchids and nest epiphytes. The latter, with their long narrow leaves, form conspicuous clumps on tree branches. They gradually build up impressive masses of black humus largely from the decay of their old roots and leaves. The humus is very water retentive and is a favoured site for other epiphytes to establish. Nest epiphytes probably live for many decades, but they eventually become so heavy that they fall off and crash to the ground or even cause whole branches to break away. In timber-milling days some bushmen were maimed or killed by falling epiphytes, which came to be termed 'widowmakers'.

Woody epiphytes include several small shrubs that never make contact with the ground, for example *Pittosporum cornifolium,* and a few large shrubs that eventually send a root to the forest floor, as with puka (*Griselinia lucida*). Several small to large trees start in the same way, either on tall trees or on tree ferns, but their descending roots become so massive that they are able to stand alone when their supporting trees die.

To disperse from tree top to tree top, the high epiphytes need to have seeds that don't readily fall to the shady forest floor. Some are wind dispersed as dust-like seeds (orchids), thread-like seeds (ratas) and seeds with parachutes of hairs (*Brachyglottis*). Others are carried by birds, either externally as with the sticky seeds of the pittosporums, or internally as with the seeds in berries of puka, the nest epiphytes, five-finger and others. The ferns and their allies have wind-dispersed dust-like spores.

MISTLETOES

The leafy parasites or mistletoes are quite a different story. They grow on the trunks of trees or on the branches of trees or shrubs. While epiphytes gain only good light from their high perches, the parasites demand more, drawing water and nutrients through root-like suckers from the living tissues of their hosts. However, unlike other parasites that attack the roots of trees, mistletoes do have green leaves and so are able to manufacture most of their own nutrients. (See page 194 for further information.)

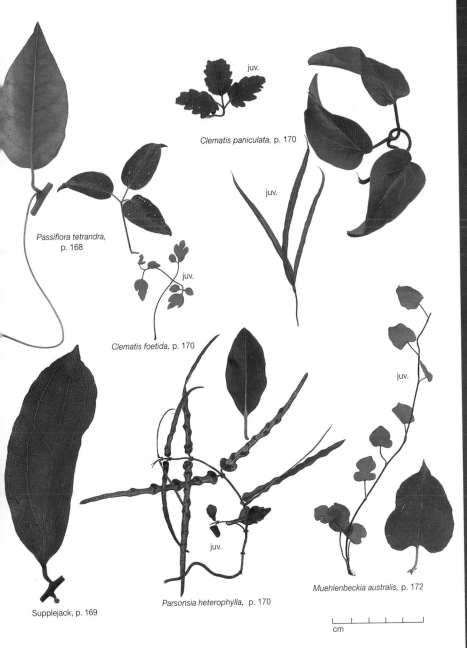

juv.

Clematis paniculata, p. 170

juv.

Passiflora tetrandra,
p. 168

juv.

Clematis foetida, p. 170

juv.

Muehlenbeckia australis, p. 172

juv.

Supplejack, p. 169

Parsonsia heterophylla, p. 170

cm

Plate 28. Climbing flowering plants.

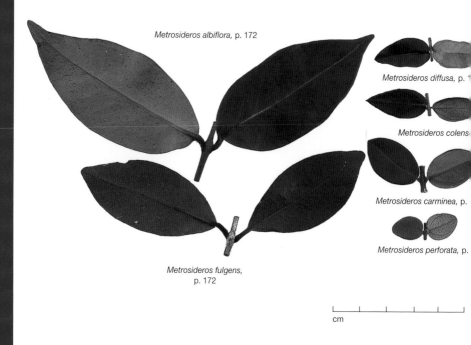

Metrosideros albiflora, p. 172

Metrosideros diffusa, p.

Metrosideros colens

Metrosideros carminea, p.

Metrosideros perforata, p.

Metrosideros fulgens,
p. 172

cm

Plate 29. Climbing flowering plants: ratas.

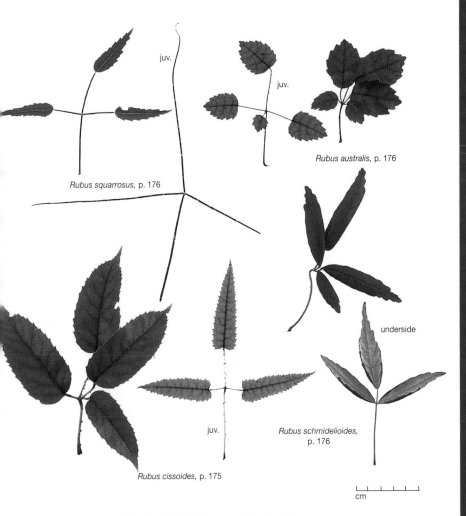

juv.

juv.

Rubus australis, p. 176

Rubus squarrosus, p. 176

underside

Rubus schmidelioides,
p. 176

juv.

Rubus cissoides, p. 175

cm

Plate 30. Climbing flowering plants: bush lawyers.

juv.

Microsorum pustulatum,
p. 178

Microsorum novae-zelandiae, p. 178

Microsorum scandens,
p. 178

juv.

cm

Plate 31. Climbing ferns.

juv.

Arthropteris tenella, p. 177

juv.

Blechnum filiforme, p. 177

Pyrrosia eleagnifolia, p. 179

Lygodium articulatum, p. 179

cm

Plate 32. Climbing ferns.

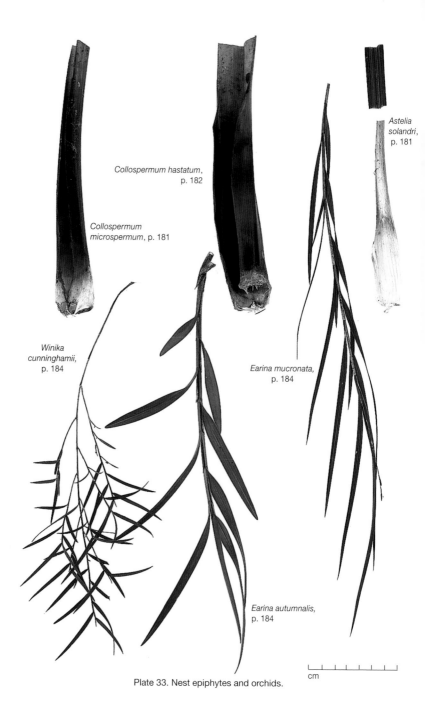

Collospermum hastatum,
p. 182

Collospermum
microspermum, p. 181

Astelia
solandri,
p. 181

Winika
cunninghamii,
p. 184

Earina mucronata,
p. 184

Earina autumnalis,
p. 184

cm

Plate 33. Nest epiphytes and orchids.

Broadleaf, pp. 145, 189

Puka, p. 188

Brachyglottis kirkii var. *kirkii*,
p. 188

underside

underside

Pittosporum cornifolium, p. 187

Pittosporum kirkii, p. 188

cm

Plate 34. Shrub epiphytes.

VINES

KIEKIE
Freycinetia banksii   **Pandanaceae**
This is a robust climber whose leaves often completely obscure the trunks of supporting trees. It may also form dense entanglements on the ground particularly in swampy sites. It is a common vine in lowland, especially swampy, forests throughout the North Island and in the northeast and west of the South Island.

The stems are about 4 cm in diameter with the older parts ringed with leaf scars. They are initially fixed to trunks by spreading roots but later separate in their upper parts and swing downwards away from the trunks. Eventually masses of a thicker type of root grow down to the ground close to the trunk. The leaves tend to be tufted towards the ends of the stems. They are up to 1.5 cm long x 2–2.5 cm wide with sheathing bases and finely toothed cutting edges.

The very small flowers, male and female on different plants, are densely crowded on finger-like stalks clustered at the ends of branches. The clusters are surrounded by broad reduced white to purplish leaves with fleshy sugary bases. The hard green fruits deriving from the female flowers are aggregated into a form reminiscent of a corn cob. Flowering occurs through spring with fruits maturing in late summer.

There are many species of *Freycinetia*, mostly in the western tropical Pacific.

Long-leaved stems of kiekie looping down from the trunk of a swamp maire. Younger kiekie spreads over the floor of the swamp.

NATIVE PASSION VINE, KOHIA (Plate 28)
Passiflora tetrandra   **Passifloraceae**
This species can be frequent in lowland forests throughout the North Island and as far as the middle of the South Island.

The mature stems of the native passion vine are up to 10 cm in diameter and often form snake-like coils on the forest floor in their lower parts but extend from there up into the forest canopy. The pointed leaves are 5–10 cm long x 2–3 cm wide, dark glossy green and often undulate at the margins. Slender tendrils up to 15 cm long are formed in the angles between the leaf stalks and the stems. These coil tightly around any slender supports they encounter.

The flowers are very modest compared with those of their cultivated relatives. They are about 1.5 cm in diameter, greenish white with a crown of yellowish filaments arising from the bases of the petals. The flowers of female plants form fruits like small

Ripening kiekie fruits.

balloons, 2.5–3 cm long, that are conspicuous with their bright orange colouring. Native birds break the fruits open to eat the seeds with their fleshy coverings. Flowering is from mid-spring through summer with fruits from autumn into winter.

The shiny leaves and bright orange fruits of kohia.

Passiflora is best represented in tropical America but there are some species in the tropics and subtropics elsewhere.

SUPPLEJACK, KAREAO (Plate 28)

Ripogonum scandens   Smilacaceae

Supplejack is found throughout the country in lowland forest. Because its entanglements are sometimes almost impenetrable, it can be a conspicuous feature of the understorey.

The twining stems are 1.5–2 cm in diameter, dark brown to black, strongly jointed like bamboo, with pairs of elongate black scales at each joint. Non-twining stems are formed in the better light of the canopy. These are about 5 mm in diameter and bear green leaves in opposite pairs, 5.5–10 cm long x 2–6 cm wide, each with a pair of strong lateral veins flanking the midrib.

The flowers are small, 6–10 mm across. What appear to be petals are in fact plump stamens. The berries are bright red and about 1 cm in diameter. Flowering is in early summer with berries present most of the year.

Ripogonum is a small genus with species in New Guinea and Australia as well as New Zealand.

An entanglement of supplejack stems.

Red berries and veined leaves of supplejack.

VINES, EPIPHYTES & MISTLETOES   169

PUAWHANANGA (Plate 28)

Clematis paniculata   **Ranunculaceae**

C. paniculata is the best known native clematis with its masses of pure white flowers lighting up the forest roof in the spring. It is found throughout the country in lowland and lower mountain forests.

The stems are up 10 cm or more in diameter at the base. The leaflets are dark green, 5–10 cm long x 3–5 cm wide, smooth margined or with a few rounded teeth towards the tip. The leaflet stalks twine around supports. All plant parts are hairless even when young.

The leaves of young plants are quite unlike those of the adults. The first leaves are thin, long and narrow, and undivided, then come leaves with 3 long and narrow leaflets, followed by leaves with deeply lobed leaflets. There is then a gradual transition to the adult state.

The flowers are white, those of male plants 5–10 cm in diameter and of female plants somewhat smaller. The clustered seeds with their plumes of hairs are about 2 mm long. Flowering is from late winter through spring with seeds maturing from mid-spring to mid-summer.

The genus *Clematis* is widespread, mostly in temperate regions.

Large pure white male flowers of *Clematis paniculata*.

Clematis foetida (Plate 28)

This is another tall vine whose foliage spreads over the forest canopy. It is found throughout the country in lowland forests.

The stems are up to 6 cm in diameter at the base. The leaflets are dark green, 2.5–6 cm long x 2–4 cm wide, smooth margined or with rounded teeth. Young leaves and stems and the flowers are covered with yellow hairs. Juvenile leaves have deeply lobed leaflets.

The flowers are yellow, those of male plants up to 2.5 cm in diameter and of female plants up to 1.5 cm in diameter, pleasantly perfumed despite the species name. The seeds are about 3 mm long. Flowering occurs through spring with seeds maturing from late spring to mid-summer.

KAIHUA, NEW ZEALAND JASMINE (Plate 28)

Parsonsia heterophylla   **Apocynaceae**

This pleasantly perfumed climber, sometimes known as New Zealand jasmine, is found throughout the country in coastal to lower mountain forest.

The twining stems are up to 10 cm in diameter. The adult leaves are thick and dark green, mostly 3–7 cm long x 1–4 cm wide, with smooth margins.

The distinctive seedheads of *Clematis paniculata*.

Abundant yellowish flowers of *Clematis foetida*.

The jasmine-like flowers of *Parsonsia heterophylla*.

The smaller leaves of juveniles vary widely in shape from long and narrow to short and round, and are lobed or smooth margined. All forms can be found on the same plant.

The many flowers are in downwardly curved groups. They are white to yellow and 7–8 mm long. The dry long and narrow fruits hang downwards and when they split open they release many seeds, each about 5 mm long and with a tuft of hairs about 10 mm long for wind dispersal. Flowering occurs through spring and summer with fruits through summer into autumn.

A second New Zealand species, **P. capsularis**, is usually a small climber in shrubby vegetation but can occur at forest margins. The leaves vary considerably in form but are mostly narrower than those of *P. heterophylla,* and the white, yellow or dark red flowers are 4 mm long or less.

The genus ranges from tropical Asia through Australasia to the Pacific Islands.

Long hanging pods of *Parsonsia heterophylla*.

POHUEHUE
Muehlenbeckia australis (Plate 28)
Polygonaceae
This climber is found throughout the country in lowland and mountain forests.

The stems are up to 10 cm in diameter. The adult leaves are thin, 2–8 cm long x 1–3 cm wide with smooth margins. As is typical of the family, there is a membranous outgrowth from the base of the leaf stalk that encloses the stem above. The juvenile leaves are much smaller and often fiddle-shaped.

The numerous flowers are greenish and 4–5 mm in diameter. The black and shiny 3-angled seeds are enclosed by the persistent petals that sometimes become white and fleshy. Flowering and fruiting occur from late spring to autumn. *M. australis* loses its leaves in winter. Its foliage often smothers tree crowns in regenerating forest.

M. complexa is a smaller vine mostly found in shrubland or forming tangled masses when growing on its own. It can also grow at forest margins. The leaves are smaller than those of *M. australis*, 5–20 mm long x 2–15 mm wide.

Muehlenbeckia is also found in Australia and South America.

Metrosideros fulgens (Plate 29)   **Myrtaceae**
This vine is found in coastal and lowland forest

CLIMBING RATAS

The climbing ratas (*Metrosideros*) with their attaching roots can climb quite large trunks. The almost-round leaves of *M. perforata* have prominent oil glands on the undersides. *M. carminea* has thick leaves, often widest in the middle. In *M. colensoi* and *M. diffusa* the leaves are widest near the base, and the leaves and twigs of the former are quite hairy. Of the 2 larger-leaved species, *M. albiflora* has the leaf tips drawn out to a narrow point, whereas those of *M. fulgens* are rounded.

throughout the North Island and in the west of the South Island.

The stems are up to 10 cm or more in diameter with red-brown flaking bark. The leaves are 3.5–6 cm long x 1–2.5 cm wide and mostly rounded at the tip.

The bright red or orange flowers, in terminal groups, are 2.5–3.5 cm long. The capsules are about 1 cm long. Flowering is from late summer to spring. The capsules take about a year to mature and seeds are released in spring and early summer.

Metrosideros albiflora (Plate 29)
M. albiflora is found in lowland forests south to the Bay of Plenty, mostly in kauri forests.

Left: Very small flowers and thin leaves, with distinctively pointed tips, of *Muehlenbeckia australis*. Right: *Metrosideros fulgens* with flower buds, open flowers with yellowish petals and bright red yellow-tipped stamens.

The stems are several centimetres in diameter with pale fawn bark separating in thin flakes. The leaves are 3.5–9 cm long x 2–3.5 cm wide and pointed at the tip.

The white flowers, in terminal groups, are 1.5–2 cm long. The capsules are 6–9 mm in diameter. Flowering occurs through summer to early autumn with the capsules ripening from late summer through autumn.

Metrosideros perforata (Plate 29)

This species is found in coastal and lowland forest throughout the North Island, in the west of the South Island and to Banks Peninsula in the east.

The stems are up to 15 cm or more in diameter with dark brown stringy bark. The leaves are 6–12 mm long x 5–9 mm wide and almost round, with conspicuous oil glands on the undersides.

The small white flowers, in terminal groups, are about 1 cm long. The capsules are 4–5 mm in

Right: Massive, cable-like stems of the climbing rata, *Metrosideros perforata,* hanging down from the crown of a rimu. The leaf mosaic of a young vine of the same species can be seen on the rimu trunk.

Young climbing stems of *Metrosideros perforata*.

Buds and small white flowers of *Metrosideros perforata*.

Left: Crimson flowers of *Metrosideros carminea* with yellow nectar cups. Right: Foliage, pink buds and white flowers of *Metrosideros diffusa*. The inflorescences are attached to the woody twigs—a distinctive feature.

diameter. Flowering is from mid-summer to early autumn with capsules ripening through autumn into winter.

Metrosideros carminea (Plate 29)

This is found in coastal to lowland forests in the north of the North Island south to East Cape and Taranaki.

The stems are several centimetres in diameter with pale bark separating in thin strips. The leaves are thick and very shiny above, 1.5–3.5 cm long x 7–12 mm wide, rounded to a little pointed at the tip.

The bright red flowers, in terminal groups, are 1.5–2 cm long. The capsules are 6–7 mm in diameter. Flowering is from late winter to mid-spring. Capsules ripen from late spring to early autumn.

This species is now widely cultivated for its bright display of flowers in early spring.

Metrosideros diffusa (Plate 29)

This is found in lowland to lower mountain forests throughout the country including Stewart Island.

The stems are several centimetres in diameter

Overlapping leaves and small white flowers in terminal clusters on *Metrosideros colensoi*.

with pale bark separating in thin strips. The leaves are thin and shiny above, 1–2 cm long x 3–10 mm wide, pointed to rounded at the tip.

The white to pinkish white flowers, in lateral groups on woody twigs, are 10–12 mm long. The capsules are 3–4 mm in diameter.

Flowering is from mid-spring to mid-summer with capsules ripening from mid-summer to early autumn.

Metrosideros colensoi (Plate 29)

Found locally throughout the North Island and in the north of the South Island, this species prefers fertile soils such as those of river terraces.

The stems are several centimetres in diameter with pale bark separating in thin strips. The leaves are thin and dull, hairy, 1.5–2 cm long x 7–10 mm wide, narrowly pointed at the tip.

The white to pinkish white flowers, mostly in terminal groups, are about 1.5 cm long. The capsules are about 4 mm in diameter. Flowering is from late spring through summer with capsules ripening through summer into early autumn.

BUSH LAWYERS

The lawyers (*Rubus*) attach themselves with curved hooks. *R. squarrosus* has either leaflets without blades or small blades borne on long stalks. *R. australis* has almost-round leaflets. *R. cissoides* and *R. schmidelioides* have leaflets longer than wide, but in the latter the undersides are white.

Robust stems of the common bush lawyer, *Rubus cissoides*. The armband-like corky outgrowths are typical.

BUSH LAWYER, TATARAMOA (Plate 30)
Rubus cissoides   **Rosaceae**

The common bush lawyer is found throughout the country in lowland and mountain forests.

The stems are up to 10 cm or more in diameter,

Foliage and pinky white flowers of the bush lawyer, *Rubus cissoides*.

often with corky outgrowths like armbands at intervals. The leaflets are 6–15 cm long x 2–6 cm wide, pointed at the tip and with pointed marginal teeth. The hooks are reddish.

The flowers, in much-branched groups, are white and 1–1.5 cm in diameter. The clusters of small berries are orange red and 5–10 mm long. Flowering is in the spring with the fruits ripening through summer and autumn.

The genus is widespread throughout the world and includes the blackberry and raspberry.

Rubus schmidelioides (Plate 30)

R. schmidelioides is found throughout the country in lowland forests, particularly on alluvial soils.

The stems are several centimetres in diameter, often with corky outgrowths like those of *R. cissoides*. The leaflets are 2–6 cm long x 2.5–3.5 cm wide and densely clad with reddish to grey hairs below. The tips are pointed and the margins are bluntly toothed and often partly rolled downwards. The hooks are red.

The flowers, in much-branched groups, are white and 8–15 mm in diameter. The fruits are yellow and 5–7 mm long. Flowering occurs in the spring with ripe fruit from mid-spring through summer.

SWAMP LAWYER (Plate 30)
Rubus australis

The swamp lawyer is found throughout the country in lowland and mountain forests, particularly in swampy sites.

The stems are several centimetres in diameter. Juvenile plants on the forest floor have thin round leaflets 1–3 cm long x 1–2 cm wide. Adult leaflets are thicker, 3–5 cm long x 1–3.5 cm wide, pointed to rounded at the tip with pointed marginal teeth.

The flowers, in moderately branched groups, are white and 6–12 mm wide. The fruits are yellowish and about 9 mm long. Flowering occurs in the spring with ripe fruit from mid-spring through summer.

Rubus squarrosus (Plate 30)

R. squarrosus is notable for having leaflets with midribs but no blades when young. Leaflets with blades are formed when the forest canopy is reached. It is found throughout the country in lowland to lower mountain forests.

The stems are several centimetres in diameter. Juvenile plants, especially in open sites, are a remarkable sight. The twigs, leaf stalks and leaflet midribs without blades are densely entangled and armed with bright yellow hooks. The adult leaflets are up to 7 cm long x 3 cm wide with marginal teeth towards the tips, and still with yellow hooks.

The flowers, in much-branched groups, are yellowish and 8–10 mm wide. The fruits are orange-red and about 6 mm long.

Flowering occurs in the spring with ripe fruits from late spring to autumn.

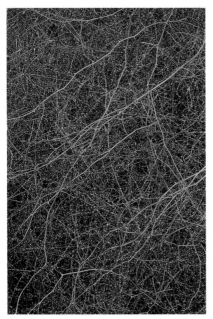

A daunting entanglement of the leafless, yellow-prickled juvenile stems of *Rubus squarrosus*.

CLIMBING FERNS

The climbing ferns, like most ferns, prefer moist, shady sites, so they are usually found climbing tree trunks below the forest roof. Their stems are slender and soft tissued and, with one exception, they cling to the trunks by slender branching roots. Mangemange climbs by twining. (See also page 221.)

THREAD FERN (Plate 32)
Blechnum filiforme   **Blechnaceae**
This is the only New Zealand *Blechnum* that climbs. It is found throughout the North Island in coastal and lowland forest and at the northern fringe of the South Island.

Initially the scaly stems, 2–5 mm in diameter, branch and spread over the forest floor forming a carpet. At this stage and at the base of tree trunks the fronds are small, on average about 16 cm long x 2 cm wide, with up to 20 pairs of leaflets, each toothed, about 1 cm long and rounded at the tip. As the stems grow up the tree trunk the fronds steadily increase in size to a maximum a few metres above the ground. They look quite unlike those of the juvenile stage and are up to 60 cm long x 15 cm wide, with up to 30 pairs of leaflets, each up to 9 cm long x 1.5 cm wide, toothed and drawn out to pointed tips. It is only at this stage that the distinctive fertile fronds are formed. Their leaflets are long and thread-like, hence the common name.

Blechnums are widespread throughout the world. *B. filiforme* is restricted to New Zealand.

Arthropteris tenella (Plate 32)   **Davalliaceae**
A. tenella is found in coastal and lowland forest in the North Island and in the north of the South Island.

It has slender scaly sparsely branched stems only a few millimetres in diameter. As with *Blechnum filiforme*, the fronds near the base of a tree are much smaller than those higher up. The smallest juvenile fronds are 5–10 cm long and often have an unusual appearance: there are 1–2 pairs of small round leaflets and a much larger elongate terminal leaflet narrowing to a point at the tip. Going up the trunk the fronds become progressively larger with many narrow pointed leaflets, each with rounded marginal teeth. The largest adult fronds are up to 40 cm long with leaflets up to 8 cm long x 1 cm wide.

The sori on the frond undersides are dome-like.
A. tenella also grows in eastern Australia.

Blechnum filiforme climbing a tawa trunk.

Arthropteris tenella with juvenile fronds.

Microsorum pustulatum (Plate 31)
(syn. *Phymatosorus diversifolius*)
Polypodiaceae

This fern is widespread in lowland and mountain forests throughout the country, including the subantarctic islands. As well as climbing tree trunks, it grows on the ground and on rocks in drier sites (see page 233).

The stems are stout and fleshy, 4–10 mm in diameter, green to grey green, with scattered small blackish scales. The juvenile fronds are undivided. The adult fronds, higher above the ground or in more open sites, are leathery, bright glossy green with several pairs of smooth-margined leaflets. The largest fronds are 45 cm long x 30 cm wide.

The dome-like sporangial clusters on the frond undersides are notable for their size and orange to orange-brown coloration.

M. pustulatum also grows in Australia.

Microsorum scandens (Plate 31)

This species is found in coastal and lowland forests throughout the North Island and in the north and the northern half of the west coast of the South Island.

The stems are slender, 2–4 mm in diameter, with crowded dark brown spreading scales. The juvenile fronds are undivided. The adult fronds, higher above the ground, are thin and dull green with up to 20 pairs of smooth-margined leaflets. The largest fronds are 50 cm long x 18 cm wide.

The dome-like sori on the frond undersides are small and brown.

M. scandens is also found in Australia.

Microsorum novae-zelandiae (Plate 31)

In mountain forests tree trunks are often covered with mosses, lichens and similar plants, and this fern often establishes itself among them rather than on the ground. It is found in the North Island from Coromandel to Wellington.

Its stems may be elongated and sparingly branched, stout, 4–10 mm in diameter, and densely covered with large straw-coloured scales. There are no distinctive juvenile fronds. The fronds are leathery, dark green, with up to 25 pairs of leaflets. The largest fronds are 1.2 m long x 35 cm wide.

The dome-like sori on the frond undersides are large and brown.

M. novae-zelandiae is restricted to New Zealand.

Stems of *Microsorum pustulatum* flecked with dark scales. The fronds are the simple juvenile type.

Microsorum scandens on a nikau. Fronds nearest the ground are simple, those above are compound.

LEATHER LEAF FERN (Plate 32)

Pyrrosia eleagnifolia **Polypodiaceae**

P. eleagnifolia is widespread throughout the country in coastal to mountain forests.

The fronds are undivided, fleshy and smooth margined, from almost round to elongate, densely covered with stellate hairs on the undersides, 3–20 cm long x 0.5–2 cm wide. The slender stems are freely branched and spread widely over the branches and trunks of trees. The dome-like sori often largely cover the leaf undersides.

With the water stored in the fleshy leaves and the reduction of evaporation by the covering of hairs, this fern is very drought tolerant. It also grows abundantly on introduced trees and can often be found on rocks in well-lit places.

P. eleagnifolia is restricted to New Zealand but other species are found in Africa, Asia and the Pacific Islands.

MANGEMANGE (Plate 32)

Lygodium articulatum **Schizaeaceae**

This climbing fern has an unusual way of growing. What appear to be stems are technically fronds of indefinite growth that twine around slender supports and often reach the forest canopy. The true stems are quite short and remain attached to the ground. It is a common species in lowland forests in the north of the North Island from North Cape to the Bay of Plenty.

The sterile leaflets branch by 2–3 equal forkings to form smooth-margined secondary leaflets up to 10 cm long x 2 cm wide. The fertile leaflets fork many times and have lobes at their tips with sporangia along the margins.

L. articulatum is restricted to New Zealand. Other species are found in tropical and subtropical regions.

Fronds of leatherleaf fern, *Pyrrosia eleagnifolia*, arising from a network of stems attached to a tree trunk.

Mangemange, *Lygodium articulatum*.

An entanglement of mangemange (*Lygodium articulatum*) against a kauri trunk background.

EPIPHYTES

NEST EPIPHYTES

Some large trees have their branches densely loaded with nest epiphytes and from a distance they certainly do look like large nests, rather like those made by storks in Europe or white herons closer to home.

Nest epiphytes in the tropics belong to several families, including ferns and, in the American tropics, the distinctive bromeliads. Our 3 species belong to the lily family and have long narrow leaves densely tufted in large clumps. In *Astelia solandri* the leaves do not have a fan-like arrangement and the leaf bases are silvery and strongly folded and flattened. In the 2 collospermums the leaves often have a fan-like arrangement and their black to dark brown bases are broad and strongly rounded. The funnel-like spaces between the leaf bases are able to store considerable quantities of rainwater. In all the species the flowers are male or female on different plants.

The nest epiphytes *Collospermum hastatum* (below) and a young *Astelia solandri* (above).

KOWHARAWHARA (Plate 33)

Astelia solandri **Liliaceae**

A. *solandri* is found, mostly as an epiphyte, in lowland forest throughout the North Island and as far as south Westland in the South Island. It is the only New Zealand species of *Astelia* that is consistently epiphytic. Our other species grow on the ground, some in forests, others in open habitats from the coasts to the mountains.

The leaves are in dense drooping tufts, 1–2 m long x 2–3.5 cm wide, with the 2 sides of each leaf tightly folded together at the base. The upper sides of the leaves are bright green, the undersides silvery.

The inflorescences are branched with many small yellowish to maroon flowers. The berries are spherical, 4–5 mm in diameter and translucent green to yellowish brown. Flowering is from mid-spring to early winter with berries present at most times of the year.

The genus occurs elsewhere in southeast Australia and on islands in the Pacific, including Hawaii, as well as islands in the south Indian and south Atlantic oceans.

Collospermum microspermum (Plate 33)
Liliaceae

C. *microspermum* is found only in the North Island

as a common epiphyte in forests above about 300 m altitude. With its narrow leaves it could be mistaken for *Astelia solandri,* but its dark rounded leaf bases make it easy to distinguish.

The leaves are densely tufted, drooping, 0.4–1.5 m long x 1–2.5 cm wide, often arranged in fans, with black to dark brown, broadly rounded bases. The 2 leaf surfaces are dull green.

The inflorescences, 5–15 cm long, are branched with many small whitish flowers. The berries are spherical, milky white and 4.5 mm in diameter. Flowering is from late spring through summer, with berries from late summer to early winter.

Opposite: A profusion of epiphytes on a northern rata, which also began life as an epiphyte. At the upper left is a nest of *Collospermum hastatum*; below that *Astelia solandri* with the fern *Asplenium flaccidum* hanging below it; and lowermost of all a spindly shrub of *Pittosporum cornifolium*. At top centre is a young specimen of the large shrub epiphyte puka, *Griselinia lucida*. On the right are more nest epiphytes, some with the fern *Asplenium polyodon* hanging below them.

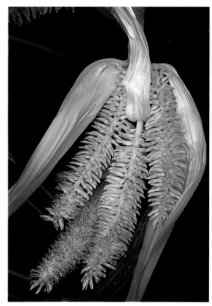

Left: A leaf fan of *Collospermum hastatum* with distinctive black bases. Rainwater is stored in the spaces between the leaf bases. Right: A pendent inflorescence of *Collospermum hastatum* with male flowers and buds.

Collospermum hastatum with colourful berries from female flowers.

KAHAKAHA (Plate 33)
Collospermum hastatum

C. hastatum is a common epiphyte in coastal and lowland forests throughout the North Island and in the north of the South Island.

The leaves are densely tufted, not drooping, 0.6–1.7 m long x 3–7 cm wide, often arranged in fans with black broadly rounded bases. The 2 leaf surfaces are dull to bronzy green.

The hanging inflorescences, 15–30 cm long, are branched with many small pale yellow flowers. The berries are spherical, translucent yellow changing to red, and about 4.5 mm in diameter. Flowering is from mid- summer to early autumn with berries through autumn and winter.

Collospermum has fewer species and a more restricted distribution than *Astelia*. Apart from our 2 species there is one in Fiji and another in Samoa.

Left: Attractive fronds of epiphytic *Asplenium polyodon*. Right: Massive hanging tassels of club moss *Huperzia varia* and (to the left and right above) *Asplenium flaccidum*; both hang below a nest epiphyte. At bottom left is a young plant of the shrub epiphyte puka.

Asplenium polyodon   Aspleniaceae

This is a common species of epiphytic fern in lowland and mountain forests throughout the North Island and mostly in the west of the South Island.

Its roots frequently anchor into the soil below a nest epiphyte and its attractive divided leaves hang downwards. As well as its association with nest epiphytes, it may also attach to trunks and branches.

The frond blades are up to 1 m long, leaflets are wedge-shaped and shiny dark green, 5–12 cm long x 1–3 cm wide, with large teeth each divided into a number of smaller teeth. The tufts of fronds are attached to very short concealed stems, and the frond stalks are densely covered with scales. The elongated sori lie between the leaflet margins and the midribs.

A. polyodon also grows in Australia and in the tropics from Madagascar to the Pacific.

Asplenium flaccidum

A. flaccidum is a common epiphytic fern throughout the country in coastal to mountain forests. It is also frequently found on tree fern trunks.

The frond blades are up to 1 m long with dull green toothed leaflets 2–20 cm long x 0.5–2 cm wide. The lowermost leaflets may themselves be divided into leaflets. In comparison with *A. polyodon*, it has much more slender, almost string-like leaf divisions. The leaf stalks are sparsely scaly. The sori are near the margins of the teeth.

The species is also found in Australia.

Huperzia varia
(syn. *Lycopodium varium*)   Lycopodiaceae

This is a common species of club moss (see page 236) that occurs throughout the country in lowland to lower mountain forests. It is also found in Australia. Like the aspleniums, *Lycopodium varium* often hangs below nest epiphytes. The stems fork freely to form large and heavy masses that sway in the lightest breeze. A smaller form grows on tree fern trunks.

The small leaves are close set, undivided, spirally arranged and up to 2 cm long x 2–3 mm wide. The sporangia are formed singly in the angles of often reduced leaves at the branch tips.

The genus *Lycopodium* is widespread throughout the world in cold to tropical regions.

EPIPHYTIC ORCHIDS
Orchidaceae

In New Zealand we have about 120 native orchids, of which 7 are epiphytes. They are attached by their roots to mossy branches or trunks.

When there are no distinctive flowers to be seen, orchids can be recognised by their exposed white roots that sometimes develop chlorophyll and become partly green. See also forest floor orchids, pages 216–219.

Further reading: *The Nature Guide to New Zealand Native Orchids*, Ian St George.

Earina mucronata (Plate 33)

E. mucronata is found throughout the country in coastal and lowland forests where it often festoons more or less horizontal branches.

The hanging unbranched stems can be up to 1 m long and are quite strongly flattened. The thin grassy leaves are 6–15 cm long x 4–6 mm wide.

The branched terminal inflorescences hang downwards. The flowers are 1–1.2 cm in diameter, perfumed, mostly greenish cream but with the strongly lobed lip petal yellow to apricot. Flowering mostly occurs through spring to early summer.

Earina is restricted to New Zealand, New Caledonia, Fiji, Samoa and Tahiti.

Earina autumnalis (Plate 33)

This species is found throughout the country in coastal and lowland forest, sometimes in association with *E. mucronata*.

The stems can be up to 1 m long, as in *E. mucronata*, but are usually shorter and are rounded to a little flattened. The stiff leaves are 4–12 cm long x 5–8 mm wide, sheathing at the base.

The branched terminal inflorescences turn upwards. The flowers are about 13 mm in diameter, strongly perfumed, waxy white with an unlobed lip petal, yellow at the base. Flowering mostly occurs from late summer through to early winter.

Winika cunninghamii (Plate 33)
(syn. *Dendrobium cunninghamii*)

W. cunninghamii is found throughout the country in lowland forest, often in branch forks of tall trees.

The much-branched masses of stems and leaves hang downwards and can be up to 1.5 m long. The

Earina mucronata with hanging clusters of green and orange flowers.

Earina autumnalis with white, yellow-centred flowers in upward-turning clusters.

Strongly perfumed *Earina autumnalis* in full flower.

stems look like those of a slender bamboo and the older lower parts are shiny as if polished and are sometimes coloured bright yellow. The leaves are 3–5 cm long x 3 mm wide.

The flowers are formed in small groups near the branch tips. They are mostly white with the lower lip petal partly rose purple, 2–2.5 cm in diameter. Flowering is mostly through spring to early summer.

Winika is restricted to New Zealand.

Drymoanthus adversus

This small tufted plant with conspicuous widely spreading roots is found throughout the country in lowland forests mostly on tree trunks and well-lit branches. The leaves are up to 6 cm long x 1.5 cm wide.

The small inflorescences occur in the leaf angles. The flowers are about 7 mm across, greenish white with red flecks, the lip petal cup-shaped. The seed capsule is much larger than the flower at about 1.5 cm long x 3.5 mm wide. Flowering occurs from mid-spring to early summer.

Winika cunninghamii.

A second species of *Drymoanthus* has recently been described: **D. flavus**. In general appearance the 2 species are similar, although *D. flavus* is smaller, has yellow flowers and tends to have spotted leaves rather than spotted flowers. It is uncommon but has been collected at scattered localities from near Rotorua to Stewart Island.

The genus is restricted to eastern Australia and New Zealand.

Bulbophyllum pygmaeum

B. pygmaeum is found throughout the country in coastal to lowland forest but is most abundant in the north. It is also found on Lord Howe Island.

Its slender branching stems form dense spreading mats on branch surfaces and sometimes on coastal rocks in Westland. The spherical bulb-like swellings at the leaf bases are 3–5 mm in diameter; the leaf blade is 4–10 mm long x 2–4 mm wide. The small flowers form singly from below the bulbs. They are whitish and 1.5–2 mm long, and appear in early summer.

The genus Bulbophyllum includes more than 1000 species, mostly in the tropics of America, Africa and Asia.

Bulbophyllum tuberculatum

This species is found at scattered localities in lowland forest in the North Island and near Collingwood in the northwest of the South Island.

It forms smaller mats than B. pygmaeum. The elongate bulb-like swellings at the leaf bases are 6–7 mm long x 3–4 mm wide; the leaf blade is up to 5 cm long x 5 mm wide but usually less. The flowers are generally in small groups from below the bulbs. They are mostly whitish but with a red lip petal and about 4 mm long. Flowering occurs in late autumn.

Above: Drymoanthus adversus with pale spreading attaching roots.
Centre: Bulbophyllum pygmaeum, a very small epiphytic orchid.
Below: Bulbophyllum tuberculatum showing 'bulbs', leaves and flowers.

EPIPHYTIC TREES & SHRUBS

Three small shrubs—*Pittosporum cornifolium*, *P. kirkii* and *Brachyglottis kirkii* var. *kirkii*—are found as epiphytes; they never send roots to the ground.

Five large epiphytic shrubs or trees eventually send a root or roots down to the ground. Only 2 of them are almost always epiphytic and widespread in their distribution: puka (*Griselinia lucida*) and northern rata (*Metrosideros robusta*). Southern rata, broadleaf and mountain five-finger are also widespread but are more often terrestrial than epiphytic. They mostly grow in wet mountain climates where it is relatively easy for them to establish on moss-laden branches.

Pittosporum cornifolium (Plate 34)
Pittosporaceae

This species is found in lowland to lower mountain forests throughout the North Island and in the north of the South Island.

It is a rather spindly shrub, often hanging below nest epiphytes. The leaves are 3.5–7.5 cm long x 1.5–3.5 cm wide, smooth margined, stiff but not fleshy, with pointed tips and short stalks.

The spindly stems and foliage of *Pittosporum cornifolium* hanging below an epiphyte nest.

Left: Leaves and brightly coloured open capsules of *Pittosporum cornifolium*. Right: The small epiphytic shrub *Pittosporum kirkii* with terminal clusters of yellowish flowers.

The flowers, in terminal clusters, are each about 1 cm long with pale red to yellowish petals. The capsules are rounded and about 15 mm in diameter. The open capsules have an orange- red interior with black seeds embedded in a bright yellow sticky fluid and are attractive to birds. Some of the seeds not eaten can become attached to the birds and transported to other trees. Flowering occurs through winter to early spring with capsules opening from mid-spring to early autumn.

Pittosporum kirkii (Plate 34)

P. kirkii is found in lowland to lower mountain forests from the far north to the central North Island.

It is a more or less erect shrub. The smooth-margined leaves are thick and somewhat fleshy, 5–10 cm long x 2–3 cm wide, with rounded tips and stalks about 1 cm long.

The flowers, in terminal clusters, are each about 2 cm long with yellow petals. The capsules are elongated, 2.5–4 cm long and strongly flattened. The open capsules have seeds embedded in a sticky yellow fluid. Flowers and capsules are present from late spring to mid-summer so presumably the latter take a year to ripen.

Brachglottis kirkii var. *kirkii* growing on a tree trunk.

Brachyglottis kirkii var. kirkii (Plate 34)
Asteraceae

This plant is found in lowland to lower mountain forest throughout the North Island.

It is an erect shrub. The leaves are alternate, soft and rather fleshy, 4–10 cm long x 2–4 cm wide, generally with a few large teeth towards the ends of the blades.

The flowers, in crowded terminal heads, are pure white and up to 5 cm in diameter. The dry seed-like fruits have parachutes of hairs for wind dispersal. Flowering and fruiting are from mid-spring to mid-autumn.

PUKA, SHINING BROADLEAF (Plate 34)

Griselinia lucida   **Griseliniaceae**

The name puka is applied to several unrelated species, notably the widely cultivated *Meryta sinclairii*.

Puka mostly establishes itself in nest epiphytes or at branch forks. Eventually it sends a root to the ground that presses close to the bark of the supporting tree and branches near to the ground. Once ground contact is made, the roots enlarge in size and develop distinctive longitudinal ridges and grooves. Near the top of the main root horizontal

A puka growing on a large cabbage tree.

Distinctive longitudinally grooved puka roots.

Epiphytic puka can grow on the ground in sunny sites.

girdling roots develop and encircle the supporting trunk several times to firmly anchor the puka. The descending main root can be 10 cm or more in diameter, but this would not seem sufficient for the puka to stand alone, so it probably falls with its supporting tree.

G. lucida is found throughout the country in lowland forests although it is more common in the north. In some forests puka can be very abundant.

It is a shrub to small tree up to 8 m tall. The leaves are bright green, shiny, thick and leathery, 7–18 cm long x 4–10 cm wide, broadly rounded at the tip with one side shorter than the other at the base, giving a lop-sided appearance.

The flowers are very small and greenish, in clusters on the twigs. The berries are 5-10 mm long, dark purple. Flowering is from mid-spring to early summer with berries ripening through the following summer, autumn and winter. (See also pages 145, 183, 190.)

Broadleaf, ***Griselinia littoralis***, sometimes grows as an epiphyte. It is similar to puka, although it lacks its distinctively grooved roots. For description see page 145.

NORTHERN RATA
Metrosideros robusta   Myrtaceae

Northern rata doesn't appear to associate with nest epiphytes but mostly establishes itself on branch surfaces or trunks. Young plants often have swollen tuber-like modifications of their roots that may store water. A slender root eventually grows downwards and this often branches near the ground to form a basal tripod or some more complex arrangement. Horizontal girdling roots also form and sometimes extend for the full length of the main descending root. In time the main roots enlarge greatly and fuse together to form a massive and contorted 'pseudo-trunk', able to stand on its own when the supporting tree within dies and rots away. The space left by the supporting tree is like a narrow cave.

Northern rata has sometimes been referred to as 'strangling rata' with the implication that it kills the supporting tree, usually a rimu or another conifer. However, when the light-demanding northern rata establishes itself in a tree crown, the supporting tree is already mature and it may just die of old age by the time the northern rata is itself a mature tree. That death is probably hastened, however, by the rata crown shading that of the supporting tree and by the roots of the interlocked trees having to compete for water and nutrients. For description see page 94.

VINES, EPIPHYTES & MISTLETOES   189

Left: A rimu heavily burdened with epiphytes. At the top is the crown of a northern rata in flower. Below that is the shiny-leaved crown of a puka and clumps of nest epiphytes. Right: A young stage of a northern rata on a rimu. The main descending root is on the right with a series of horizontal girdling roots.

Where southern rata, ***Metrosideros umbellata***, grows as an epiphyte the end result is similar to that of northern rata. Little is known about the earlier stages and in particular whether girdling roots are formed. For description see page 95.

Metrosideros bartlettii was found only in the 1970s, in forest patches near North Cape. Like northern rata it is frequently epiphytic but is found on tree ferns as well as on trees such as puriri. Northern rata occurs in the same area but the 2 are easily distinguished. The pseudotrunk of *M. bartlettii* has pale soft bark separating in thin flakes, while northern rata has darker thicker bark. The leaves of *M. bartlettii* are quite thin and pointed at the tip and its small white flowers are quite different from those of the other tree ratas.

The pseudotrunk, comprising coalesced roots, of a mature northern rata. The original supporting tree has long since died and rotted away.

EPIPHYTES & VINES ON TREE FERN TRUNKS

The trunks of tree ferns provide a home for several epiphytes and vines. In some cases the decaying frond bases offer niches where epiphyte seeds or spores can easily lodge, as well as a fibrous medium, not unlike potting mix, in which they can germinate and become established. This is especially the case with ponga and wheki, whose old fronds drop away from their persistent stalk bases very readily leaving the way open to invaders. In the gully tree fern the stalk bases are pressed tightly to the trunk so it is difficult for seedlings to gain a foothold. In other tree ferns the entire old fronds (wheki-ponga) or their midribs (*Cyathea smithii*) hang downwards and persist as thick skirts that prevent the establishment of epiphytes and vines. However, in tall older specimens of these species, the skirts no longer reach the ground and seedlings can take root below them in the fibrous layers of fine roots that make up the bulk of the lower trunks.

Mamaku do not have persistent old fronds, except very untidily when young. The old leaves separate, leaving hard shield-like scars that form an armour-like surface over the trunk that is unsuitable for the establishment of seedlings.

Tree fern trunks are partly or completely shaded by their often enormous umbrella-like crowns, so the epiphytes and vines have to be reasonably shade tolerant. Some trees that begin life as tree fern epiphytes eventually push their crowns through the fronds to reach the light. When the tree fern dies, the trees often remain standing on roots that extend to the ground within the remains of the tree fern trunk.

FORK FERNS

Tmesipteris   Psilotaceae

These are not ferns at all but belong to a small group of spore-producing plants that are believed to have descended from a group of primitive early land plants that are only known from fossils.

There are 4 species of *Tmesipteris* in New Zealand, one of them rare (*T. sigmatifolia*). The genus is also found in eastern Australia, Tasmania, New Caledonia and some high islands in the central Pacific. They grow mostly on tree fern trunks and their hanging stems are usually unbranched. The leaves are small, flattened and simple. The distinctive sporangia, divided into 2 compartments, are each attached near the end of a short stalk from which a pair of leaves diverge.

T. tannensis is widespread but mostly in the west in lowland and mountain forests. It is sometimes also epiphytic on trees.

The stems are 5–80 cm long and are unbranched. The leaves, in many planes, are about 2 mm wide and the sporangia are drawn out and pointed at each end.

T. elongata is widespread in the North Island, but mostly in the west of the South Island in lowland to mountain forests. It also grows in Australia.

The stems are 5 cm–1 m long and sometimes fork a few times. The leaves, in many planes, are about 1.5 mm wide and the sporangia are rounded.

T. lanceolata is found in coastal to lowland forest in the northern half of the North Island with a few records from the northwest of the South Island. It also grows in New Caledonia and Queensland.

The stems are 4–20 cm long and unbranched. The leaves, flattened in one plane, are about 4 mm wide and the sporangia are rounded.

The fork fern *Tmesipteris tannensis* growing on a tree fern trunk. Sporangia can be seen here and there.

Lycopodium varium

A small form of this club moss is frequent on tree fern trunks. See page 183 for the description.

FILMY FERNS

Filmy ferns are a distinctive group that are often found growing on tree fern trunks. Their spreading stems are wiry and slender and are attached to the trunks by short roots. (See also pages 234–236.)

Trichomanes venosum is abundant in wetter coastal to mountain forest throughout New Zealand.

The frond blades are narrow and up to 14 cm long with light green translucent conspicuously veined primary leaflets. There may also be a few secondary leaflets at the base of the blade.

Hymenophyllum ferrugineum is found in lowland to mountain forests throughout the North Island, in the west of the South Island and in Stewart Island.

The spreading stems are thin and bear olive-green fronds whose blades, up to 20 cm long, are densely covered with reddish brown stellate hairs.

H. flabellatum is found throughout the country in moister lowland to mountain forests.

The thin stems bear tufts of yellow hairs as do the frond stalks. The frond blades are yellow green, hairless and up to 25 cm long.

A ponga tree fern trunk with epiphytic ferns, a fork fern, *Tmesipteris tannensis*, and a very small filmy fern.

Rumohra adiantiformis   Dryopteridaceae

Found throughout New Zealand in lowland to mountain forests, this fern is widespread in the Southern Hemisphere.

The climbing stems are densely covered with golden brown scales and are attached to tree fern trunks by short roots. They bear leathery much-divided fronds up to 50 cm long. The black dome-like sori are very prominent on the undersides.

FIVE-FINGER

Pseudopanax arboreus   Araliaceae

For description see page 78.

Five-finger seedlings usually establish themselves among frond bases just below a tree fern crown. Branching roots then gradually make their way down through the dense zone of wiry roots to the ground. At the same time the tree fern has been increasing in height, but not as rapidly as the stem of the five-finger, which now holds its crown well above the fronds of the tree fern. The five-finger ends up with a pseudotrunk comprising its own fused roots combined with the trunk of the tree fern, until the tree fern dies and rots away.

Rumohra adiantiformis on a tree fern trunk.

Left: A tree fern with 2 young five-fingers. Right: On the left a mature five-finger is growing on a tree fern. In the background a towai is growing on a collapsed tree fern.

KAMAHI

Weinmannia racemosa   Cunoniaceae

For description see page 86.

In cooler forests seedlings of kamahi are frequently observed on tree fern trunks. Larger specimens mostly seem to develop in the fibrous root zone near the base of a tree fern. Roots grow the short distance to the ground and a trunk curves upward towards the forest canopy. Kamahi often branch near the base to form several to many spreading trunks. If you look in among the trunks of a mature kamahi you may find the stump of the original tree fern on which the kamahi started its life. On Mt Taranaki and Mt Ruapehu there are examples of large kamahi, each with a tall tree fern among their trunks still bearing a living crown of fronds.

Towai (*Weinmannia silvicola*, page 87) and makamaka (*Ackama rosifolia*, page 87) have also been observed growing as low tree fern epiphytes in the north of the North Island.

A tree fern bearing a large kamahi trunk on its base and another smaller kamahi higher up.

VINES, EPIPHYTES & MISTLETOES   193

MISTLETOE PARASITES

The word 'mistletoe' evokes images of druids or kisses at Christmas. This is the European mistletoe and, despite its role in folklore, it is a modest plant with small whitish flowers and white berries. Some New Zealand species too have inconspicuous flowers but others are spectacular with relatively large bright red or yellow flowers.

Mistletoes can be divided into 2 groups — large shrubby species with well-developed leaves and much smaller dwarf species whose leaves are reduced to scales. The former mostly parasitise small to large trees and the latter, shrubs.

The mistletoes can be recognised as parasites by their foliage being clearly different from that of the host and, at the point or points of attachment, by their stems being anchored by outgrowths penetrating the host. In shrubby species with stems spreading over the host surface, the suckers or haustoria can often be clearly seen.

Native birds visit the larger brightly coloured mistletoe flowers for nectar and bring about their pollination. At the bud stage these flowers have bulbous tips and birds such as tuis have been observed to tweak the tips, causing the long petals to separate explosively, scattering pollen on to the birds before curling back to expose the nectar.

Native bees have also been observed to perform this trick although, as they are smaller than the flower buds, it takes them rather longer to achieve. They tweak the bud tips with their mandibles and eventually the buds open.

Birds are also involved in seed dispersal. They swallow the berries and eventually excrete the sticky seeds unharmed, sometimes onto a suitable branch. Also when squeezed, or even without such encouragement, the berries expel their single seeds with some force. The seeds with their glue-like coating attach to nearby branches, or to feathers and beaks, later to be preened off to stick firmly to branches of sometimes distant trees.

Ileostylus micranthus with bright yellow berries.

The greenish yellow flowers, in groups of up to 15, are 3–5 mm in diameter. The berries are 5–7 mm long and white to pink with purple spots. Flowering is from mid-spring to early summer with berries ripe through summer and autumn

The genus with its one species is found only in New Zealand.

Ileostylus micranthus   Loranthaceae
This species is found throughout the country on a wide range of hosts including coprosmas, lacebarks, manuka and totara. It is also occasionally found on a number of introduced trees and shrubs.

It is a shrub up to 1 m in diameter with a few stems forming suckers spreading from the initial point of attachment. The leaves are 2–8 cm long x 1–3 cm wide.

The greenish yellow flowers, in groups of up to 10, are about 5 mm in diameter. The berries are bright yellow and 5–8 mm long. Flowering is from mid-spring to early summer with ripe berries through summer and autumn.

The one species of this genus is found only in New Zealand and on Norfolk Island.

Tupeia antarctica   Loranthaceae
T. antarctica is found throughout the country, mostly on five-finger, species of *Coprosma* and putaputaweta. It also attacks the introduced broom and may parasitise other shrubby mistletoes.

It is a shrub up to 1 m in diameter. The leaves vary in form on the same plant and are mostly 3–5 cm long x 1–3 cm wide. This species is unique among the shrubby mistletoes because it has only one point of attachment to its host.

Peraxilla tetrapetala on a mountain beech.

Peraxilla tetrapetala   Loranthaceae

This species is found throughout the country, particularly on mountain beech but also on *Quintinia*.

It is a freely branched bushy shrub up to 1 m or more high with many stems, which form suckers and spread down the branches of the host and often onto its trunk. New clumps of leafy stems arise, here and there, from the network of spreading stems. Leaves are mostly 1.5–3.5 cm long x 1–1.5 cm wide.

The flowers are single or in groups of 2–3, 25–35 mm long, bright red to orange with the petals splitting right to the base. The berries are yellow to orange, 4–5 mm long. Flowering is from mid-spring to mid-summer with berries forming through the summer.

The genus of 2 species is restricted to New Zealand

Peraxilla colensoi

P. colensoi is found throughout the country but is more common in the south, where it often grows on silver beech. It can also be found on ratas and pittosporums as well as some introduced trees.

This species has a very similar habit of growth to that of *P. tetrapetala*. The leaves are mostly 4–6 cm long x 3–4 cm wide.

An impressive display of *Peraxilla tetrapetala*. Its spreading stems can be seen on the trunk of the beech tree.

VINES, EPIPHYTES & MISTLETOES   **195**

Left: *Peraxilla colensoi* with eye-catching crimson flowers. Centre: Yellow buds and orange to red flowers of *Alepis flavida*. Right: *Korthalsella lindsayi* at the top growing on *Melicope simplex*.

The flowers are in groups of 3–10, 3.5–5 cm long, crimson with the petals splitting right to the base. The berries are orange, 6–8 mm long.

Flowering is from late spring through summer with berries through summer into autumn.

Alepis flavida   Loranthaceae

This mistletoe can be found from about Auckland southwards mostly on mountain beech, sometimes sharing trees with *Peraxilla tetrapetala*.

It is a sparsely branched shrub up to 1 m high. The spreading sucker-forming stems are not as extensive as those of the peraxillas and usually do not reach the trunk of the host. Leafy shoots do not arise from these stems. The leaves are mostly 3–5 cm long x 7–10 mm wide with the leaf veins readily visible below.

The flowers are in groups of 6–15, 1–2 cm long, bright yellow to orange yellow or red with the petals splitting only halfway to the base. The berries are yellow to orange and 4–5 mm long. Flowering is through summer with berries from mid-summer through autumn.

Korthalsella lindsayi   Viscaceae

This species is found from the central North Island southwards mostly on small-leaved species of *Coprosma* and *Melicope simplex*. It is sometimes difficult to detect on the latter as the flattened stem segments are quite similar to the leaves of the host.

The plants are flattened in one plane, branching at wide angles and mostly 3–5 cm long and wide. The stem segments are flattened and leaf-like, 5–12 mm long x 3–9 mm wide.

The minute flowers are borne on clusters of narrow branchlets. The berries are greenish and about 2 mm long. Flowering and fruiting is from late spring through summer.

The genus *Korthalsella* is widespread elsewhere in the world.

The Forest Floor

THE FOREST FLOOR

The forest floor is the shadiest and most sheltered place in the forest and here are found mostly small to very small plants, including herbaceous flowering plants, ferns, and hundreds of species of mosses, liverworts, lichens and fungi that often require microscopes to reveal their detailed structures. Most people do not notice these miniature plants individually unless they are brightly coloured, as with some of the fungi, or have colourful berries. In mist-shrouded cloud forests, where the ground and trunks and branches of trees may be blanketed with ferns, mosses, lichens and a few flowering plants, these small plants are noticeable because they are growing in mass rather than individually.

In this section we will consider the larger ferns and flowering plants, individually or in groups, and open the door on the many smaller plants, defining their groups and how they live, highlighting interesting and attractive examples, and giving references to more comprehensive accounts for those readers who want to explore particular groups in more detail.

A soft carpet of mosses with a *Corybas* orchid.

GRASSES & OTHER TUFTED PLANTS

All the plants of this group have long narrow parallel-veined leaves. Not all are true grasses (Poaceae). Others are sedges (Cyperaceae) or rushes (Juncaceae), but share with grasses their small crowded wind-pollinated flowers and dry seeds. Others again, included for their tufted appearance, belong to the lily and related families and have larger insect-pollinated flowers with the seeds mostly embedded in fleshy berries.

Further reading: *The Cultivation of New Zealand Native Grasses*, Lawrie Metcalf.

Kauri grass (*Astelia trinervia*) in a kauri forest.

KAURI GRASS

Astelia trinervia   **Liliaceae**

Kauri grass is common in kauri forests in the north of the North Island and reappears in west Nelson in the South Island. The leaves are 1–3 m long x 2–4.5 cm wide. The 2 halves of the leaves, just above the sheath, are tightly folded together. There are 3 conspicuous veins on each side of the midrib and parallel to it.

The flowers are dull maroon and the deep crimson berries are seated on the shrivelled remains of the flowers. Flowering occurs through autumn to early winter with berries present for much of the year.

The astelias have separate male and female plants.

Astelia fragrans

This species is found throughout the country in coastal to lower mountain forests. The leaves are 0.5–2 m long x 2.5–7.5 cm wide. Unlike *A. trinervia*, the leaf bases are not tightly folded, and there is a single prominent vein on each side of the midrib.

The flowers are greenish fawn to dark green and the berries, orange flecked with red, are seated on the fleshy orange remains of the flowers. Flowering occurs in late spring with berries present through summer and autumn.

Astelia nervosa

This distinctive species is found throughout the country in mountain to subalpine forest and tussock grassland. In the latter habitat some forms of the species are so white with scales that they appear to be covered with frost. The leaves are 0.5–1.5 m long x 2–4 cm wide. The veins are obscured by thick

Astelia fragrans in beech forest.

Green (unripe) and orange berries of *Astelia fragrans*.

layers of scales that can sometimes be ruffled up into a white shaggy fur. The leaves are so thickly covered with scales that they are often bronze to white rather than green, particularly on the undersides.

The flowers are greenish fawn to dark maroon and the berries, orange to almost red, are partly enclosed by the fleshy remains of the flowers. Flowering occurs from spring to early summer with berries from late summer through autumn.

Astelia solandri, normally epiphytic, often grows as a ground plant as well (see page 181).

Astelia banksii

A. banksii is mostly found in coastal forest and shrubbery south to the Bay of Plenty. The leaves are 1–2.5 m long x 3–4.5 cm wide. The several parallel veins on each side of the midrib are evenly spaced and not very conspicous. The undersides of the leaves are white with scales.

The flowers are pale greenish cream and the berries are at first bright green, then whitish, and when ripe are partly or completely magenta. Flowering is through autumn into winter and berries can be found at most times of the year.

Astelia nervosa: growing in mountain shrubland (left); a silvery form (right).

Astelia banksii with a small inflorescence.

Luzula picta var. pallida showing the characteristic cobwebby hairs.

Luzula   **Juncaceae**

Of the 11 species of *Luzula* in New Zealand, only one variety of *L. picta* grows in forests. The other species inhabit rock outcrops or tussock grassland.

This rush is found through most of the North Island and locally in Nelson and the east of the South Island. It ranges from sea level in the far south up to 1200 m further north.

L. picta var. pallida is a tufted grass-like plant up to about 30 cm high when in flower. The leaves are about 5 mm wide with distinctive scattered long soft hairs. The pale cream flowers are in several rounded clusters. Flowering in the luzulas is from spring to early summer and the capsules ripen from late spring to mid-summer.

Luzula is widespread in temperate regions and also on mountains in the tropics.

TURUTU, BLUE BERRY, INK BERRY
Dianella nigra   **Liliaceae**

D. nigra is found throughout the country except for Stewart Island. It grows on the forest floor, banks and the edges of bush tracks.

The plants form tussocks up to 50 cm or more in height. The flowerheads are much and widely branched with delicate slender stalks. The flowers are greenish white and 6–9 mm in diameter, while the berries are up to 1 cm in diameter and often coloured a vivid blue purple. Picking for a vase is never successful as the delicately attached berries fall off readily.

Flowers appear from late spring to early summer and berries through summer to autumn.

Dianella is widespread in the southern hemisphere but there is only one species in New Zealand.

Libertia   **Iridaceae**

Two of our 4 species of *Libertia* grow on the forest floor: *L. grandiflora* and *L. pulchella*.

L. grandiflora grows along streams and on the forest floor through the North Island and in the north of the South Island. It forms tussocks up to 50 cm or more in height.

The flowerheads are freely branched with white flowers 1.5–3 cm in diameter. The seed capsules are up to 10 mm in diameter and are almost black when mature. The flowers open in the spring and capsules ripen from mid-summer into autumn.

L. pulchella is much the smallest of our species and is most frequently encountered in wet mossy forests in the mountains. It is found throughout the

Dianella nigra with handsome purple berries attached to slender stalks.

Libertia grandiflora in flower.

Libertia pulchella growing among mosses in cloud forest.

country and is also native to Tasmania, eastern Australia and New Guinea.

Often there are only a few leaf fans per plant and they are characteristically flattened towards the ground. The leaves are up to 5 cm long. The flowerheads are little branched with white flowers 1–1.5 cm in diameter. The capsules are up to 4 mm in diameter. Flowering is in late spring and early summer with capsules ripening from late summer to early winter.

Gahnia   **Cyperaceae**

The most distinctive feature of *Gahnia* species is the way in which the filaments of the pollen-producing stamens become greatly elongated and entangled as the seeds develop. When the latter are released many of them are snared by these threads and hang suspended for some time. The seeds can be attractively coloured from red brown or orange to black.

Most species of *Gahnia* are of tussock form from 0.5 to 1.5 m high. The leaves are stiff and rough to the touch from small projections along the margins. The inflorescences are much branched with small crowded wind-pollinated flowers.

The gahnias are quite wide ranging in their habitats from forest to shrubland and bog. The forests they prefer are those where the floor is reasonably well lit, e.g. kauri and beech forests. In darker forests they are generally restricted to better-lit tracks.

There are 5 species of *Gahnia* that include forests among their habitats. They are widespread in the North Island, although in some cases less common or absent in some regions. Some of them extend to Marlborough, Nelson and Westland.

G. *lacera* alone has erect flower- or seedheads; in the other species they are drooping.

The tussocks of **G. pauciflora** and **G. procera** are usually less than 90 cm high. The flower scales of the former are dark brown and of the latter purple black.

The tussocks of **G. setifolia** and **G. xanthocarpa** are usually much more than 90 cm high. The seeds of the former are less than 4.5 mm long and red brown or yellow cream. The seeds of the latter are more than 5 mm long and black.

The inconspicuous small flowers open variously from spring through to autumn. The seeds are present most of the time.

The genus *Gahnia* is centred in New Zealand and Australia but extends to the Pacific Islands and through southeast Asia to China and Japan.

HOOKGRASS

Uncinia   Cyperaceae

The uncinias make sure that they are not passed by unnoticed by attaching their seeds firmly to clothing, fur, feathers and, somewhat painfully, to hairy legs. For this reason they are sometimes referred to as 'bastard grass'. This effective means of dispersal is achieved by a single slender hook, attached to each seed, that is shaped like a shepherd's crook.

There are about 17 species of *Uncinia* in New Zealand that grow on the forest floor, often in quite

An inflorescence of *Gahnia procera* showing the long persistent filaments of the stamens.

shady places; 10 of these are restricted to forests and the other 7 can also be found in shrubland. Many of the forest species occur throughout the country

Left: *Gahnia procera* with seeds dangling from threads. Right: *Gahnia xanthocarpa* with drooping inflorescences.

and range in altitude from sea level to 1300 m.

The uncinias form tussocks or tufts ranging in height from 5 to 75 cm. The leaves often have minute projections that make them rough to the touch. The flowers are small and scaly, and crowded into narrow spike-like heads borne singly at the tops of slender stalks. Flowering generally takes place in the spring and seeds ripen during the summer.

The genus *Uncinia* is widespread in the Southern Hemisphere with the exception of South Africa.

Carex   Cyperaceae

Four of the forest species, including *C. testacea,* are widespread through the country and range from sea level to 600–1200 m. The remaining 2 are largely restricted to the North Island.

Carex is similar to *Uncinia* but lacks the distinctive seed hooks and generally has a few lateral as well as terminal flower spikes. The tufts or tussocks range from 10 cm to 1 m in height.

It is a very large genus with more than a thousand species in cold and temperate regions and mountains in the tropics. Of our 73 species, 6 grow on the forest floor as well as in open habitats.

C. testacea, along with a few other species of mostly open habitats, is remarkable in that the flowering stems at the seed stage lie along the ground and, with renewed growth, extend away from the plant for as much as 3 m, spreading the seeds as far away from the parent plant as possible.

Carex mostly flower from late spring to mid-summer with the seeds maturing from mid-summer to early autumn.

Above: *Uncinia uncinata* with seedheads.
Centre: *Uncinia* seedhead showing the distinctively hooked stalks attached to each seed. The hooks are a very effective device for seed dispersal.
Below: *Carex dissita* with seedheads.

SNOW GRASSES

Chionochloa **Poaceae**

The snow grasses, as the common name suggests, are mostly found on mountain slopes. Where they dominate, their sometimes large tussocks provide a very attractive texture to the landscape. A few species are largely restricted to coastal rocks and cliffs, and 2 grow in forests as well as sheltered open habitats.

The forest species of *Chionochloa* differ from the other forest grasses in the large size of their tussocks. They are up to 1 m high and the stout flowering stems are up to 2 m high. The latter have prominent swollen joints and look rather like the stems of a slender bamboo. The flower- and later seedheads are much and openly branched and have an attractive feathery appearance.

The 2 forest species, ***C. conspicua*** and ***C. cheesemanii***, are similar in general appearance, but the most easily observable difference is the wider leaves of the former, up to 7mm, than the latter, up to 4 mm. *C. cheesemanii* is also a smaller plant than *C. conspicua*.

One subspecies of *C. conspicua* is widespread in wetter areas of the South Island and in Stewart Island. The other subspecies is found through the axial ranges of the North Island, in Northland, Coromandel Peninsula and Mt Pirongia. Both subspecies occur in a range of forest types and in shrubland from sea level to 1500 m.

C. cheesemanii has scattered populations along the North Island axial ranges and in the far north of the South Island. It grows in beech forest and grasslands from 900 to 1500 m.

Flowering then seed formation take place from spring through summer. The genus *Chionochloa* is also represented in Australia.

Carex testacea.

Chionochloa conspicua with many feathery flowerheads.

BUSH RICE GRASS
Microlaena avenacea   Poaceae

This grass is widespread throughout the country and can sometimes form large patches on the forest floor. The altitudinal range is from sea level to about 750 m. It has slender tufts of grey-green leaves, mostly 30–60 cm tall. The flowerheads are narrowly branched and drooping.

Flowering is during the summer with the seeds ripening during the autumn.

Microlaena is found in New Zealand and Australia.

Oplismenus hirtellus var. *imbecillus*   Poaceae

This grass is unlike others in this group in having slender spreading prostrate stems forming roots near the base and bearing scattered leaves. The leaves are relatively broad, the flowerheads are short and little branched.

O. hirtellus var. *imbecillus* is widespread through the North Island at low altitudes. A second variety is restricted to northern Northland.

The genus ranges widely through tropical and warm temperate regions.

Arthropodium candidum   Liliaceae

This is a diminutive relative of the better-known *A. cirratum* (rengarenga). The plants are delicate in texture and often form small colonies. They die down in the winter to small tubers and resprout in the spring.

The leaves are about 10–30 cm long x 3–10 mm wide, and green, although there is also a coppery bronze form. The flowerheads are unbranched or little branched. The flowers are white with stamen filaments that are densely hairy in their upper parts. The capsules are about 3 mm in diameter.

The species is widespread from south of Auckland in forest and shady open habitats from sea level to about 1000 m.

Species of *Arthropodium* are also found in Australia, New Guinea, New Caledonia and Madagascar.

Above: Bush rice grass, *Microlaena avenacea,* with seedheads.
Centre: *Oplismenus hirtellus* spreading over the forest floor.
Below: The bronze-leaved form of *Arthropodium candidum.*

HERBS

Botanically, herbs are small non-woody flowering plants. The forest-floor herbs in this group mostly have broad, net-veined leaves.

BUTTERCUP
Ranunculus   Ranunculaceae
The several dozen native species of *Ranunculus* are almost all found in open mostly alpine habitats. The exceptions are the forest species *R. reflexus* (formerly *R. hirtus*) and *R. urvilleanus*. The genus *Ranunculus* is widespread in temperate regions.

R. reflexus is found throughout the country in lowland to subalpine forest.

The leaves have stalks up to 10 cm long and hairy leaflets that are coarsely toothed and sometimes deeply lobed.

The flowerheads are branched and bear reduced leaves. The flowers are about 10 mm in diameter with yellow petals. Spherical clusters of flattened dry seeds form at the centre of each flower. Flowering is through spring and summer and the seeds ripen from mid-spring to early autumn.

R. urvilleanus differs from *R. reflexus* in its long petioles, mostly much longer than 10 cm. It is found in coastal and lowland damp places, and open places in forest in northern Northland.

Ranunculus reflexus.

BITTER CRESS
Cardamine   Brassicaceae
Of our 6 species of *Cardamine,* only **C. debilis** grows in forest as well as shrubland and stream margins. The species is widespread at lower altitudes.

The rosette leaves are up to 10 cm long with 2–7 pairs of leaflets and a terminal one. The leaflets are broad and smooth margined to lobed and toothed. The flowerheads are branched and have reduced leaves on their lower stems. The flowers are white with 4 petals and up to 1 cm wide. The capsules are long and narrow. Flowering occurs mostly in spring and summer but also at other times of the year.

The genus has many species in temperate regions of the world.

Cardamine debilis with seed capsules.

FORGET-ME-NOT

Myosotis   **Boraginaceae**

The 30 or so species of *Myosotis* are mostly found in open habitats. Of the few that occur in forests, **M. forsteri** is the most widespread. It is found from the Bay of Plenty southwards in lowland and mountain forests and along streams.

The leaf rosettes of *M. forsteri* are single, not in groups. The leaf blades are almost circular, up to 4 cm long and covered with stiff hairs. The leaf stalks are similar in length to the blade. The flowerheads are distinctively coiled, as is typical for *Myosotis*. The flowers are white, 4–6 mm in diameter and they each form 4 seeds. Flowering is from mid-spring to mid-autumn with seeds maturing from late spring through summer and autumn.

M. venosa is similar but has rosettes in small groups and longer leaves with softer hairs. It is found along the axial ranges of the North Island and in northwest Nelson.

M. petiolata, ranging from Auckland through the eastern side of the North Island to northwest Nelson, can also be found in forests. The leaf rosettes are solitary. The leaf blades are similar to those of *M. forsteri* but smaller, mostly up to 1.5 cm long.

The genus is widespread in temperate regions.

A very modest forget-me-not (*Myosotis forsteri*) with tiny white flowers.

Lagenifera   **Asteraceae**

Lageniferas are mostly found in open habitats but 3 of the 5 species also grow in light forest where the floor is not too shady. None of the 3 grows in Northland, but they range throughout the rest of the country, including the subantarctic islands in the case of *L. pumila*. They grow in lowland to mountain open sites and open forest. Other species are found in Australia, southern Asia and South America.

L. pinnatifida usually has single rosettes of often deeply lobed, softly hairy leaves measuring 2–6 cm long x 1.5–2.5 cm wide. The daisy-like flowers, formed singly at the ends of long stems, are white and 10–15 mm in diameter. Clusters of seeds develop at the centre of the flower.

L. petiolata and **L. pumila** differ chiefly in having spreading stems that form patches of rosettes and shorter, often almost round leaf blades with rough hairs. These 2 species are closely related. *L. petiolata* has leaf blades 1–2 cm wide and leaf stalks mostly 2–3 cm long. *L. pumila* has leaf blades 7–10 mm wide and leaf stalks mostly 10–15 mm long.

The lageniferas flower from spring into summer and the seeds develop from summer into autumn.

GUNNERA   **Haloragaceae**

Our 10 native species of *Gunnera* grow in moist to boggy, mostly open places from the lowlands to the mountains. Four of the species are also found in forests. They range widely through the country, although only *G. strigosa* is found in Northland. By means of spreading slender stems they sometimes form quite extensive patches of rosettes. The flowerheads are branched or unbranched and bear small densely crowded flowers followed by berries.

G. albocarpa and **G. strigosa** have leaf blades about as long as wide, round to kidney-shaped. Both have branched flowerheads. *G. albocarpa* is sparsely hairy, has white berries and is found in lowland to mountain forests. *G. strigosa* is distinctly hairy, has bright red berries and is found in lowland forests.

G. prorepens and **G. flavida** have leaf blades up to twice as long as wide and unbranched flowerheads. *G. prorepens* has leaves that may be sparsely hairy, red to purplish berries and is found in lowland to subalpine forests. *G. flavida* is hairless with yellow berries and has a similar altitudinal range.

Flowering is from spring into summer with berries ripening from summer into autumn.

The genus *Gunnera* ranges through South America, South Africa, New Zealand, eastern Australia, New Guinea and Indonesia.

Jovellana **Scrophulariaceae**
Our 2 species of *Jovellana* grow on shady banks and cliffs along streams, often within or below overhanging forest.

J. sinclairii has slender sprawling branches up to 50 cm long. The leaf blades are broad, coarsely toothed and 2–8 cm long. The branching flowerheads are at the stem tips and the flowers, about 1 cm wide, are white with purple spots. The petals are fused together and have a 2-lipped cup-like form. The seeds develop in a dry capsule.

This species is found in the North Island from East Cape southwards in lowland and lower mountain sites.

J. repens is a smaller plant with creeping and rooting stems up to 20 cm long. The leaf blades are smaller, mostly 1–2 cm long. It ranges from Bay of Plenty to the northern South Island.

Jovellana sinclairii with white purple-spotted bell-like flowers.

Both species flower then fruit from mid-spring through summer.

This is a small genus with a few species in Chile and New Zealand.

Gunnera prorepens with colourful clusters of berries.

The small stinging nettle *Urtica incisa*, showing small yellow flowers and white stinging hairs on the leaf stalks.

A much larger nettle, *Urtica ferox*, with conspicuous stinging hairs.

STINGING NETTLES
Urtica   Urticaceae

Stinging nettles are widespread in temperate and subtropical regions. Their most notable feature is the unpleasant sting they can inflict with specialised hairs on their leaves and stems. The hairs are pale and stiff and stand at right angles to the plant surfaces. When touched the tips break off, leaving sharp points that easily penetrate the skin and inject the stinging fluid like a hypodermic needle.

Of our 6 native species of *Urtica,* only **U. incisa** is truly a forest dweller. It is up to 60 cm tall with coarsely and prominently toothed leaf blades 2–5 cm long and wide. The flowers are very small and crowded on spikes. They open through spring and summer, followed by small dry seeds.

U. incisa is found throughout the country in lowland and mountain forests, and also in Australia.

A more spectacular species, found at coastal and lowland forest margins and in shrubland, is **U. ferox** (ongaonga, tree nettle). 'Tree' is an exaggeration but it is definitely a shrub, sometimes up to 2 m tall. With its many stinging hairs, it is a daunting sight and contact should be avoided. At least one person is known to have died after brushing past this plant.

U. ferox is found at low altitudes through the North Island and in the east of the South Island. Flowering is from late spring to early autumn.

Nertera   Rubiaceae

The nerteras catch the eye in the forest shade with their scatterings of brightly coloured berries. Five of our 7 species grow in moist places on the forest floor.

Nerteras are related to coprosmas but are herbaceous and mat forming, not woody shrubs. Like coprosmas the flowers are small and wind pollinated. Other species are found in Central and South America, and Australia through to southeast Asia.

N. depressa and **N. cunninghamii** have hairless leaves with blades that are longer than wide. The berries too are hairless and bright to dark red. The leaf blades of *N. depressa* are 3–15 mm long x 2–10 mm wide and narrow abruptly to the stalk. They often have an unpleasant smell when crushed. The leaf blades of *N. cunninghamii* are 5–8 mm long x 1–3 mm wide and are gradually narrowed to the stalk. They do not have an unpleasant smell when crushed. Both species are widespread in coastal to mountain forests. *N. depressa* also occurs in South

Nertera villosa with hairy leaves and orange berries. The other plant is *Schistochila*, a leafy liverwort.

America, Australia and Indonesia.

N. dichondrifolia, N. villosa and *N. ciliata* have hairy leaves with blades that are about as long as wide. The berries too are hairy, at least when young. The leaf blades of the first 2 are 6–15 mm long x 5–13 mm wide and hairy on both surfaces. The berries are red to orange. *N. villosa* has long straight erect hairs on the leaf blades, while those of *N. dichondrifolia* are short and curved. The leaf blades of *N. ciliata* are 3-5 mm long x 3-5 mm wide with the hairs mostly restricted to the margins. The berries are orange.

N. dichondrifolia is found throughout Northland and south to Bay of Plenty and Kawhia, while *N. villosa* ranges from near Auckland to Stewart Island in all lowland and mountain types of forest that are sufficiently moist. *N. ciliata* is found in similar habitats in the central and southern South Island.

The forest nerteras flower from spring into summer with berries ripening from summer through autumn.

Galium   **Rubiaceae**

Our galiums, with their whorls of 4 leaves, are small modest plants with very small flowers, each forming a pair of dry rounded seeds. An introduced species, known as cleaver or goosegrass, is better known as a sometimes troublesome weed that clings to clothing with its abundant curved hairs.

Our 3 species are found throughout the country in moist places in lowland to mountain forests but also in wetter open habitats.

G. tenuicaule has leaves 6–15 mm long, while those of *G. propinquum* and *G. perpusillum* are less than 6 mm long. *G. propinquum* has widely spaced leaf groups. In *G. perpusillum* they are closely spaced and sometimes overlapping.

Flowers then seeds are produced from late spring into winter.

Galium is widespread throughout the world.

Anaphalioides
(syn. *Gnaphalium*)   Asteraceae

The 2 species of *Anaphalioides* grow in moist places in lowland to mountain forest, especially on banks near streams and on cliffs. They can also be found in moist shady open habitats.

A. trinervis has stems that are woody at the base and extend into branches that are upright or hugging the ground. The leaves have no stalks and measure 4–10 cm long x 0.3–2 cm wide. The undersides are white. The flowerheads at the ends of branches are much branched with white daisy-like flowers up to 1.5 cm in diameter. Clusters of seeds, each with a tuft of hairs at the top, develop at the centre of each flower.

This is a variable species that is found throughout the North and South Islands.

A. rupestris also has prostrate stems but the leaves are only 1.5–3 cm long x 5–10 mm wide. The flowers are up to 1.5 cm in diameter. This species is found in the South Island, mostly along western coasts, and in Stewart Island.

Both species flower from spring into summer and the seeds ripen from late spring to autumn.

Parietaria   Urticaceae

Our only species, *P. debilis*, is one of our few annual plants. It occurs throughout the country in coastal and lowland light forest and shrubland. It is upright in growth with weak slender stems and thin leaves with long slender stalks up to 3 cm long and blades 1–4 cm long x 1–2.5 cm wide. The small flowers are densely crowded on short branches of the flowerheads.

Flowers then seeds are formed from mid-spring to mid-summer.

P. debilis is found in many other parts of the world.

Australina   Urticaceae

A. pusilla is found here and there in coastal to lowland forest throughout the country. It has slender prostrate stems that spread and root to form patches. The leaf blades are rounded, 1–1.5 cm long x 1–1.5 cm wide, with rounded marginal teeth. The leaf stalk is very slender and up to 1.5 cm long. The small flowers are in small groups in the leaf angles,

Above: *Anaphalioides trinervis* in flower in its typical habitat, a moist rocky bank.
Centre: A nettle relative but without stinging hairs, *Parietaria debilis*.
Below: Another non-stinging member of the nettle family, *Australina pusilla*.

Luzuriaga parviflora: pure white flowers (left); a dense patch with hanging flowers (right).

Parataniwha: on the forest floor, (left); handsome foliage (right).

each flower forming a single seed.

Flowers then seeds are formed from late spring to mid-summer.

Australina also occurs in Africa and Australia.

Luzuriaga   Liliaceae
Our sole species, **L. parviflora** (nohi), is found throughout the country, mostly in cool wet mountain forests notable for their profusion of mosses and lichens. It is a small low-growing plant with wiry 4-angled stems. The leaves are 7–27 mm long x 3–6 mm wide with short twisted petioles. The flowers are solitary at branch tips, pure white and 2–3 cm in diameter. The berry formed from each flower is also white, spongy and about 1 cm in diameter. The flowers open through summer to early autumn and the berries are present much of the year.

A few other species of *Luzuriaga* are found in western and southern South America.

PARATANIWHA
Elatostema rugosum   Urticaceae
Parataniwha is one of our most attractive forest plants, not for its flowers but for its large prominently veined leaves toned from green to red or purple. Although there is no relationship, the leaves are reminiscent of those of some of the ornamental begonias.

There are many species of *Elatostema* in the Asian and African tropics. We have just the one species but it is among the most attractive.

Parataniwha is found only in the North Island. It is most abundant in the north of the island but occurs locally as far south as the Tararua Ranges. It favours moist shady places in lowland to mountain forests, particularly near streams. It is most impressive where it grows on cliffs near waterfalls, forming extensive curtains of overlapping foliage.

The robust stems of parataniwha are woody at the base and spread and root over the ground. They turn up at the ends and are then fleshy and sometimes 1 m or so high. The tips of the stems curve over and the leaves tend to lie in one plane parallel to the ground. The leaves, 8–25 cm long x 2.5–6 cm wide, are strongly and sharply toothed, often wider on one side of the midrib than the other and curved towards the narrower side. The whole vein network is dark coloured and the leaf tissue bulges strongly upwards between the veins. There are no leaf stalks.

The flowers are minute and in small dense clusters at the bases of the leaves. Each flower forms

Berries of *Pratia angulata*.

Creeping *Pratia angulata* with its asymmetrical flowers.

a single small seed. Flowers then seeds are produced from spring through to autumn

Pratia   **Lobeliaceae**
Of our 5 species of *Pratia*, 2 are found in forests.

P. angulata is a common species found throughout the country in damp lowland to subalpine forests and open places. Its slender spreading and rooting stems form extensive patches. The small leaves have short stalks and broad blades, 3–12 mm long x 1–8 mm wide, with coarse marginal teeth. The flowers are single from the leaf angles, 7–20 mm long, white, with the petals partly fused into a tube that is split to the base at the back. The eye-catching berries are 7–12 mm in diameter and purple red. The flowers are followed by berries from mid-spring to mid-autumn.

P. physaloides is restricted to the north of Northland. It contrasts strongly with our other pratias and it is sometimes treated as a separate genus, *Colensoa*. It is almost a shrub and up to 1 m high. The leaves are soft with stalks up to 10 cm long and strongly toothed blades 7–15 cm long x 4–6 cm wide. The flowerheads are terminal on branchlets and comprise about a dozen flowers. The flowers are 3–5 cm long and vary from pale violet to dark blue purple. The berries are 1–1.5 cm in diameter and often an intense blue purple. Flowers and berries develop from spring through to autumn.

This species is found in coastal and lowland forest in the far north, particularly along streams.

Pratia is related to the better-known *Lobelia*. There are other species in Australia, Asia and South America.

The much larger upright *Pratia (Colensoa) physaloides*, with elongated purplish white flowers above and brilliant blue-purple berries below.

The distinctive leaves of *Hydrocotyle elongata*.

PENNYWORTS
Hydrocotyle   **Apiaceae**
Two of our species of *Hydrocotyle* grow throughout the country in coastal to lower mountain forest and also in moist open sites. Their creeping stems form patches up to 40 cm in diameter.

H. elongata has leaves with hairy stalks and blades. The blades have marginal lobes bearing pointed teeth. **H. americana** is hairless and has lobed blade margins with rounded teeth.

Hydrocotyle is widespread throughout the world.

ORCHIDS

There is no ready way to identify a plant as an orchid by its leaves, although some on the forest floor have a single often-broad leaf, which helps. So we have to rely on the flowers, which fortunately are distinctive. They are mostly very asymmetric with the uppermost petal often curved forward as a sort of hood and the lowermost or lip petal sometimes elaborately modified to form a landing stage for pollinating insects. More distinctive still is a peg-like structure, or column, at the centre of the flower, which produces the pollen and bears the sticky stigma that receives pollen from another flower.

The minute seeds of orchids are remarkable in being dust-like and produced in thousands in dry capsules. The seeds can only develop into new plants after their cells have been invaded by the filaments of a fungus from the soil. The embryo obtains soil mineral nutrients from the fungus which enable it to develop into a young plant. Once the orchid forms chlorophyll it manufactures sugars and the fungus gets a share as its reward. Some orchids are indirect parasites, obtaining sugars from tree roots via the filaments of their associated fungi. See *Corybas cryptanthus* (below), *Gastrodia*, page 218 and *Danhatchia*, page 219.

We have 130 native species of orchid in New Zealand and of these about a third are shared with Australia. Getting carried by wind across the Tasman Sea would be no great problem for dust-like seeds. Of the terrestrial (not epiphytic) species, about two-thirds are restricted to open, including alpine, habitats. Of the approximately two dozen species that can be found on the forest floor, about 10 also grow in open habitats. All orchids are members of the family Orchidaceae.

The forest floor orchids that are most often noticed are species of *Corybas* (spider orchids), *Pterostylis* (greenhood orchids) and the strange non-green species of *Gastrodia*.

See pages 184–186 for epiphytic orchid species.

Further reading: *The Nature Guide to New Zealand Native Orchids*, Ian St George.

A spider orchid, *Corybas trilobus,* with its broad leaves and strongly cupped flowers.

SPIDER ORCHIDS
Corybas

Spider orchids are found throughout the country, including the subantarctic islands, on the forest floor and suitable open sites. They arise from small tubers below the leaf litter. Some species produce their leaves from autumn through winter, others from spring through summer. There is only one leaf per

Corybas rivularis with conspicuous 'antennae'.

Tutukiwi, *Pterostylis banksii.*

plant, although sometimes several to many plants form patches. The leaves are broad, deeply notched at the base and often flecked with red or purple. After the leaves a single relatively large flower is formed, sometimes below the leaf, sometimes sitting on top of it. The hood petal is often dark red to purple. The lip petal is similarly coloured, unusually large and sometimes curved into a tunnel-like form. The remaining petals are drawn out into long thin appendages reminiscent of the legs of some spiders.

The most widespread and most commonly encountered forest species of *Corybas* is **C. trilobus**. As the name indicates, the leaf is 3-lobed, the central lobe being smaller than the other 2 and pointed.

C. cryptanthus is quite unlike the other species. It has no chlorophyll and is an indirect parasite. It grows in association with native beech and manuka at scattered localities in both main islands. Even when in flower it is difficult to spot as it is partly covered by litter and the ghost-like flowers are pale with red and brown flecks.

GREENHOOD ORCHIDS
Pterostylis
The greenhood orchids also arise from tubers but are otherwise very different from the spider orchids.

A distinctive greenhood orchid, *Pterostylis alobula.*

The latter grow close to the surface of the leaf litter while the greenhoods have erect stems up to 20–35 cm high to which several long and narrow or short and broad leaves are attached.

The flowers are single at the stem tips and, as the common name suggests, a brightish green, sometimes with whitish stripes. The flowers are very distinctive in form. The hood petal is strongly developed and, in association with 2 lateral petals, curves forward into a beak-like form, The beak-like appearance is accentuated when the hood petal is drawn out at the tip into a long and narrow point that is often attractively pink. The lowermost petals are partly fused together and their 2 lobes may also be drawn out into pink 'antennae' that angle upwards like arms held aloft. The lip petal is most remarkable of all. It is long and narrow, sometimes dark coloured at the tip, and angles out from the flower like a partly lowered drawbridge. When touched by a finger, or in nature a landing insect, it suddenly swings inwards on a sort of hinge, dropping the insect inside the flower and cutting off its retreat. The only way out for the insect is to climb up the column. If it has already visited another greenhood flower, pollen will be removed by the sticky stigma below. The flower's own sticky pollen will be then picked up near the top of the column before the insect escapes from the flower. The lip petal resumes its ready position after about half an hour, so if the first insect visitor didn't bring pollen with it from another flower, there will be another chance.

The most commonly encountered forest floor greenhood orchid is **P. banksii** (tutukiwi). It grows throughout the country, including the Chatham Islands, and flowers from October to December. Other forest species are found throughout the North Island and the northern South Island or are restricted to the north of the North Island. Their flowering times are earlier than *P. banksii*.

Gastrodia

Although the gastrodias can be up to 1m tall, but usually less, they are not easy to spot because they lack chlorophyll and their colouring blends in with the background of tree trunks and leaf litter. However, despite their camouflage colouring, they are the most easily observed of the indirectly parasitic orchids as they stand well above the litter. The stems vary in colour from pale brown to dark brown or almost black. Sometimes they are shiny as if polished and may have flecks of pale and darker

A tall slender *Gastrodia cunninghamii*.

Strangely coloured *Gastrodia cunninghamii* flowers.

THISMIA RODWAYI
Burmanniaceae

T. rodwayi belongs to a family that is closely related to the orchids. It is a small plant and, like some of the orchids, lacks chlorophyll and is indirectly parasitic on the roots of trees. It is found on the volcanic plateau of the central North Island and in a few places further north. The tubular flowers with curved-over petals are up to 15 mm high and stand just above the litter. They are translucent red and have been likened to small lanterns.

T. rodwayi also grows in Tasmania.

The small but highly attractive flower of *Thismia rodwayi* arising from leaf litter.

brown to give an attractive wood-grain appearance. The leaves are reduced to dry scales and the apparently only partly open flowers are spread along the top of the stem. The flowers are similar in colour to the stems and sometimes droop downwards.

As with most other forest floor orchids, the stems arise from underground tubers, but in this case they can be quite large, several centimetres long and wide. They provided a special food item for the Maori.

Without chlorophyll, how do the gastrodias sustain themselves? It has been discovered that the fungal threads that invade the underground parts are connected to adjacent tree roots, so the gastrodias, as well as drawing essential mineral nutrients from the fungus, also help themselves to the sugars the fungus has obtained from the tree. These strange orchids then are indirect parasites.

We have 3 native species, of which 2 grow on the forest floor, often in very shady places. The most widespread species is **G. cunninghamii** (Huperei), which is found throughout the country including the Chatham Islands. The flowers open in spring and summer. Other species of *Gastrodia* are found in Australia, the Himalayas and Japan.

Danhatchia australis

This orchid has no chlorophyll and its pink to brownish coloration makes it difficult to see against leaf litter. The stems with brownish white flowers can be up to 12 cm high. It has been found through Northland and the Coromandel Peninsula, and in northwest Nelson in the South Island. In Northland it grows in association with taraire (page 139) and it is probably an indirect parasite on the roots of that tree.

The genus with its one species is found only in New Zealand.

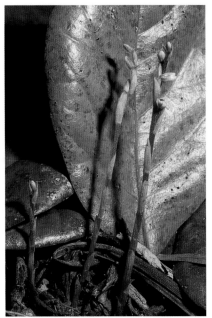

Danhatchia australis.

A STRANGE PARASITIC PLANT

Dactylanthus taylori (pua reinga) is a direct parasite on the roots of a number of native trees and, although difficult to see among the leaf litter, it has been observed at several localities through the North Island. The germinating seed of this parasite attaches itself near the tip of a host root, if one happens to be nearby. As it grows it stimulates the root to enlarge into a ball-like shape. Radiating flanges of the parasite penetrate into the host tissue and draw water and nutriment from it. The parasite eventually enlarges into a rounded gall-like structure covered with warty protuberances. In summer and autumn shoots grow out from between these protuberances and push above the leaf litter. These are covered with pinkish brown scale-like leaves that aggregate into cup-like structures at the shoot tips, and within these there are clusters of stems bearing small close-packed male flowers in some plants and females in others. The 'cups' contain a good amount of nectar, and recently it was discovered that the native short-tailed bat visits to lap it up and is the pollinating agent for the flowers (see page 288).

Unfortunately, the possum is also partial to the nectar and causes considerable damage. Further depredations are made by people who dig up the parasite still attached to the host roots, boil the combination to separate the 2 components and sell the disc-like radially flanged ends of the roots as 'wooden roses'.

Dactylanthus has one species and is restricted to New Zealand.

Brown scaly inflorescences of *Dactylanthus taylori*.

A 'wooden rose' caused by *Dactylanthus taylori*.

FERNS

The leaves of ferns are commonly called fronds. They are usually much divided, often with several orders of leaflets, and are coiled into a tight spiral when young.

Ferns reproduce by microscopic single-celled spores. Produced in great quantities, these are readily spread by the wind, but only those that settle in moist, preferably shady sites are able to germinate and form small plantlets that bear the sex organs. For sperm to reach the eggs, they must be able to swim through a film of water and this is the main reason why ferns grow mostly in moist shady places. Fertilisation results in a new fern plant.

Fern spores are formed in special organs known as sporangia. These mostly have slender stalks with a more or less spherical head or capsule that contains the spores. On drying, a line of thickened cells around the rim of the capsule slowly bends backwards, so opening the capsule, then suddenly snaps forward to expel the spores as if from a catapult (see page 234).

Often the sporangia are aggregated in distinctive groups (sori), which are easily observable, especially with a hand lens. The position, arrangement and protective coverings (indusia), if any, of the sori are often useful in the identification of ferns.

Tree ferns are described on pages 67–71; climbing ferns on pages 177–179.

Further reading: *New Zealand Ferns and Allied Plants*, Patrick J. Brownsey and John C. Smith-Dodsworth.

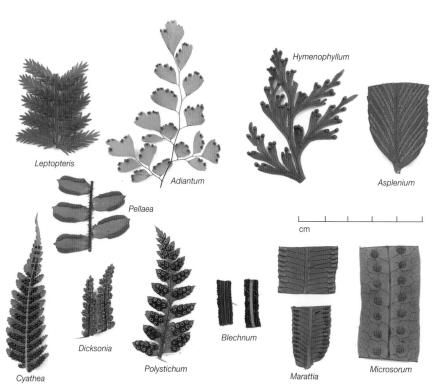

Hymenophyllum

Leptopteris

Adiantum

Asplenium

Pellaea

cm

Dicksonia

Blechnum

Polystichum

Marattia

Microsorum

Cyathea

Plate 35. Sori of ferns.

The umbrella fern *Sticherus cunninghamii* with new fronds developing.

Sticherus flabellatus.

Handsome large fronds of the king fern, *Marattia salicina.*

UMBRELLA FERNS
Sticherus
Gleicheniaceae

Umbrella ferns grow mostly in open habitats and, particularly in the tropics, are frequent as early pioneers following fire. The frond stalks end in a bud which, after a period of dormancy, grows up into a second tier of forking leaflets. This process may be repeated so that in some species fronds reach several metres in height.

Our 2 umbrella ferns grow on shady roadside banks in forest or on the forest floor where it is reasonably well lit. They can also occur in shrubby vegetation.

In **S. cunninghamii** the fronds are in 1–3 tiers, each forking 3–4 times. The ultimate frond segments are up to 1.5 cm long x 3 mm wide and the undersides of the leaflet stalks are very scaly.

In **S. flabellatus** the fronds are in 1–2 tiers, each forking 2–3 times. The ultimate frond segments are up to 4 cm long x 3 mm wide and the undersides of the leaflet stalks are generally without scales.

S. cunninghamii is found throughout the country in lowland to mountain forests but is uncommon in the east and south of the South Island. *S. flabellatus* is found at lower altitudes in forest and shrubland south to the Bay of Plenty in the North Island and in northwest Nelson and north Westland in the South Island. This species also grows in Australia, New Caledonia and New Guinea.

KING FERN
Marattia salicina
Marattiaceae

The king fern was once abundant in the North Island south to Taranaki in deep densely forested gullies. The massive stem is filled with starch, which was prepared by the Maori for food. Since European settlement, pigs in particular have greatly reduced this species.

The fronds of *M. salicina* are thick, dark green, up to 4 m long and are attached to massive but short scaly hemispherical stems. They are divided into primary and secondary leaflets. The sori near the margins on the frond undersides each overlie a vein and are very distinctive. The sporangia are fused together in 2 rows and the compartments they form can usually be discerned externally (Plate 35).

The king fern is also found in Queensland.

Leptopteris   Osmundaceae

With their filmy fronds, *Leptopteris* resemble the true filmy ferns although they are not, in fact, closely related. With blades up to 1 m long, the fronds are much larger than those of the filmy ferns and the sporangia are underneath the fronds, not on the margins. The fronds are thin and translucent, and are attached to slender trunks up to 1 m in height.

The stalkless sporangia are not arranged in clearly marked groups and are sometimes attached singly (Plate 35).

There are 2 species in this genus, each with 3 orders of leaflets.

L. hymenophylloides has blades that taper at the tip but not the base and the ultimate segments are flattened in the plane of the rest of the frond.

L. superba (crape fern, Prince of Wales feathers) has blades that taper at both ends and its ultimate segments turn up at right angles to the rest of the frond. As a result, the fronds have a very attractive fluffy texture.

Both species are found in dark and moist forest habitats throughout the country, although *L. superba* is rare in Northland. It requires cool temperatures and constant high humidity so it is abundant in Westland and at higher altitudes elsewhere. *L. hymenophylloides* can tolerate drier conditions, so where both are found at the same locality, it will extend over valley slopes while *L. superba* is confined to valley bottoms near streams. At such sites the 2 species often hybridise.

Other species of *Leptopteris* are found in New Caledonia and New Guinea.

Leptopteris superba.

L. hymenophylloides (above) has the segments all in the same plane. *Leptopteris superba* (below) showing the upturned segments giving the fluffy texture to this species.

The leathery fronds of *Blechnum colensoi*. A fertile frond with very narrow segments is on the right.

Blechnum discolor showing central fertile fronds surrounded by sterile fronds.

A grove of *Blechnum discolor*.

Blechnum fraseri with short slender trunks.

HARD FERNS

Blechnum   Blechnaceae

Blechnum is a widespread genus well represented in the southern hemisphere. It is easily recognised because 2 types of frond are present on plants: sterile fronds of normal appearance and without sporangia on the undersides; and centrally placed fertile fronds with 2 lines of sporangia on the undersides of narrow rolled-up, often dead-looking leaflets (Plate 35).

Of the 19 native species, 12 commonly grow on the forest floor or on banks and cliffs in forest. With the exception of *B. fraseri,* they are widespread through the country, in some cases including the subantarctic islands. *B. fraseri* also stands apart in having 2 orders of leaflets, the others having primary leaflets only. Leaf dimensions in the following are of the sterile fronds.

B. chambersii (formerly *B. lanceolatum*) has frond blades strongly tapering to the base and measuring 13–50 cm long x 1.5–12 cm wide. The longest leaflets are 0.8–6 cm long x 0.4–1.2 cm wide. The stems are short and erect. This species is also found in Australia and possibly some of the tropical Pacific islands.

Large fronds of *Blechnum novae-zelandiae* growing on a moist cliff. Young fronds are red to pink in colour.

Blechnum fluviatile with fertile fronds developing at the centre.

B. colensoi (formerly *B. patersonii*) is notable for its handsome dark green leathery frond blades, undivided or with few broad leaflets. The blades are 25–50 cm long (sometimes more) x 12–30 cm wide and the leaflets are 10–20 cm long x 2–4 cm wide. The stems are short and creeping. This species favours the darkest and dampest places in forests, often near streams or waterfalls.

B. discolor (crown fern) is a conspicuous species as it often forms extensive colonies on drier forest floors that exclude other plants. It has short trunks crowned by spreading fronds with blades 20–100 cm long x 5–16 cm wide and the longest leaflets 2.5–8 cm long x 6–14 mm wide.

B. filiforme is a common climbing fern (see page 177) but it can also form extensive mats on the forest floor, where it bears the small juvenile type of leaf.

B. fluviatile is an attractive small species with long and very narrow fronds with many short rounded leaflets. The blades are 15–75 cm long x 2–6 cm wide and the leaflets 1–3 cm long x 8–12 mm wide with minutely toothed or smooth margins. The stems are short and erect. *B. fluviatile* also grows in Australia.

B. fraseri has short trunks and the fronds have primary and secondary leaflets. The blade is 15–40 cm long x 8–25 cm wide, the primary leaflets 4–15 cm long x 1–3 cm wide and the secondary leaflets 5–23 mm long x 2–25 mm wide. The fertile fronds are not greatly different from the sterile. They are smaller and the secondary leaflets are narrower. *B. fraseri* is found in lowland forest from North Cape to north Taranaki and in the South Island in coastal forest in the northwest. It also grows in Indonesia and the Philippines.

B. membranaceum, with its narrow fronds with short rounded leaflets, is similar in appearance to *B. fluviatile* but the blades are shorter, 6–25 cm long x 1–4 cm wide, and the leaflets, 5–20 mm long x 4–8 mm wide, have conspicuous teeth. The stems are short and erect. This fern grows along stream-sides or on banks in better-lit forests. It is related to *B. chambersii* and the 2 hybridise freely in nature.

B. novae-zelandiae (kiokio) is the largest and most striking blechnum with bright green frond blades 20–250 cm long x 8–60 cm

Blechnum vulcanicum.

wide and leaflets 5–35 cm long x 1–3 cm wide. The stems are short and creeping. It is a common species in lowland to mountain forests, where it can be abundant on road banks, stream edges and cliffs, where it can cover extensive areas with curtains of overlapping fronds. This handsome fern was formerly included in *B. capense*, along with 2 other related but smaller species. **B. montanum** grows

Blechnum procerum.

in forest near the treeline from the central North Island southwards. **B. triangularifolium** grows on dry banks in coastal forest and scrub in the North Island and northern South Island.

B. nigrum has very dark green oddly shaped fronds. It is common on the wetter western sides of both islands, where it grows in very dark, very wet places in lowland to mountain forests. The fronds have a large terminal leaflet and much smaller leaflets below, except for the basal pair, which can be as large as the terminal one. The leaflets are irregularly lobed. The frond blade is 5–20 cm long x 1.5–5 cm wide and the leaflets 8–30 mm long x 7–20 mm wide. The stems are short and erect.

B. procerum is a common species in drier fairly open forest but can also be found in shrubland and tussock grassland above the treeline. The frond blade is 9–55 cm long x 5–22 cm wide. There are only 2–12 pairs of leaflets, each 2.5–15 cm long x 1–3.5 cm wide. The stems are short and creeping.

B. vulcanicum is found throughout the country at cooler altitudes and latitudes mostly on banks in open forest or at forest margins. The frond blade is 8–35 cm long x 4–14 cm wide with 10–25 pairs of leaflets. The lowermost pairs of leaflets are distinctively sickle-shaped. The stems are erect or short-creeping.

MAIDENHAIR FERNS

Adiantum   Pteridaceae

Maidenhair ferns are widespread throughout the world. Because of their delicate often much-branched fronds with slender polished stalks, a number of species are popular as house plants. Five of our 7 species are found in forests and 3 of these grow elsewhere in the southern hemisphere and sometimes Asia.

The most abundant and widespread species, from the Kermadecs to Stewart and Chatham Islands, is **A. cunninghamii**, which grows in coastal and lowland forests, where it is often a decorative feature of cliffs and banks. The fronds have up to 3 orders of leaflets and the blade measures 10–35 cm long x 5–24 cm wide. The ultimate leaflets are irregularly fan-shaped, up to 2 cm long and toothed on one side.

The arrangement of the sori is very distinctive. They form on the undersides of rounded marginal flaps, which protect the immature sporangia by folding under and pressing against the underside of the frond. In this position the flaps are often distinctively kidney-shaped (Plate 35).

Blechnum nigrum, a very dark green low-growing species that is found in shady moist places.

Sori of maidenhair fern (*Adiantum*).

Pellaea rotundifolia showing the characteristic shape and position of the sori.

Anarthropteris lanceolata. Note the sori on the overturned frond.

Pellaea   Pteridaceae

Pellaea is a widespread genus throughout the world with 3 native species in New Zealand, 2 of which occur in forests. The fronds have primary leaflets only and the stalks and leaflet undersides bear scales and hairs.

P. rotundifolia (button fern, tarawera) is our commonest and most widespread species, growing in rocky sites in lowland to mountain forests. The frond blade is 15–40 cm long x 1.8–4 cm wide and the rounded leaflets are 8–20 mm long x 5–13 mm wide. The 2 marginal bands of sporangia on the leaflet undersides are dark brown and conspicuous (Plate 35).

P. falcata is found in Northland in open coastal habitats and pohutukawa forest. The leaflets are elongate, 1.5–4 cm long x 7–15 mm wide. This species is also found in Australia and New Caledonia and perhaps southeast Asia.

Pteris   Pteridaceae

There are 4 native species in this genus. *P. macilenta* is the one most commonly encountered in drier and more open coastal and lowland forests. Its frond blades have 3 orders of thin leaflets and measure 25-90 cm long x 15-50 cm wide. The ultimate leaflets are up to 1.5 cm long x 5 mm wide with marginal teeth. The bands of marginal sporangia are partly protected by inrolling of the margins.

P. macilenta is common in the North Island but is largely restricted in the South Island to the north and northwest coasts.

Pteris is a widespread genus, particularly in the tropics.

LANCE FERN
Anarthropteris lanceolata   Grammitidaceae
A. lanceolata grows on rocks in forest or on lower parts of tree trunks. It is found throughout the North Island at lower altitudes and near the coast in the northern half of the South Island.

It has tufts of rather thick undivided narrow pointed fronds with large almost circular sori on the undersides. The fronds have poorly defined stalks and measure 7–30 cm long x 7–23 mm wide. This species is unusual in that the roots are able to give rise to new tufts of fronds, a very effective way of forming quite extensive mats.

Ctenopteris heterophylla   Grammitidaceae
C. heterophylla grows on rocks or as a low epiphyte in lowland to subalpine forest throughout New Zealand. It is also found in Australia.

With the frond blade divided into toothed leaflets, this fern stands apart from the others in the family. The frond blades are 4–30 cm long x 5–50 mm wide.

FINGER FERNS
Grammitis   Grammitidaceae
These have narrow finger-like undivided fronds, rounded to pointed at the tip and with poorly defined

Ctenopteris heterophylla growing on a bank.

stalks. The narrowly oval sori form a distinctive herringbone pattern on the undersides. The forest species in New Zealand have short stems and tufted leaves.

Of our 9 species of *Grammitis,* most range widely through the country, including the subantarctic islands. Six are found in forests, although 2 are restricted to high-altitude forest and extend into open alpine habitats. In the forests these ferns grow on rocks, sometimes on the forest floor, or as low epiphytes. Two of the forest species are frequently encountered.

G. billardieri is found in lowland and mountain forest and subalpine shrubland throughout the main islands, the Chathams and the subantarctic. It grows mostly as a low epiphyte but can also be found on rocks. It also occurs in Australia.

The fronds are 3–20 cm long x 3–9 mm wide, completely hairless or with a few hairs near the base.

G. ciliata is a smaller species with fronds 2–9 cm long x 2–6 mm wide. They are mostly conspicuously hairy and always have hairs intermingled with the sporangia.

G. ciliata grows in lowland and mountain forest through the North Island and in the northern South Island. It is restricted to New Zealand and mostly grows on damp earth and rocks and rarely as a low epiphyte.

Grammitis billardieri growing on a bank.

Pneumatopteris pennigera showing the deeply divided leaflets.

GULLY FERN
Pneumatopteris pennigera
Thelypteridaceae

P. pennigera (gully fern) is a common fern in damp very shady places in lowland to mountain forest in the North Island and in coastal and lowland forest in the South Island.

Its slender trunks are up to 1 m in height and the fronds have primary leaflets that are deeply and regularly divided into segments that almost qualify as secondary leaflets. The frond blade is 30–150 cm long x 10–40 cm wide and the longest leaflets are 6–20 cm long x 1.5–3 cm wide. The sori are dome-shaped without indusia.

This genus is widely dis-tributed throughout the world with one New Zealand species. This species is also found in Australia.

Lastreopsis
Dryopteridaceae

Lastreopsis is widespread throughout the world. The sori have umbrella-like kidney-shaped indusia.

L. glabella has a short erect stem. The fronds have few scales but distinctive red-brown hairs on the upper sides of the stalks and leaflet midribs. The frond blades are 10–35 cm long x 5–25 cm wide. The species is found throughout the country in damp coastal and lowland forest.

L. microsora has creeping stems. The fronds have few scales but abundant soft whitish hairs on the midribs and veins. The frond blades are 15–35 x 10–25 cm. Found in coastal and lowland forest in the North Island, it is much less common near the coast in the South Island. The species is also native to Australia.

L. hispida has creeping stems. The fronds are notable for their

Lastreopsis microsora.

Lastreopsis velutina.

rough texture and the abundance of black bristle-like scales on the stalks, veins and midribs. The frond blades are 18–50 cm long x 15–40 cm wide. It is common in coastal to lower mountain forest in the North Island and coastal forest in the South Island, and is also found in Australia.

L. velutina has short erect stems. The fronds are densely covered with soft brown hairs on all surfaces, giving it a distinctive velvety texture. The frond blades are 15–55 cm long x 15–45 cm wide. This attractive fern is not common. It is found in drier coastal and lowland forest in the North Island and in coastal forest of the eastern South Island.

SHIELD FERNS
Polystichum
Dryopteridaceae

Polystichum is widespread throughout the world. The sori have umbrella-like hemispherical indusia (Plate 35). Two of our 4 species are frequently encountered in forests as well as in open sites.

P. richardii has leathery fronds with leaflet tips that are rather prickly to the touch. There are narrow scales, with fringes of hairs at the base, covering the stalks. The blades are 10–50 cm long x 4–25 cm wide and the primary leaflets 2–13 cm long x 1–5 cm wide. The indusia have black centres. Found in drier habitats in coastal to mountain forests in the North Island and in the east of the South Island, it also grows in the open on rocks and in shrubland.

P. vestitum has softer fronds. There are larger broader scales, lacking marginal hairs, that are abundant on the stalks. The blades are 20–100 cm long x 6–25 cm wide and the primary leaflets 3–15 cm long x 1–2.5 cm wide. The indusia do not have black centres. Except for Northland, this species is found throughout the country including the subantarctic islands. It grows best in cool moist forest where it develops short fibrous trunks that sometimes become very broad and irregular in

Polystichum richardii showing sori on the underside of the frond.

The softer fronds of *Polystichum vestitum* showing the scales on the midrib and undersides.

shape. The species also grows in tussock grassland and shrubland.

Lindsaea   Dennstaedtiaceae

L. trichomanoides is the most likely of our 3 species to be found in forests. The stems are creeping and the fronds have red or chestnut-brown stalks and blades with 2–3 orders of leaflets. The blade is 5–25 cm long x 2–8 cm wide and the ultimate segments 4–10 mm long x 2–7 mm wide, fan-like with the elongated sori curving around inside the outer margin. The indusium is open towards the margin. *L. trichomanoides* grows in drier lowland to mountain forests throughout the North Island and in the Marlborough Sounds and the west coast of the South Island. It is also native to Australia.

Asplenium bulbiferum with plantlets on the upper sides of the fronds.

Asplenium bulbiferum with a well-developed plantlet.

Asplenium oblongifolium.

SPLEENWORTS

Asplenium   **Aspleniaceae**

Asplenium is a large genus found throughout the world. Of our 16 native species, 5 are commonly encountered on the forest floor and 2 others (*A. flaccidum* and *A. polyodon*) are epiphytic (see pages 182–183). **A. polyodon** can also grow on the forest floor.

Two of the forest-floor species are common, large and conspicuous. The sori are elongated with an indusial flap attached to one side (Plate 35).

A. bulbiferum (hen and chickens fern) is found throughout the country in lowland to lower mountain forest. It is also present in Australia. The stems are short and erect with rather soft fronds. The frond blades, 12–120 cm long x 5–50 cm wide, have 2–3 orders of leaflets. The primary leaflets are 3–35 cm long x 1–12 cm wide. The sori are 2–4 mm long. A notable feature of the species is the development of small plantlets (the 'chickens') on the upper sides of many but not all fronds. This is an additional means of reproduction.

A. lamprophyllum has a similar appearance to *A. bulbiferum* but differs in having creeping stems, generally smaller fronds, 15–60 cm long x 6–25 cm wide, no plantlets and sori up to 1 cm long. It grows mostly on rocky sites in forest from Northland to the central North Island.

A. oblongifolium (formerly *A. lucidum*) is quite different in appearance. The stems are short and more or less erect. The frond blades have only primary leaflets and measure 10–100 cm long x 7–45 cm wide. The leaflets are 4–25 cm long x 7–45 cm wide with drawn-out tips. They are thick, dark green and shiny above. The sori are up to 3 cm long. This handsome species grows in coastal to lower mountain forests, shrubland and coastal cliffs throughout the North Island and in coastal sites in the northern South Island.

There is a group of smaller species with much-divided fronds, 3–45 cm long x 1–22 cm wide, that have some similarity to the epiphytic *A. flaccidum* — **A. richardii**, **A. hookerianum** and **A. terrestre** — and they are often difficult to distinguish. Natural hybrids between these and other species of *Asplenium* further complicate the situation.

COMB FERN
Schizaea dichotoma
Schizaeaceae

S. dichotoma is found mostly in kauri forests through Northland and the Coromandel Peninsula and also around thermal sites near Rotorua and Taupo. It is also widespread in the tropics and subtropics from Madagascar to the Pacific.

The stems spread for short distances on the forest floor. The frond stalks are unusually tall, up to 30 cm, and branch towards the ends by several forks into a fan-like arrangement. At the tip of each stalk branch are 2 short rows of leaflets that are folded towards each other to provide a comb-like appearance. The sporangia are in 2 rows at the edges of the leaflets.

This fern is not conspicuous but may catch the eye with its strange appearance.

In better-lit forest sites the climbing fern, *Microsorum pustulatum,* can grow luxuriantly on the forest floor (see also page 178).

Schizaea dichotoma. At the tip of its stalk each frond has a fan-like arrangement of narrow segments with crescent-shaped sori.

FILMY FERNS
Hymenophyllaceae

Filmy ferns are a very distinctive group and they are strongly represented in New Zealand with 27 species, all growing in forests. The fronds are delicate, tissue-paper thin and translucent. However, they are not as delicate as they look. During dry spells they shrivel up but quickly revive when it rains.

Unlike most other ferns, where the sori are on the undersides of fronds, in filmy ferns they develop directly from the margins, usually at the tips of the ultimate leaflets. The sporangia are attached to short or long stalks and when young they are protected by a pair of membranous flaps, one above and one below (Plate 35).

Almost all our filmy fern species grow throughout the country, including the subantarctic islands. They generally range from lowland to mountain forests in damp dark places. Eight of the species are also found in Australia and some of them further afield.

Marginal sori of the kidney fern.

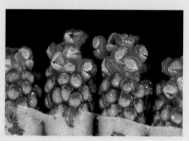

A close view of kidney fern sporangia.

Two filmy ferns, *Trichomanes reniforme* (kidney fern) and *Hymenophyllum demissum*.

Hymenophyllum

Of the 21 species of *Hymenophyllum*, 11 grow on the forest floor or on rocks and of these 3 are sometimes epiphytic; the remainder are generally epiphytic.

Our largest filmy fern, **H. dilatatum**, has bright green fronds with 3–4 orders of leaflets and blades 8–40 cm long x 4–15 cm wide. The frond stalk is strongly winged. At the other extreme are several diminutive species with fronds only a few centimetres long. The latter often grow intermingled with mosses and liverworts and are sometimes mistaken for leafy liverworts.

Our commonest species, **H. demissum**, grows mostly on the forest floor. Its pale green fronds have 3–4 orders of leaflets. The frond blades are 7–25 cm long x 3–15 cm wide. The frond stalks are not winged.

Trichomanes

Of the 6 species of *Trichomanes*, 5 grow on the forest floor or on rocks and only one is usually epiphytic. All are small plants and all but one of them have divided fronds.

The remaining species is one of our most remarkable and attractive ferns. **T. reniforme**

Close-up of a translucent filmy fern frond, *Hymenophyllum demissum*, showing sori with protective flaps.

A carpet of kidney ferns in hard beech forest.

Kidney fern showing marginal sori.

(kidney fern) has fronds with slender stalks up to 25 cm long and kidney-shaped to round undivided shiny blades 3–10 cm long x 4–13 cm wide. It often forms extensive and attractive mats on the forest floor and on rocks and sometimes extends on to the bases of tree trunks. The crowded sori form a fringe around the frond margin projecting beyond the prominent protective cups.

CLUB MOSSES
Lycopodiaceae

Club mosses are small plants comprising a few hundred species represented in most parts of the world. The heyday of the group was several hundred million years ago in the Carboniferous or Coal Age, when ancestral forms were trees in swamp forests.

They differ from ferns in that their leaves are small and undivided, and the sporangia develop singly in the angles of some of the leaves. Where the sporangia-bearing leaves are grouped at the ends of branches, they may form distinct cones. *Lycopodium volubile* is a common club moss at forest margins.

Lycopodium volubile with hanging cones.

Lycopodium volubile

This is a common and very attractive plant throughout the country at low to middle altitudes. Its long branching stems scramble in shrubland and along forest margins. In earlier times masses of this lycopodium were gathered to decorate country dance halls. It is also found in South east Asia, New Guinea and New Caledonia.

The slender stems branch by equal forkings and can extend over the ground or through shrubs for 5 m or more. There are 2 rows of larger leaves, up to 5 mm long, that are flattened in one plane. They are pointed and rather sickle-shaped. Smaller narrower leaves, up to 2 mm long, are closely pressed to the upper sides of the stems between the rows of larger leaves.

Pendulous spore-producing cones, up to 8 cm long, are formed at the tips of special stems sparsely covered with the smaller type of leaf.

Attractive foliage of *Lycopodium volubile*.

MOSSES & LIVERWORTS

Mosses and liverworts are mostly small plants of cool, moist and shady places, where they grow close to the ground or other surfaces. They often form dense cushions or mats that retain water like a sponge.

There are hundreds of species of these plants in our forests and they occupy a wide range of habitats. Many grow on the forest floor on soil, leaf litter, logs, exposed tree roots or rocks; a smaller number grow on rocks in and alongside streams. Many species occur as epiphytes, mostly on tree trunks and branches, but there are others on tree fern trunks and on twigs, where they may form conspicuous swaying curtains.

In high-rainfall forests mosses and liverworts are often present in great profusion and grow intermingled with lichens and filmy ferns. It is a rich and fascinating miniature plant world that can only be fully appreciated with a microscope.

Mosses and liverworts have small undivided leaves or no leaves at all. Like ferns, they reproduce by means of spores. However, the sporangia that contain the spores are relatively large and are not closely grouped together. Fern sporangia are much smaller and are often crowded in groups (sori).

The difference between mosses and liverworts can usually be seen in the sporangia. Those of mosses have slender wiry stalks and the capsules are covered by a loose hood, which drops away and the capsule then opens by a terminal lid to release the spores. Most liverwort sporangia have delicate translucent stalks, and the capsules usually split into 4 valves to release the spores.

Mosses and liverworts also reproduce vegetatively. Detached leaves and bits of stems of mosses readily grow into new plants, and some of the thallose liverworts too form plantlets in special cups.

There are 2 main groups of liverworts. Thallose liverworts have no leaves but instead a fleshy layer, known as a thallus, that sits close to the ground; the distinctive hornworts with their quill-like sporangia belong to this group. The second group, the leafy liverworts, includes most of the species found in forests.

Further reading: *The Mosses of New Zealand,* Jessica Beever, K.W. Allison & John Child; *The Liverworts of New Zealand,* K.W. Allison and John Child.

Sporangia of the moss *Ptychomnium aciculare* have slender wiry stalks.

Sporangia of the liverwort *Schistochila* with delicate translucent stalks and black spore capsules.

MOSSES

Dawsonia superba is our tallest moss and one of the tallest in the world. It also grows in Australia and New Guinea. Its unbranched stems can be up to 50 cm tall and its colonies in shady but well-drained sites on the forest floor have been likened to clumps of young pine seedlings.

Dendroligotrichum dendroides grows in similar sites to *Dawsonia* but mostly at higher altitudes. It is also a tall moss, sometimes up to 40 cm but mostly about 20 cm. The stems branch at the top into an attractive tree-like form.

Polytrichum is related to but smaller than *Dawsonia superba*. The leafy stems are erect and crowded together to form mats or cushions. The species are mostly found in moist open habitats.

Breutelia pendula is a distinctive moss. It has red upright stems that are densely covered with brown hairs on their lower parts. The stems often branch at the top into an umbrella-like form.

Leucobryum candidum or milk moss (page 127) is mostly encountered in beech forests, where it forms large clumps on the forest floor and the exposed roots of beech trees. When dry it is notably whitish in colour.

The species of **Dicranoloma** are common in New Zealand forests, both on the ground and on tree trunks, and are also well represented in open habitats. The curved leaves are drawn out into long twisted tips and have yellow or orange patches at the base. A number of the species are yellow green to golden in colour.

Macromitrium is a genus of mosses that form spreading patches that grow closely pressed to smooth tree trunks.

Hypnodendron and **Hypopterygium** are the attractive umbrella mosses of shady moist forest-floor sites. The erect stems are short and branch freely at the top into a fluffy umbrella-like form. To quote from *The Mosses of New Zealand*, 'A patch of fronds, their edges just overlapping, each frond a slightly different shade of green from its neighbour, forms a memorable mosaic.' In *Hypopterygium* there are 2 rows of lateral leaves and a third row of smaller leaves along the stem undersides. *Hypnodendron* does not have a third row of leaves.

Ptychomnium aciculare is a common and attractive moss that grows on the forest floor and logs and also epiphytically on tree trunks. Its stems are red and the spreading leaves with twisted points become papery and crumpled when dry.

Weymouthia mollis is a very distinctive moss. It is pale green to fawn in colour and hangs curtain-like from twigs of trees, particularly at higher altitudes in 'goblin forest', where mists are frequent.

Sphagnum or **bog moss** is found throughout the world and is often the dominant plant in bogs in cooler climates. Our sphagnum bogs are frequently in open sites, including forest clearings, but in high-rainfall areas, such as the west coast of the South Island and Stewart Island, sphagnum can be abundant on the forest floor. It is pale green in colour, soft and almost woolly in texture. The leaves are very distinctive in that they have a mixture of very small narrow green cells and much larger colourless cells. These are without living contents and have a remarkable capacity for absorbing and retaining water, thus ensuring ensures that the living sphagnum at the surface of a bog never dries out. Because of its water-retaining ability, sphagnum plays an important role in horticulture. It is used as a packing medium for plants and is added to potting mix and compost to make them more water retentive. Collecting and selling sphagnum has become a small industry on the West Coast in recent years.

Bog moss (*Sphagnum*) dominating a small bog surrounded by mountain beech forest.

Dawsonia superba, one of the world's largest mosses.

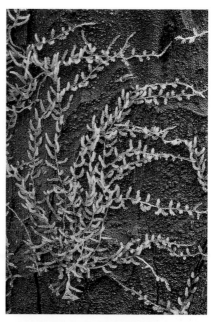

An epiphytic moss, *Macromitrium longipes*.

One of the umbrella mosses, *Hypnodendron kerrii*.

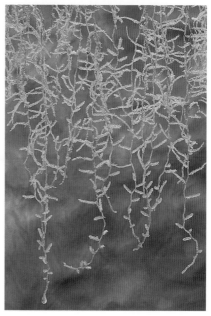

The 'old man's beard' moss, *Weymouthia mollis*.

A dense colony of an umbrella moss.

A species of *Polytrichum* with sporangia.

Breutelia pendula with sporangia.

Dicranoloma billardieri.

LIVERWORTS

THALLOSE LIVERWORTS

These occur mostly on moist sites in forests or in the open and can sometimes cover extensive areas.

Marchantia is the best-known genus, in which air chambers can be seen on the upper surface of the thallus as a network of hexagonal outlines. At the centre of each hexagon is a prominent and often whitish pore.

A distinctive feature of marchantias is the cup-like structures on the upper surface, within which small flattened 2-lobed plantlets form. This is a non-sexual mode of reproduction and the plantlets are often splashed out by rain drops.

In *Lunularia* the plantlet-forming structures are crescent-moon shaped. This appears to be the primary form of reproduction.

Asterella has smaller thalli that often branch to form circular rosettes. There are no plantlets formed.

Monoclea is an impressive thallose liverwort. Its fleshy dark green thallus, among the largest of any of the liverworts, can form a continuous cover over many square metres along stream edges in dark forest. The capsules of the sporangia each open by one longitudinal split.

Other thallose species are mostly small, thin and delicate. Some grow pressed to the substrate and

Marchantia showing cups containing plantlets.

are branched or unbranched and with or without midribs. Others spread by slender stems, some of which turn upwards and branch at their tips into an umbrella-like thallus. They can be mistaken for small filmy ferns.

The thalli of the **hornworts** are thin and dark green. The sporophytes are very distinctive, being quill- or bristle-like, several centimetres long and forming spores through their whole length. When the sporophytes are mature they split at the tip into 2 valves, which gradually separate downwards to release the spores. This group includes several genera of which *Anthoceros*, with several New Zealand species, is best known.

LEAFY LIVERWORTS

This is the largest group and most of the species are found in forest habitats.

They usually have rounded leaves overlapping in 2 rows and flattened into one plane, often with a row of smaller leaves on the stem undersides. The leaves sometimes have smooth margins but more often they are lobed, toothed or are divided into long fine segments.

The sporophytes have long delicate white stalks that elongate quite rapidly, and round to elongate black or dark brown capsules. They look something like wax matches.

Plagiochila has about two dozen New Zealand species that often grow in great profusion and include the largest species of this group. The stems are wiry and dark brown to black. The leaves are toothed and there is no third row of small leaves on the stem undersides.

Trichocolea has only 3 native species but they are so distinctive in appearance that they are often noticed. The leaves are deeply incised into many long and hair-like segments that are densely interlocked so that the plant looks and feels densely woolly. This a means of retaining moisture.

Thallose liverwort *Marchantia foliacea* with reproductive structures raised up on long stalks.

A hornwort, *Anthoceros flabellatum*, with quill-like sporangia, some with spores visible at their tips.

A leafy liverwort, *Plagiochila*, with *Nertera villosa*.

Hymenophyton with thalli, raised up on stalks.

A fluffy water-retaining mat of *Trichocolea*.

Left: *Lepidozia microphylla*, a delicate leafy liverwort forming a curtain on a cliff next to a waterfall.

Monoclea forsteri, which can form extensive sheets in moist shady forest sites.

FUNGI & LICHENS

Slimes, jellies, mushrooms and toadstools, puffballs, mildews, yeast—these and more are all fungi, a strange group of organisms. Most of the year in the forest you would hardly know they were there, but come the autumn, when temperatures are still mild and the weather is moist, they suddenly appear as if from nowhere. It is not surprising then that in earlier times they were believed to be supernatural. Many fungi are brilliantly to delicately coloured and some are extremely beautiful.

Like animals, fungi have no chlorophyll and so must obtain their nutriment from dead remains of plants or from living plants and sometimes dead or living animals. They really only become visible when they reproduce. Before that they comprise slender branching whitish filaments growing through soil and other substrates, or within living tissues in the case of parasitic species. Sometimes if you lift off a bark flake from a dead log you can see a mass of these filaments looking a bit like white candy floss. They feed themselves by secreting enzymes into their surroundings that break down the complex molecules into simpler compounds that can be absorbed.

The parts that are visible — the mushrooms, toadstools, puffballs and so on — are known as fruiting bodies. These are composed of densely compacted filaments and they differ greatly in size, form and colouring, but all produce very small spores in countless numbers. The spores spread widely on the wind, so many of the species are found in different parts of the world.

Lichens are basically fungi, mostly cup fungi. Like fungi in general, they are unable to manufacture their own food but they have overcome this problem very successfully by trapping algae within their tissues and helping themselves to the sugars they manufacture. They therefore function in much the same way as green plants do and can grow in a much wider range of habitats than other fungi.

Lichens are a conspicuous feature of our forests. They grow on the ground, on litter, logs, tree trunks, branches, twigs and rocks. In moist higher-altitude forests, pale swaying curtains of old man's beard lichens (*Usnea*) drape the twigs of trees and shrubs.

Further reading: *Mushrooms and Toadstools,* Marie Taylor.

A bracket fungus, *Ganoderma applanatum*, on a tree trunk. The lower surface is white with spores.

Crustose lichens growing on a young kahikatea trunk.

FUNGI

SLIME MOULDS

These curious organisms are doubtfully included in the fungi as they seem to straddle the boundary between fungi and animals. When not forming spores, a slime mold is a jelly-like mass that branches and spreads over leaf litter, twigs and logs like a large amoeba. Its spreading movement can sometimes be observed with the naked eye. When it encounters any nutritive material it engulfs it and digests it internally like an animal.

When reproduction takes place portions of the jelly often grow upwards, forming slender stalks with heads containing the spores. Some slime moulds are brightly coloured orange or yellow.

SOOTY MOULDS

Although they don't form visible fruiting bodies, the sooty moulds are conspicuous when their black tufts of filaments densely cover tree trunks, notably those of manuka and black beech, and the twigs and leaves of shrubs. The way is prepared for them by scale insects and sometimes aphids, which tap into the sap of the plants and excrete sugary drops known as honey-dew. (See also page 246).

CUP FUNGI

This is a large group in which the fruiting bodies are mostly in the form of discs, saucers, cups or flasks with narrow openings. The spores are produced on the upper or inner surfaces. Many cup fungi grow on decaying plant material but others are quite specialised parasites of both plants and animals.

The genus **Peziza** is a large

An orange slime mould spreading over dead leaves and a piece of bark.

A golden slime mould on a fallen beech log.

Cookeina colensoi, a cup fungus.

HONEYDEW, SOOTY MOULDS & WASPS

When you walk through a beech forest in northwest Nelson in summer there is a low-pitched humming sound which is puzzling until you notice that the tree trunks are swarming with wasps. This is a story with several players.

First on the scene are scale insects (see also page 293), which are able to penetrate the bark of tree trunks and branches with their long mouth parts to suck up sap and at the other end to excrete drops of sugary honeydew through long tubes. Scale insects can be abundant on the trunks of beech trees and the honeydew they produce is an important food source for a number of native organisms, the most conspicuous being sooty moulds, whose dark filaments turn the tree trunks black. Honeydew is also provides food for native bees, introduced honey bees and other insects, lizards and nectar-feeding birds such as tui, bellbird and kaka. Since wasps have become established in New Zealand this situation has changed dramatically.

Apart from the danger that people will be stung, the wasps are also a serious problem for the native animals that feed on the honeydew; after the wasps have finished there is little left for them.

Droplets of honeydew excreted by scale insects.

Wasps feeding on honeydew on a beech trunk.

Beech trunk covered in sooty mould and honeydew.

Peziza, a colouful cup fungus.

Scutellinia colensoi.

one in which the cups may be several centimetres across in a variety of colours including brown, yellow and orange.

Scutellinia colensoi is an attractive and unusual little species with clusters of stalked orange-red discs, each fringed with black hairs. An even smaller *Scutellinia* forms stalkless and hairless discs, blue green in colour, on rotting wood. The wood becomes blue-green stained too and this persists after the discs have disappeared.

The earth tongue, **Trichoglossum hirsutum**, is jet black and club-shaped with a velvet texture. It grows in soil or among mosses.

Cyttaria gunnii, the strawberry fungus, parasitises silver beech. The fungus filaments growing in the living tissues of the beech cause rather unsightly galls from which stalked golf ball-like fruiting bodies emerge in the spring. The spores form in crowded cup-like indentations over the surfaces of the fruiting bodies. (See page 126).

The earth tongue, *Trichoglossum hirsutum*.

PARASITIC FUNGI

Two notable species of cup fungi parasitise the immature stages of 2 native insects. The filaments of **Cordyceps robertsii** invade the buried caterpillar of a moth, killing it and feeding on it. Later a wiry often unbranched stalk of the fungus grows out from the head of the caterpillar and above the ground. Towards the end of the stalk spores are formed in flask-like cavities. At this stage the whole structure is known as a vegetable caterpillar.

The vegetable cicada forms in a similar way but the stalks are shorter and much branched.

Left: An excavated vegetable cicada with the dead cicada pupa below and the fungus growing out from its head. Right: An adult cicada that has succumbed to a different parasitic fungus.

GILL FUNGI

This is the best-known and probably the largest group of fungi, generally referred to as mushrooms and toadstools. The fruiting bodies are umbrella-like in form with an erect stalk crowned with a cap. On the underside the cap develops close-set radiating flanges known as gills and on these the spores are formed.

There are many species of gill fungi in New Zealand forests. They range in form from small and delicate to large and robust, and in colour from pale and ghostly to modest brown tones and a kaleidoscope of bright colours — yellow, red, blue, green and sometimes combinations of two or more. Some species grow on decaying logs and leaf litter; a number have their filaments associated with tree roots, obtaining sugar for themselves and providing water and mineral nutrients to the trees; and some are parasites of trees. The filaments of these parasites spread through the living tissues of the trees and eventually kill them. The fungi continue to grow on the dead trees and at this stage form their fruiting bodies.

The robust yellow-brown fruiting bodies of species of **Armillaria** grow out from the lower trunks and roots of trees they have killed.

Growing on dead wood or leaf litter are small species known as **wax-gills** because of their translucent waxy texture. A number of them are brightly coloured yellow, orange, red, blue and green.

Species of **Russula**, also often brightly coloured, can be identified by their brittle texture. A bent stalk snaps or crumbles like chalk.

The milk caps, **Lactarius**, exude a milky fluid when broken.

One of the species of **Entoloma** (E. hochstetteri) is particularly notable for its attractive appearance. It has a pointed conical cap and both cap and stalk are sky blue.

Flammulina velutipes has a tough and rubbery

The gill fungus *Armillaria limonea*, which parasitises trees.

The wax-gill *Hygrocybe viridis*.

Left: A very delicate, pure white gill fungus appropriately named *Delicatula*. The common name is parachute mushroom. Right: *Mycena interrupta*, a gill fungus.

A gill fungus, *Flammulina velutipes*, growing on the cut end of a log. The cut surface is white with spores from the fungus

A bright red wax-gill, *Hygrocybe rubro-carnosa*.

A yellow wax-gill, *Hygrophorus salmonipes*.

cap that is slimy when young. The stalk is extremely velvety in texture. This species grows in clumps on tree stumps and is widespread throughout the world.

Cortinarius is a large and often colourful genus and can be identified by the cobwebby veil attaching young caps to the stalks. As the cap expands the cobweb is broken.

The **ink caps** (*Coprinus*) are very unusual gill fungi. They often have deeply conical caps, which, at maturity, completely dissolve into an inky-black fluid containing the spores. The fluid and its black spores are spread by passing slugs and the like.

BOLETES

These are fungi of mushroom form but with pores, not gills. The form of the fruiting body is the same as that of the gill fungi but instead of gills there is soft spongy tissue. This tissue is penetrated by close-set vertical pores within which the spores are produced.

Several native species are found in forest litter or on the bases of tree fern trunks. *Porphyrellus novae-zelandiae* and *P. niveus* are light brown with distinctive raised network patterns on their stalks.

Tilopilus formosus is quite different in appearance. It is larger and the top of the cap and the stalk are almost black and velvety.

POUCH FUNGI & PUFFBALLS

Some pouch fungi have stalks and caps, but the caps do not expand away from the stalks and the spore mass remains enclosed within. Other species are similar but lack stalks. The puffballs also lack well-defined stalks but they eventually form pores at the top

Two gill fungi: *Russula* (left) in leaf litter and *Entoloma hochstetteri* (right).

Two gill fungi: *Cortinarius* (left) and an inkcap, *Coprinus comatus* (right).

through which the spores puff out with pressure from gusts of wind. Forest fungi in this group grow mainly in leaf litter.

Among the stalked pouch fungi there are several that catch the eye with their bright colouring. **Weraroa erythrocephala** has a rounded bright red cap. **W. virescens** is pale blue with a more elongate, sometimes oddly shaped cap. **Thaxterogaster porphyreum** is bright violet, including the stalk, with a rounded cap.

The common puffballs (**Lycoperdon**) are well known in pastures and lawns but some also grow on the forest floor.

The **earthstars** are more unusual. When young their puffballs are enclosed by a fleshy coat, which eventually splits into several segments that spread widely into a star or flower-like pattern. The puffball is then able to release its spores.

More curious still are the **birdsnest fungi**. These are small species that grow on leaf or bark litter. At first the fruiting bodies are closed, but then they disintegrate at the top to assume a cup-like form. This might suggest they belong to the cup fungi, but their microscopic details place them in a different group. Instead of a single spore mass in each cup there are a dozen or more, each compressed into a pill-like form. Raindrops landing in the cups splash the 'pills' in all directions.

Above: A puffball, *Lycoperdon*. Note the pores at the tips.
Centre: An earthstar, *Geastrum*, a fancy sort of puffball.
Below: A birdsnest fungus, *Nidula candida*.

Brilliant *Weraroa erythrocephala,* a pouch fungus.

A less flamboyant species of the same genus,
Weraroa virescens.

The purple pouch fungus, *Thaxterogaster porphyreum,*
growing in beech litter.

STINKHORNS

The stinkhorns are notable for their strange forms and sometimes meat-red coloration but also for their smell, delightful to flies but repulsive to humans. When young the fruiting bodies are like soft white eggs. Under moist conditions the 'eggs' eventually swell and split to release a rapidly expanding spore-bearing structure that may be spike-like, flower-like or basket-like in form. Flies are attracted to the meaty colour of some species but more particularly to the rotten-meat smell of the spores. The latter are in mucus-like blobs or films and they are dispersed when flies are smeared with some of the sticky liquid. Two fairly large species are often noticed. **Aseroe rubra** has a hollow tube crowned by radiating red petal-like segments bearing blobs of dark spore fluid at their bases. The **basket fungus** has a ball-like network of vein-like segments completely covered with spore fluid on the inside.

SPINE OR TOOTH FUNGI

Some of these have a mushroom form, but instead of having gills or tubes below the caps they have pointed spines that bear the spores. They range in colour from fawn to brown or dark purple. In the northern hemisphere they are sometimes called

A spine fungus known as fungus icicle, *Hericium clathroides*.

Left: The stinkhorn *Aseroe rubra*, with flies attracted by the smelly spore-filled fluid. Right: Stinkhorns growing out from soft egg-like structures, which can be seen at left.

'forest hedge-hogs'.

A quite different fungus with spines is known as a **fungus icicle** or stalactite fungus. It grows attached to rotting wood and is pure white in colour, branching like a miniature tree.

CORAL FUNGI

These are erect and often much branched like coral, as their name suggests. The spores form all over the surface. Some species are white, others are yellow, red, purple or pink.

JELLY FUNGI

These grow on wood and range from very soft and jelly-like to tough and leathery. White translucent much-lobed species of *Tremella* are well represented, and the ear fungus, *Auricularia*, is abundant on rotting wood. *Auricularia* has large irregular brown cups that form spores on the upper surfaces.

Above: Basket fungus, a stinkhorn.
Centre: An attractively coloured coral fungus.
Below right: Ear fungus, *Auricularia polytricha,* growing on rotting wood.
Below: A jelly fungus, *Tremella fuciformis.*

CRUST AND BRACKET FUNGI

Some of these fungi grow on dead wood and bark while others are parasites on the trunks and branches of trees.

Many of the bracket or shelf fungi form their spores in pores on their undersides. They grow for some years and each year add a new layer of pores below. The upper surface of the shelves is patterned in concentric zones, sometimes attractively varying in colour. Each zone is formed by the upturned edge of a spore-producing layer on the underside.

A common smaller bracket fungus growing on dead wood is *Coriolus versicolor*. It is thin and leathery, and the upper surface is attractively zoned in shades of dark blue, grey and brown.

One of the large bracket fungi growing on trees is *Ganoderma applanatum* (see page 244), which grows for many years and is hard and woody in texture. It is so firmly anchored to the tree that it is almost impossible to detach.

A small stalked bracket fungus, *Favolaschia calocera*, catches the eye, in the North Island particularly, because of its bright red-orange colour. It has quite large pores on the under-sides. Some think that this is an introduction from the tropics as it appears to have spread widely in milder regions in recent years.

Pynocoporus cinnabarinus is a brightly coloured bracket fungus that grows on fallen wood. The species name likens it in colour to the mercury-bearing ore cinnabar.

Above: A thin attractively patterned bracket fungus, *Coriolus versicolor*.
Centre: A small introduced bracket fungus with large pores, *Favolaschia calocera*.
Below: A spongy, strikingly coloured bracket fungus, *Pycnoporus cinnabarinus*.

LICHENS

Lichens can be grouped according to the form of their thallus.

Crustose lichens form circular patches that press close to the surface to which they are attached — tree trunks, logs, rocks and even glass. They are attached by fungal filaments, often so intimately that they cannot be detached without removing some of the surface. The attaching filaments secrete acids that dissolve the surface of rocks and release mineral nutrients required by the lichen. By this means some crustose lichens become firmly etched into rocks so that rock and lichen are virtually one.

Foliose lichens have a leafy look. Some are attached all over their lower surfaces but have many, more or less erect leaf-like lobes. Others are attached loosely at one point. The latter are termed foliose and include some of the largest species, sometimes up to 50 cm in diameter.

Much-branched **fruticose** (shrubby) **lichens** may be erect on the ground, rocks or logs, or hanging on twigs, sometimes with liverworts and mosses.

Lichens grow very slowly, increasing in diameter

A crustose lichen spreading slowly at its margins.

Left: (Above and below) a fruticose lichen; (left) a small foliose lichen; and on the branch a grey crustose lichen with spore cups of the fungal component. Right: A foliose *Pseudocyphellaria* species with orange fungal spore cups.

by 1–10 mm per year, so a large crustose lichen growing under extreme conditions must be centuries old.

The lichen thallus is often grey, the colour of the fungal component, although sometimes when wet the green of the alga shows through. Some species are more brightly coloured and even when the thallus is grey the spore-producing structures may be coloured red, yellow, brown or black. These pigments of lichens can be extracted and used as dyes for wool.

Lichens reproduce by means of spores, which are formed in discs, cups or flasks, sometimes elevated above the thallus on stalks (pixie cups). Most lichens also reproduce vegetatively, either by portions of the thallus breaking away, or by the more specialised means of a cluster of algal cells, wrapped around by a few fungal filaments, detaching from the thallus and being washed or blown away.

A foliose lichen with spore cups but also many smaller outgrowths made up of fungal filaments and algal cells. These outgrowths readily wash or blow away and are an efficient non-sexual mode of reproduction.

'Pixie cups' of a species of Cladonia.

Birds

BIRDS

It has been estimated that before humans arrived in New Zealand there were more than 60 species of birds that made the forests their home. Since human settlement about 40 percent of these birds have become extinct.

Our forest bird fauna is not large, especially compared with that of tropical forests or even the forests of England, which are noisy with bird song. This is generally the case for islands remote from continents as, despite their ability to fly, forest birds rarely traverse wide ocean gaps. A visiting ornithologist was struck by our general lack of bird song and spoke of 'New Zealand's silent forests'. Nevertheless, our forest birds are an interesting group that play an important role in the forest ecology.

New Zealand's isolation has led to some interesting evolutionary directions for our forest birds. A number of them are flightless, although in some cases — for example the moa and kiwi — this may have evolved before New Zealand separated from the ancient southern continent of Gondwana. Loss of flight is common among the birds of isolated islands and this is attributed to the absence of mammal predators.

It has also been suggested that in the absence of foliage-eating browsing mammals, some birds evolved to fill that niche — for example the large flightless moa and some of the smaller flying birds such as the two parakeets, the pigeon and the kokako.

Our national icon, the kiwi, is also a curious product of evolution. With its long beak it probes deep into the soil to extract some of its diet of invertebrates.

Ornithologists group forest birds based on what they eat and at what level in the forest they mostly find their food. In many cases, if the preferred food is unavailable or in short supply, birds will widen their diets.

The **honeyeaters** in New Zealand include the tui, bellbird and stitchbird. These birds have long tongues, branched and feathery at the tip, for sweeping up nectar from flowers. The flowers they visit have a tubular or cup-like form to hold the copious nectar and they are generally brightly coloured, mostly red but sometimes yellow, to catch the eyes of birds. Most of these flowers are found in the canopy of the forest on ratas and pohutukawa, rewarewa, the kowhais, the tree fuchsia and puriri. The birds act as pollinators for these flowers, and the stamens are arranged so they dust pollen on the heads of the birds as they reach in for the nectar.

The **arboreal herbivores** include the two parakeets, the native pigeon and the kokako. They eat some or all of buds, leaves, flowers, fruits and seeds. They also eat invertebrates in the breeding season.

The **arboreal insectivores** are a large group of 10 species including the rifleman, brown creeper, whitehead, yellowhead, grey warbler, fantail, tomtit, saddleback and 2 cuckoos. Most of them eat other invertebrates as well as insects, and a few add lizards and birds to their diet as well.

The **ground herbivores** once included 7 species of moa but now the rare kakapo is the only representative.

The **ground insectivores** are a small but varied group, including the weka, New Zealand robin and the 3 species of kiwi. Some species are nocturnal, others are active by day and night, and others again during daytime only. Some are flightless and others fly.

The **predators** include the New Zealand falcon, the kingfisher and the morepork.

There are 2 birds — kaka and silvereye — whose diet is so consistently varied that they could be termed the **generalisers**.

GHOSTS FROM THE PAST

The most notable of the extinct birds are the 11 species of flightless **moa**. Some of them weighed 85–170 kg and were able to reach to 2–3 m or more above the ground; others weighed 20–30 kg and probably reached to under 2 m. The last moas became extinct only a few centuries ago and information about their diets has been obtained from gizzards of some species preserved in swamps. This shows that they ate twigs, leaves and fruits of a wide range of conifers, flowering plants and some ferns.

With its very short tail, the **bush wren** (*Xenicus longipes*) was similar to the rifleman, but larger, with a dark yellowish green colouring above and ash grey below. It worked its way along branches in search of invertebrates. The call was a repetitive, whirring 'seep'. The bush wren was once widespread throughout the country, but the last sightings were in the 1960s.

The **piopio** (*Turnagra capensis*) was once widespread but rapidly declined following European settlement. The last confirmed sighting was in 1902. It was 26 cm long, plump and with a short beak. The upperparts were olive brown grading to a rust-red tail. The underparts of the North Island form were olive grey and of the South Island form brown and white streaked. The piopio fed on invertebrates, sometimes on the forest floor, but also on berries and foliage.

The **huia** (*Heteralocha acutirostrus*) was a larger bird, averaging about 47 cm in length. It was once widespread in the North Island but by European settlement it had become restricted to the southern half. A steady decline resulted from forest destruction, introduction of predators and, finally, over-collecting for museums. The last accepted record was in 1907. The colour of the huia was glossy black with a bluish iridescence. The tail was white tipped and there were orange wattles at the base of the beak. An unusual feature was the long downwardly curved beak of the female, which was about 10 cm long while that of the male was only slightly curved and about half as long. The call was a shrill whistle. The huia made only short flights and mostly travelled by long leaps in the canopy or over the ground. The diet was mostly invertebrates, the male foraging on the surfaces of trunks and branches or splitting rotting wood with its beak, and the female probing deeper for a wider range of insects.

The **New Zealand owlet-nightjar** (*Megaego-theles novaezelandiae*) is not an owl, but with its large round eyes, flat face and short beak it would certainly have looked like one. This bird was probably extinct before the arrival of Europeans.

The extinct flightless **snipe-rail** (*Capellirallus karamu*), although a much smaller bird than the kiwi, also had a remarkably long and slender beak that it probably used to probe for invertebrates in the subsoil.

The extinct North Island **stout-legged wren** (*Pachyplichus jagmi*) and the related South Island *P. yaldwyni* are thought to have been poor fliers and may have used their strong legs to break open decaying logs to find invertebrates.

The **laughing owl** (*Sceloglaux albifacies*) was once widespread throughout the country but had become rare by the time Europeans arrived. It was last seen in the late 1800s. It was about twice the size of the morepork, yellowish brown in colour heavily streaked with dark brown. The face was white. Its call was described as a 'series of dismal shrieks', perhaps like demented laughter. Its diet was probably similar to that of the morepork.

The **harrier**, *Circus eylesi*, was about 7 times the weight of the falcon. It is thought to have perched in the forest then rapidly pursued passing prey.

The **New Zealand eagle** is the largest eagle known and therefore the largest bird of prey. The maximum wing span was nearly 3 m and the weight averaged 11 kg. This large bird must have been a fearsome sight to its prey, the moa and other large birds.

Two **adzebills**, *Aptornis*, one in the North and the other in the South Island, were probably flightless and fed on the forest floor. They had stout beaks, stood about 80 cm tall and may have weighed 12 kg. Their diet probably included large invertebrates, frogs, lizards, tuatara and petrels.

The **New Zealand crow** fed on dead moa, petrels, seals and similar prey, as well as on large insects, lizards and fruit.

TUI, PARSON BIRD
Prosthemadera novaeseelandiae

The tui is found only in New Zealand and is widespread on the main islands and in the Auckland, Chatham and Kermadec Islands.

It is 30 cm long. The colour is almost black with an iridescent sheen. The most conspicuous feature is a tuft of white feathers on the neck, which led to the colonial name 'parson bird'. In the juvenile these feathers are lacking. The beak is slightly downwardly curved and the tail is long and broad. The flight is noisy and whirring, and the song — one of the great delights of the forest — is mostly of fluid melodic notes, sometimes strangely intermingled with short coughs and clicks.

Individual birds establish feeding and breeding territories and defend them vigorously. The nests are built at branch forks or on the outer branches. They are made with twigs and sticks and lined with grass. The eggs are about 3 cm long, white or pale pink with reddish brown spots or patches.

The tui feeds and breeds mainly in forests but will visit town gardens to take nectar from plants, both native and introduced. It also eats medium-sized berries and insects.

BELLBIRD, KORIMAKO
Anthornis melanura

The bellbird is restricted to New Zealand and is widespread south of Northland, including the Auckland Islands. It became extinct in Northland in the 1860s, although it is still to be found on the offshore islands.

This is a smaller bird than the tui at about 20 cm long and is only about a third of its weight. The male is olive green with bluish black wings and tail. The female is browner in tone and has a narrow white stripe extending from the bill on each side. Both sexes have a short slightly curved bill, a tail forked at the tip and red eyes.

The flight is noisy and whirring, and the song is of loud melodic ringing notes, particularly impressive at dawn and dusk at places where the bellbird is common.

Like the tui, the bellbird establishes breeding and feeding territories. The nests are sited at branch forks and are similar to those of the tui. The eggs are about 2.5 cm long, pinkish white with reddish brown spots and blotches.

The bellbird also finds nectar plants in towns, as well as berries and insects.

A tui with its distinctive tuft of white feathers.

STITCHBIRD, HIHI
Notiomystis cincta

The stitchbird has never been found in the South Island but was once widespread in the North Island. By the late 1800s it had disappeared from everywhere except Little Barrier Island but has recently been reintroduced to islands off Northland and the Bay of Plenty, as well as Kapiti Island further south.

The stitchbird has a similar length and weight to the bellbird. The male has a white tuft behind each eye, but its head and adjacent parts are velvety black bordered with golden yellow. The rest of the body, including wings and narrow tail, are pale brown. The female is greyish brown with a white band at the bases of the wings. The bill of this species is short and a little curved and its call is a loud explosive whistle and also a note that sounds like 'stitch'.

Stitchbirds nest in holes high in mature trees, which is unusual for honeyeaters. The nest is a platform of sticks with a cup of wiry tree fern roots, lined with tree fern scales and feathers. The eggs are about 2 cm long and white.

As well as nectar, stitchbirds also eat berries and insects. They are not as aggressive as tuis and bellbirds and sometimes have difficulty getting a fair share of nectar.

Above: A male bellbird, a small bird for such a loud song.
Centre: A male stitchbird, similar in size to the bellbird but less tuneful.
Below: Female stitchbird.

PARAKEETS, KAKARIKI

Cyanoramphus novaezelandiae
(red-crowned parakeet)
C. auriceps
(yellow-crowned parakeet)

The parakeets were once common through the main islands but were reduced in numbers with the introduction of mammal predators in the 1800s. This is particularly the case with the red-crowned parakeet, which, unlike its yellow-crowned relative, forages on the forest floor as much as in the canopy. It is common, however, on some of the smaller islands. Both species are found on the Chathams and subantarctic Islands, and the red-crowned parakeet extends to the Kermadecs, Norfolk Island and New Caledonia. The parakeets are usually single or in pairs but can form flocks in the winter.

These 2 species are very similar. Both have long pointed tails and a general bright yellow-green coloration with violet-blue edging to the wings. The red-crowned parakeet has a bright red head above the beak, with narrow extensions to the eye and beyond on each side. The yellow-crowned parakeet has a bright yellow head above the beak bordered below with a narrow red band that extends to each eye but not beyond. The former averages 26.5 cm long and 75 g in weight. The latter is smaller at 24 cm and 45 g. The flight of both is swift with rapid wing movements and is accompanied by a high-pitched chatter.

The parakeets do not form proper nests but live in holes in tree trunks and branches or ground burrows where they lay their eggs, which are about 2.5 cm long and white.

They feed on seeds, berries, flowers, leaves and also insects.

Top: Yellow-crowned parakeet. Above: Red-crowned parakeet.

NEW ZEALAND PIGEON, KERERU
Hemiphaga novaeseelandiae

This is a large plump bird about 50 cm long and weighing about 650 g. It is widespread in the main islands and the Chathams, and was once found in the Kermadecs and Norfolk Island but is now extinct there. The upper parts and the upper breast are a metallic blue green with a purplish sheen. The underparts are white and the eyes, beak and feet are red. The diving and sweeping flight is accompanied by a noisy swishing of the wings. The call is a soft cooing.

The nest is a simple platform of sticks on a horizontal branch fork or in a tangle of vines. Only one egg is laid at a time but several times in a season. The egg is white and about 6 cm long.

The pigeon eats fruits and leaves and is particularly important in the distribution of the large berries of miro, tawa, taraire, puriri and karaka.

The New Zealand pigeon, the heavyweight of our flying forest birds.

KOKAKO
Callaeas cinerea

At the time of European settlement the kokako was widespread in the North Island and also in the western South Island, Banks Peninsula and Stewart Island. It is now probably extinct in the South Island and Stewart Island, and in the North Island is found in low numbers in forests in Northland to Taranaki and more abundantly in forests of the Bay of Plenty, King Country and the northern Ureweras.

This bird is about 38 cm long and weighs about 230 g. The colour is dark bluish grey with a black mask extending beyond the eyes. The beak and legs are black. A distinctive feature is the presence of pairs of fleshy rounded appendages, known as wattles, attached near the base of the beak. In the North Island the wattles are blue and in the South Island orange. The kokako jumps around in tree crowns and makes only short flights. Its song,

A kokako with distinctive blue wattles.

generally at dawn, is a slow string of very loud mournful organ-like notes.

Individuals or pairs defend a territory, which may be held for many years. The nests are built in dense foliage, where they can't be seen from above, or in epiphyte nests. They have a twig base and a cup of epiphytic orchids, filmy ferns, twigs of rata and other vines, lined with tree fern scales. The eggs are about 3.5 cm long, pinkish grey with brown and mauve spots and blotches.

The kokako feeds on leaves at all levels in the forest throughout the year, on berries when available and on insects during the summer.

A plump rifleman, New Zealand's smallest bird.

RIFLEMAN
Acanthisitta chloris
At 8 cm long and about 6 g in weight, this is our smallest bird. It is found only in New Zealand and is widespread except in the north of the North Island.

Both male and female are whitish below, the former is yellow green above and the latter streaked light and dark brown. Both have white stripes above the eye. The beaks are finely drawn out and a little upturned, and the tails are barely discernible. The rifleman's call is a high pitched 'zip-zip-zip-zip'.

A brown creeper pair in their nest.

Breeding pairs remain in their territory all year but often have unpaired birds as helpers for chick feeding. Riflemen make their nests in tree holes. They are lined with leaf skeletons, tree fern roots, twigs and feathers and have a small side entrance. The eggs are about 1.5 cm long and white.

The rifleman works its way up the stems and branches of trees and shrubs finding invertebrates in bark crevices and clumps of mosses and lichens.

BROWN CREEPER
Mohoua novaeseelandiae
This bird is found only in New Zealand and is restricted to the South Island and Stewart Island, where it is widespread. It is about 13 cm long and averages 12 g in weight. The head, wings and tail are reddish brown, and the face and a zone continuous with it behind the head are ash grey. The underside of the body is pale fawn. The brown

in the forest canopy. Their call is a mixture of slurs, musical whistles and harsh notes. Breeding pairs defend their territory all year. The nests are deep cups in the canopy foliage and are made of bark, twigs, mosses and leaves bound together with cobwebs and lined with grasses and feathers. The eggs are about 2 cm long, white to dark pink, speckled reddish brown.

The brown creeper feeds on a range of invertebrates mostly gleaned from leaves and small branches in the canopy. Some berries are eaten in the autumn.

WHITEHEAD
Mohoua albicilla
This relative of the brown creeper is also native only to New Zealand but in this case it is restricted to the North Island. Since European settlement the whitehead has largely disappeared from the northern North Island. It is a little larger than the brown creeper at 15 cm long and averaging 16 g in weight. The head and undersides are white and the wings and tail are pale brown. The beak, eyes and legs are black. In other respects the whitehead is similar to the brown creeper.

The whitehead of the North Island.

YELLOWHEAD
Mohoua ochrocephala
The yellowhead was never found in the North Island but was once widespread in forested areas of the South Island and Stewart Island. It is now restricted to the southwest of the South Island and isolated pockets elsewhere.

The yellowhead is somewhat heavier and much more colourful than the 2 preceding species of its genus. Its length is about 15 cm and the weight averages about 27 g. The head and underparts are bright yellow and the wings and tail yellowish brown. The beak, eyes and legs are black. In other respects the yellowhead is similar to its less colourful relatives.

GREY WARBLER
Gerygone igata
The grey warbler is restricted to New Zealand and is found throughout the country.

At about 10 cm long and 6.5 g in weight, it is not quite so small as the rifleman and it also has a well-developed tail with white-tipped feathers. The colouring is brown grey above with a pale grey to white face and underparts. The song is a distinctive long musical wavering trill.

The grey warblers' nests are different from the

The yellowhead is the most colourful bird of its group.

The grey warblers' nests are different from the dishes and bowl shapes of those of other birds. They are made of moss, lichen and other soft materials and are lined with feathers and tree fern scales. The nests mostly hang from twigs and are enclosed except for a small side entrance hole.

In flight the grey warbler fans its tail feathers, which enables it to flit and hover among outer foliage in search of invertebrates.

FANTAIL
Rhipidura fuliginosa

The fantail is perhaps our best-known and most attractive bird. Its appeal lies in its large fan-like tail and erratic darting movements that often bring it quite close to the observer. It is not just ours, however, as it also inhabits eastern Australia and Tasmania, the Solomons, Vanuatu, New Caledonia, Lord Howe and Norfolk Islands. It is widespread within New Zealand except for the subantarctic islands.

Because of its long widely fanned tail, equalling the rest of the body in length, the fantail seems larger than it actually is. It is 16 cm long and weighs 8 g. The head and beak are small, and the common form has a grey head with a white eyebrow, a brown back and yellow underparts. The 2 central feathers of its fanned tail are black, the others white. A completely black form, except for a white spot behind the eye, is found mainly in the South Island. The call is a penetrating 'cheet' and the song is harsh and 'saw-like'.

Mating pairs are strongly territorial during the mating season but sometimes gather in flocks during the winter. The nests are situated at forks of

A grey warbler and its distinctive nest.

understorey shrubs or on tree fern fronds and are neat cups of grass, bark, moss and cobwebs lined with fern fibres and feathers. A tail of material hangs from the bottom of each nest for about 10 cm. The eggs are about 1.5 cm long, white and speckled with pale brown spots.

The fantail mostly captures insects and other invertebrates on the wing and uses its fanned tail to stop in mid-air before darting in another direction.

A restless fantail about to take flight.

TOMTIT
Petroica macrocephala

The tomtit is found throughout the country, including the sub-antarctic islands. It is restricted to New Zealand.

It is a small bird with a large head and short tail, and weighs 11 g with a length of 13 cm. In the male the head, upper parts and upper breast are black, except for white bars on the wings and tail and a small white spot above the beak. In the North Island they are white below and in the South Island yellowish grading to white. The females have brown heads and upper parts and grey-brown underparts grading to white. The male song is a loud jingle and its call a high-pitched 'swee'. The females call is 'seet'. The territorial song of the male is a loud 'ti oly oly oly oh'.

Breeding pairs remain on their territory all year. The nests are fairly bulky and are built in tree cavities not far above the ground, on tree fern trunks or in tangles of vines. The materials include bark, twigs, mosses and leaves, lined with grasses and feathers. The eggs are about 2 cm long and cream with yellowish purple spots.

The tomtit perches on a low branch or on a trunk and flies to the ground or to tree trunks to catch invertebrates it detects. On the ground it encounters members of the ground insectivore group, to which it partly belongs.

The tomtit, an efficient insect catcher.

The saddleback with its distinctive colour pattern.

SADDLEBACK
Philisternus carunculatus

The saddleback is restricted to New Zealand and was once widely distributed throughout. In the North Island it disappeared from everywhere except the offshore Hen Island and in the South Island survived only on Big South Cape and other islands off Stewart Island. In recent times the species has been reintroduced to several other islands in the north and the south.

The saddleback is a larger bird than other arboreal insectivores, measuring 25 cm long and weighing on average 75 g. It has a slender pointed beak and is glossy black in colour except for a bright chestnut 'saddle' over the back and similar coloration at the base of the tail, and small orange-red wattles at the base of the beak. The saddleback mostly jumps from branch to branch and flies only short distances and then very noisily. The call is a long note followed by a long series of short notes.

The saddleback is a noisy inquisitive bird that strongly defends its territory. Its nests are located in tree holes, tree fern crowns and among nest epiphytes. They are made of tree fern rootlets, leaves and twigs with a lining of grasses and tree fern scales. The eggs are about 3 cm long, grey or white with dark blotches or streaks.

with dark blotches or streaks.

The saddleback rummages in litter on the forest floor and digs into rotting logs for invertebrates, so it too is in part a ground insectivore. On trunks and branches it probes crevices and prises off bark to find invertebrates, including quite large wetas.

SHINING CUCKOO
Chrysococcyx lucidus

Our 2 cuckoos are only part-time New Zealanders; they arrive in the spring to breed through the summer then depart to spend the winter in the tropics.

The shining cuckoo is widespread throughout New Zealand during the breeding season and it also breeds in Australia, New Caledonia and Vanuatu. It overwinters from Indonesia to the Solomons. Its length is 16 cm and weight 25 g. It has a short tail and is coloured metallic bronze green above and white with dark green bars below and on the face. The call is a clear descending 'see-ew' and the song a repeated 'coo-ee'. As is the custom with cuckoos, it lays its eggs in the nests of other birds, in this case the grey warbler. The host birds also feed and raise the cuckoo chicks. The eggs are about 2 cm long and olive green.

The shining cuckoo mainly eats invertebrates and especially the small green caterpillars that feed on kowhai leaves and the black hairy caterpillars of the magpie moth.

LONG-TAILED CUCKOO
Eudynamys taitensis

This cuckoo breeds only in New Zealand and overwinters in the tropical Pacific, mostly on eastern islands. It is much larger than the shining cuckoo at 40 cm in length and 125 g in weight. It is widespread throughout New Zealand during the breeding season. As the name indicates, it has a long tail as well as long pointed wings. Its upperparts are rich brown barred with black. The underparts are pale buff streaked with brown and black. The main call is a loud harsh shriek. The eggs are about 2.5 cm long, creamy white to pale pink with brownish blotches. They are laid in whitehead nests in the North Island and in brown creeper and yellowhead nests in the South and Stewart Islands.

The long-tailed cuckoo mainly feeds on large invertebrates such as weta, stick insects, spiders, beetles and bugs, and also eats some berries. Like the morepork, it also extends its diet with lizards and small birds.

The shining cuckoo, a summer visitor.

WEKA
Gallirallus australis

The weka is restricted to New Zealand and is a bird well known to trampers, as it can be very curious and if not watched can steal food and other small items. It was once common throughout the country but has largely disappeared from the North Island, although it is still well represented in a number of forested areas in the South Island. At 53 cm long and averaging about 850 g, it is a relatively large bird. The general colour is brown streaked with black. The beak and legs are short but stout and, although it cannot fly, it can run very rapidly. Its call is a shrill 'coo-eet'.

Bowl-like nests are formed on or near the ground, inside or under logs, in hollow tree bases, or under ferns or tussocks. They are made of grasses, sedges and cabbage tree leaves with a lining of grasses, moss and feathers. The eggs are about 6 cm long, creamy white or pinkish.

The weka turns over litter with its beak to find a variety of invertebrates. It also eats lizards and fallen berries and leaves.

NEW ZEALAND ROBIN
Petroica australis

This is another New Zealand-only bird that was once widespread but is now largely restricted in the North Island to a band from Taranaki to Bay of Plenty and in the South Island to the northern third and more patchily in the southern third.

It is 18 cm long and weighs 35 g. The colour is generally dark slaty grey above and pale greyish white or yellowish white below. The beak is short and the legs long and thin. The song is a long series of short descending notes.

The robin is strongly territorial. The nests are built at tree forks, often on the top of old nests of other

The weka, a very inquisitive bird.

A New Zealand robin listening for insects.

birds. They are bulky and made of twigs, bark moss and cobwebs, lined with tree fern scales, moss and grasses. The eggs are about 2.5 cm long, cream with purplish brown spots.

The New Zealand robin often perches on a low branch or low on a trunk, and when it observes movement in the leaf litter it flies down to capture its prey. It also hops around on the litter then listens for any movement. Its food includes a wide range of invertebrates.

The brown kiwi was once widespread throughout New Zealand.

The great spotted kiwi is our largest kiwi.

KIWI

Kiwi are very unusual birds in that they have long narrow beaks that probe into the soil to capture earthworms and other subsurface invertebrates. Unfortunately they have been greatly reduced in numbers by introduced predators. Dogs and ferrets kill adults, ferrets and feral cats kill chicks and possums damage the eggs.

The kiwis are all nocturnal. Family groups stay together for at least several months and on Stewart Island for much longer. The eggs are laid in burrows, in hollow logs or under dense vegetation. One or 2 eggs are laid, 11–12.5 cm long and white.

When feeding, kiwis tap the ground with their beaks to induce invertebrates to reveal their location by moving. They then take them from the subsoil, rotten logs or from leaf litter. Fallen berries are also eaten.

BROWN KIWI
Apteryx australis
Once widespread, this species is now restricted to the northern half of the North Island and the southwest of the South Island and Stewart Island.

It is 40 cm long and weighs on average 2.5 kg. Like the other kiwis, it has only vestigial wings and its feathers are dense and hair-like. The colouring is dark greyish brown with longitudinal reddish brown streaks. The long beak has nostrils at the tip. The call is a shrill ascending then descending whistle.

GREAT SPOTTED KIWI
Apteryx haastii
This species was always restricted to the South Island and is now found only in the northwest, where it can be locally common. It is 45 cm long and weighs, on average, 2.9 kg. In colouring it is light brownish grey tinged with chestnut with white horizontal bands.

LITTLE SPOTTED KIWI
Apteryx owenii
This species was once common throughout but is now restricted to the west of the South Island, where it is rare. It has been sucessfully established on Kapiti Island with smaller populations on islands in the north of the North Island. Its length is 30 cm and average weight 1.2 kg.

A kakapo at the entrance to its nesting site.

KAKAPO
Strigops habroptilus

This large flightless nocturnal parrot lives mostly on the forest floor but can clamber into the understorey. Although once wide spread, it is now very rare. The introduction of stoats led to this decline and by the 1970s only a few birds were known to exist in Fiordland and these have probably now died out. In 1977 about 100 birds were discovered in southern Stewart Island and, as they were under attack from wild cats, they were transferred to Codfish Island off Stewart Island, Maud Island in Marlborough Sounds and Little Barrier in the north.

The kakapo is 63 cm long and averages 2.3 kg in weight. In colouring it is moss green above, greenish yellow below with brown and yellow mottling. There is a brown facial mask that gives it an owl-like appearance. It is well camouflaged against its background of mosses and leaf litter. The wings are spread for balance when the kakapo is clambering into shrubs or running on the ground. The main call is a low-pitched booming that can be heard for several kilometres on a quiet night.

Kakapo breed only every 3–5 years, whenever there has been a good season for seeds and berries. Unlike other parrots, they are solitary and the males have an elaborate mating ritual. On high vantage points they clear a display area that involves a track 30–60 cm wide that connects a series of hollowed out bowls, each about 50 cm across. Females are attracted by the 'booming', which continues through the night over several months. The eggs are laid in hollow stumps, hollow dead trunks and under tussocks. They are white and about 5 cm long.

Kakapo eat berries, seeds, leaves, twigs and roots.

NEW ZEALAND FALCON
Falco novaeseelandiae

The New Zealand falcon is found mostly in the southern half of the North Island and in the forests of the western South Island as well as tussockland on the eastern side of the Southern Alps.

It has the characteristic hooked beak, long pointed wings and tail of falcons, and flies rapidly as well as soaring and gliding. It averages 45 cm long and 400 g in weight. The colouring of the upper side grades from dark brownish black to bluish black with narrow white cross barring. The underside is buff grading to dark brown with dark streaks and white bars. The underside of the tail is red brown. The call is a loud rapid 'kek-kek-kek'.

Falcons are fiercely territorial in the mating season and make dive attacks on anyone getting too close to their nests. The eggs are laid on cliff ledges, under logs or in clumps of nest epiphytes. They are about 5 cm long and buff to rich reddish brown.

Falcons swoop down on and take a wide range of smaller vertebrates and larger invertebrates, native and introduced, including birds, young rabbits and hares, grasshoppers and beetles.

The **harrier** (*Circus approximans*) mostly takes

The New Zealand falcon, a notable predator.

A kingfisher with a captured cicada.

A morepork near its nest in a hollow tree.

its prey in open habitats but also along forest margins. It is widespread in Australasia and southern Pacific.

KINGFISHER
Halcyon sancta

Our kingfisher is also represented by different forms in Australia, New Caledonia, Lord Howe and Norfolk Islands. In New Zealand it is widespread and favours wetlands and forests not too far from the coast.

It is 25 cm long and weighs 65 g. Kingfishers are plump birds with short legs and necks, large heads and beaks that seem too large and heavy for their size. Our species is a colourful bird with the upper parts grading from green on the head to bright blue elsewhere, apart from a white collar around the neck. The underparts are pale yellowish white. The call is a loud 'kek-kek-kek-kek'.

Kingfishers are solitary or in pairs. The eggs are laid in rotten tree trunks, riverbanks and coastal cliffs in which they excavate short tunnels leading to chambers.

When hunting they perch on posts, powerlines and low branches and when they spot prey they swoop down, scoop it up from the ground or from shallow water and return with it to their perch. They take a range of large invertebrates but also lizards, mice and small birds. From water they take small crabs, tadpoles, freshwater crayfish and small fish.

MOREPORK
Ninox novaeseelandiae

The repetitive night-time call of 'more pork', which gives this species its common name, is a sound very familiar to New Zealanders. The morepork is found throughout the country, on Norfolk Island and formerly Lord Howe Island. A related species is found in Australia.

This native owl differs from other members of the predator group in its nocturnal lifestyle. Its length is 29 cm and weight 175 g. The general colour is dark brown with flecks and stripes of paler brown. The large round eyes are yellow and set in a dark facial mask on the large head.

The eggs are laid in hollow trunks, in nest epiphyte clumps, under rocks, in petrel burrows or among the twists and turns of pohutukawa roots.

Its diet includes small birds, lizards, bats, mice and young rats, as well as a range of larger insects.

SILVEREYE, WAXEYE, WHITE-EYE
Zosterops lateralis

This bird is widespread in Australasia and the southwest Pacific. There are a number of subspecies and ours is the same as the Tasmanian and probably came from there. Silvereyes were present in the early 1800s and colonised the country in large numbers in the middle of that century, and are still abundant from the Kermadecs to the

A silvereye visiting nectar-filled flax flowers.

subantarctic islands.

They are 12 cm long and weigh 13 g. The upper parts are olive green except for a grey band across the base of the wings. The underparts are white below the beak, then grey, pinkish brown and finally white under the tail. The eyes are conspicuously ringed with white. The call is a rapid 'clee-clee-clee'.

Silvereye pairs are strongly territorial during the mating season but join flocks during the winter. The delicate cup-like nests are suspended from twigs at the ends of tree or shrub branches. They are made of grasses, tree fern rootlets, moss, cobweb and lichens. The eggs are about 1.8 cm long and pale blue.

Their diet includes invertebrates, fruit, nectar using their modified tongue, and anything edible provided for them in the home garden.

KAKA
Nestor meridionalis

The kaka parrot is a playful acrobatic bird that was abundant and widespread when Europeans arrived. It is much reduced in numbers now but is still to be found in forests from Coromandel southwards in the North Island and throughout the South Island and Stewart Island.

It is 45 cm in length and averages about 500 g in weight. The upper parts are mainly olive brown and the under parts dark crimson. The kaka's call is a variety of whistling and grating notes.

The eggs are laid in hollow trunks or branches. They are 4 cm long and white.

A kaka with its impressively curved beak.

Two kaka having a 'fun fight'.

The kaka is wide-ranging in its diet. It eats fruit, takes nectar with its brush-tipped tongue, eats insects, breaks up bark and decaying wood to extract grubs, and takes sap from a number of trees.

Lizards, Frogs
& Bats

FOREST LIZARDS

The lizards that most people see are sleek, often copper coloured, and are usually brought in by the family cat. But this is only a small part of the story. In New Zealand there are over 40 named species of lizard belonging to 2 large families, widespread in the world, commonly known as geckos and skinks.

New Zealand geckos and skinks are unusual in that, with a single exception, the eggs are retained by the female until they hatch and the young are born live.

In explanation it has been suggested that, as reptile eggs are normally left to fend for themselves, in cooler climates such as those of New Zealand, particularly during the Ice Age, the eggs of lizards would often be killed by the cold. Retention of the eggs in the female until hatching gets around this problem, and it is significant that our one egg-laying skink is found only in the mildest part of the country—coastal habitats and offshore islands in the northeast of the North Island.

About half New Zealand's native lizard species make the forests their home. Their diet is mostly insects and other invertebrates but they also eat berries and some drink nectar, and so play a role in the pollination of flowers and the dispersal of seeds.

The lizards have patterns of colouring that camouflage them against their backgrounds—grey shades for rocks and lichens, brown shades for bark and green for foliage. If a predator still manages to spot them and attack, they may be able to escape by shedding their tails, later to be regenerated.

Lizards emit a variety of sounds from squeeks to barks and it is thought that they also have other sounds that are not audible to the human ear.

SKINK VS GECKO

How do you tell a skink from a gecko? Geckos have rather loose skin with small, dome-like granules that do not overlap and are not shiny. The flattened undersides of their toes have ridges bearing minute hairs that enable them to climb up quite smooth surfaces. When they shed their skin every few months in the summer it comes away more or less in one piece. The pupils of their eyes are vertical slits.

By contrast, the skinks have tight skin with larger flat shiny overlapping scales as on a fish. Their narrow toes are smooth on the undersides and their skin is shed in small pieces. The pupils of their eyes are round. Distinguishing the species within these 2 groups is rather more difficult.

Geckos (left) have loose skin with small dome-like granules; their pupils are vertical slits. Skinks (right) have tight skin with shiny flat overlapping scales; their pupils are round.

GECKOS

Geckos appear to have their eyes wide open all the time and they never blink. In fact, the lower lid is permanently closed, but as it is transparent, they can still see. It is a bit like the plastic protective covers over car headlights.

As well as finding food on the ground, most geckos readily climb into shrubs and trees in search of insects as well as berries and nectar. Some, notably the green geckos, live entirely in trees.

The **forest geckos** are sombre in colour with bark-like patterns of grey, brown and sometimes green. There is considerable variation in these patterns, often between individuals of the same species.

This group is widespread through the North Island and in the northwest, southwest and southeast of the South Island. They are up to 17 cm in length and live in holes in tree trunks and under loose bark. They are found in all types of forest. The inside of the mouth and tongue are bright yellow to orange.

The **common gecko**, *H. maculatus,* and the **Pacific gecko**, *H. pacificus,* and their relatives occupy a wide range of habitats from the seashore to forests, and are similar in length and general appearance to the forest geckos. The tongue and the inside of the mouth are pink.

Duvaucel's gecko (*H. duvaucelii*) is probably our largest at 32 cm long. Fossils indicate that it was once widespread through the North and South Islands, but it is now restricted to offshore islands in the Marlborough Sounds and off the northeast North Island.

An even larger species, **H. delcourti**, is probably extinct. It

Three forest geckos: *Hoplodactylus granulatus* (top), *H. maculatus* (centre) and *H. duvaucelii* (above).

was not until 1984 that a specimen held at the Marseilles Natural History Museum for up to 150 years was recognised as belonging to this New Zealand genus. At more than half a metre in length, it was the largest gecko in the world.

The **green geckos** (*Naultinus*) are more striking in their coloration, being vivid light to dark green with spots or stripes of white or yellow. Sometimes completely yellow individuals can be encountered. This group spend most of their time among the foliage of forest trees as well as small-leaved shrubs and trees, particularly manuka and kanuka. All are active in the daytime, unlike the forest geckos, which are mostly nocturnal. The inside of the mouth of green geckos is mostly blue but sometimes pink and the tongue may be pink, red, blue or black.

The most widespread green gecko in the North Island is ***Naultinus elegans***. Its length is from 14.5 to 20 cm.

Five species of green gecko are recognised in the South Island: 2 in Marlborough, one in Nelson Province, one on the West Coast and one in parts of Canterbury and Otago. They range in length from 15 to 17 cm. Of the South Island green geckos, **N. rudis** is the most distinctive with its prominent cone-shaped scales.

Left: *Naultinus elegans* (above and centre), *N. gemmeus* (below).

Opposite: *N. stellatus* (above), *N. grayii* (centre), *N. rudis* (below).

SKINKS

Most skinks have moveable lower eyelids and in some cases they are transparent so the skink can see with its eyes closed when it pushes through leaf litter or soil. In some cases skinks, like geckos, have permanently closed but transparent lower lids, but this is not the case with the New Zealand species.

Skinks of the genus **Cyclodina** are restricted to the North Island. They are predominately nocturnal and are most often found in forest, where they live in deep leaf litter.

The **copper skink** (*Cyclodina aenea*) is widespread through the North Island and can be found in a wide range of habitats from suburban gardens to native forests. It is about 13 cm long and has a copper-coloured back, sometimes with attractive patterns of brown and light brown.

C. alani is found only in coastal forest on a few islands off the northeast North Island. It is about 25 cm long with dark brown to black patterning. This is our heaviest skink.

Three other skinks, at 22–24 cm long, are also mostly restricted to offshore islands in the northeast North Island and, in 2 cases, in the southwest as well. These are **C. macgregori, C. oliveri** and **C. whitakeri.**

The 4 species now restricted to offshore islands were widely distributed in the North Island until they were wiped out by rats. By far the largest New Zealand skink in terms of weight, **C. northlandi,** was completely eliminated.

The **ornate skink** (*C. ornata*) is widespread through the North Island and lives in holes or

crevices of logs or rocks. It is about 17 cm long and is attractively patterned with rings or patches of brown, orangey brown or dark brown.

Most of the species of **Oligosoma** favour open habitats from the coast to the mountains. An exception is *O. striatum* or the **striped skink**. This lives near or around large logs and rotting stumps but also high in the canopy, where it sometimes inhabits epiphyte gardens up to 22 m above the ground. It is about 17 cm long with a broad white or cream stripe running down each side. It has been sighted from Taranaki to the Bay of Plenty, southern Northland and Great and Little Barrier Islands.

The **chevron skink**, *homalonotum* is known only from Great and Little Barrier Islands. It is very rare, very large and lives along forested streams.

Opposite: Copper skink (above), *Cyclodina alani* (centre) and *C. oliveri* (below).

Left: Ornate skink (above), striped skink (centre) and chevron skink (below).

TUATARA
Sphenodon punctatus

Few people are likely to encounter our most famous reptile, the tuatara, in the forest. Though it was once widespread through the main islands, the introduction of predators meant it eventually became restricted to a number of offshore islands in the Marlborough Sounds and off the northeast coast of the North Island.

Although they look like lizards, tuatara belong to a separate group. Among other things, they differ from lizards in their teeth being projections of the jawbone and not set into sockets and in their lack of an external ear.

The tuatara is about 60 cm long, mostly stony grey in colour sometimes with tones of orange and red, and soft skinned. The projections on its head crest are quite flexible. It lives in burrows that it forms itself or steals from burrowing petrels while they are away at sea during the day. Its diet is mostly invertebrates, lizards, birds and birds eggs. Tuataras can probably live to 100 years old and even their eggs take more than a year to hatch.

Tuatara, *Sphenodon punctatus*.

FROGS

Like the lizards and the tuatara, native frogs are also unusual. To begin with they are small, (less than 5 cm long). They produce barely audible squeaks, and, with the exception of Hochstetter's frog, they do not have webbed feet and do not have a free-swimming tadpole stage—the adult state develops in the egg. Internally there are several distinctive features, the most notable and most primitive being the fact that their ribs are not joined to their backbones. The frogs feed on small insects and grubs at night.

Hochstetter's frog (*Leiopelma hochstetteri*) has partial webbing of its rear toes. Tadpoles of this species emerge from the eggs to swim around for several weeks before assuming the adult state. This is the only species that is at all common, being found in forests from near East Cape to the Waikato and southern Northland as well as on Great Barrier Island, where it sometimes lives under rocks on the banks of small streams. It is 4.5 cm long and its colour ranges from dark brown or almost black to a dark amber brown. Its limbs have darker ring-like bands.

Archey's frog *(L. archeyi)* is restricted to the Coromandel Peninsula and the southwest Waikato, where it inhabits wet places under rocks or rotting tree trunks. It is the smallest species, at 4.1 cm long, and its colours include greens, golds, blacks and browns.

Hochstetter's frog (above),
Archey's frog (centre) and
Hamilton's frog (below).

Hamilton's frog (*L. hamiltoni*) lives in rock stacks or boulder banks a long way from any streams on Stephens Island in Cook Strait. It is 4.7 cm long and its colouring includes gold, black and brown. It is one of the rarest frogs in the world, with fewer than 300 individuals in about 600 square metres of habitat.

L. pakeka is very similar to *L. hamiltoni* and is found only on Maud Island in the Marlborough Sounds. Other species of native frogs formerly occurred widely throughout New Zealand but became extinct when rats arrived.

BATS

Our one slender claim to having any native land mammals rests on 2 small bats, which behave more like birds than mammals and are not often seen. The wings of bats are formed by delicate leathery membranes that extend between the elongate bones of their fore-limbs and also often extend to the rear limbs. Small bats emit high-pitched sounds whose echos enable them to locate and avoid obstacles at night when they forage, or when they are in dark caves. By this means, too, they are able to locate and catch insects in flight. Bats are most often seen at dusk when they emerge from their hideaways—caves or tree hollows—to begin their nightly search for food.

Lesser short-tailed bat on *Dactylanthus taylori*.

The **long-tailed bat** (*Chalinolobus tuberculatus*) is very similar to an Australian species so may be a compara-tively recent immigrant. It is found throughout the country. The bones of its limbs are slender, it has small ears and its tail is about 3.5 cm long and contained within the wing membrane. The body length is 6–9 cm and the wing span is 25–30 cm. The colour of the body fur varies from black to reddish or chocolate brown. Its food is largely flying insects.

The **lesser short-tailed bat** (*Mystacina tuberculata*) is so distinctive that it has been placed in its own family. It has a similar body length, wing span and fur colour to the long-tailed bat but its ears are much larger and the tail, at about 1 cm long, much shorter. The bones of its limbs are unusually stout and the claws on its wings and on its relatively large feet are strongly developed. When folded, the wing tips are enclosed in small pockets at the sides of the body and the rest of the wings can function as legs. Because of this adaptation, as well as the robust limbs, large feet and specialised claws, the short-tailed bat is able to move over the ground and clamber in trees. As well as taking insects on the wing, it also captures ground insects and eats berries and nectar.

An interesting discovery in recent years is that the short-tailed bat is the pollinator of the root parasite *Dactylanthus taylori* (see page 220). Its scaly flowerheads contain considerable amounts of nectar, which is attractive to this bat. The short-tailed bat is still widespread in the North Island but is only locally common. It is now rare in the South Island and Stewart Island.

A third species, the **greater short-tailed bat**, became extinct in the 1960s. Once again, rats were the cause.

Insects & other Invertebrates

Insects and other invertebrates are among the smallest inhabitants of the forest. Invertebrates do not have an internal skeleton, although in many of them the outer tissues are tough or hard and form what is known as an exoskeleton. Ground-dwelling invertebrates mostly live in the well-aerated litter but some burrow in the soil and subsoil. Included in this group are millipedes, centipedes, wood lice, snails, beetles, insect larvae and worms. Some are carnivores but most eat the larger items in the litter and therefore play an important role, along with fungi and bacteria, in the formation of soil. They also provide an important food source for kiwi and other birds and also lizards.

Other invertebrates live at least part of their lives above the ground. These include weta, stick insects, spiders and the larvae of some of flying insects. The flying invertebrates are mostly adults of butterflies, moths, beetles, cicadas, flies, bees and wasps. Some of these play an important role in the pollination of forest flowers.

Insects are by far the largest group of organisms in the world with an estimated total of 20,000 native species in forests and open habitats in New Zealand alone. Spiders are another significant group with about 500 native species. Insects and spiders belong to the group known as arthropods, which includes animals with segmented bodies and jointed legs. The insect body is divided into a head, thorax and abdomen with three pairs of legs attached to the thorax. In spiders the head and abdomen are fused and there are four pairs of legs. In some invertebrates, such as spiders, the young are miniature versions of the adults. In many insects

PERIPATUS
a 'living fossil'

Peripatus is a notable resident of leaf litter and rotting logs. It is soft, velvety and caterpillar-like with numerous legs like millipedes, centipedes and wood lice. The legs are plump and stumpy and each ends in a pair of claws. The colouring varies from greenish or greyish green to velvety charcoal or navy blue, attractively sprinkled with golden spots. Peripatus has been famous for being a 'missing link' between worms and arthropods but is now regarded as being a very ancient type of arthropod. Fossil impressions hundreds of millions of years old that look very much like peripatus indicate that it has been around for a very long time.

Peripatus hunt for smaller arthropod prey and capture them by shooting out a jet of sticky saliva. The immobilised prey is then sucked dry.

Peripatus with golden spots and blue-tipped feet.

there is a distinct juvenile form known as a larva. In moths and butterflies, for example, this is the caterpillar and in most cases it is the longest phase of the life cycle; the flying adult, beautiful though it may be, lasts only long enough to lay eggs.

SNAILS

There are many small snails in the leaf litter, some of them attractively shaped and coloured, but they are not easily noticed. Some are so small they are said to be able to pass through the eye of a needle. They mostly eat plant material.

Other snails that make leaf litter their home are giants by comparison. Members of the **Powelliphanta** group, in South Africa, Indonesia, Melanesia, eastern Australia and some Pacific Islands, are carnivorous and eat worms and other invertebrates, including the smaller snails. The largest species is *Powelliphanta superba,* which is up to 11 cm in diameter. All species of this group have rather flattened but rotund shells that can be highly polished and attractively coloured in shades of brown, red and yellow as in *P. hochstetteri*. A few species in the South Island live in alpine tussockland.

Another genus of large land snails, **Placostylus**, is very different with a thick and hard elongate conical shell. Three species are recognised in New Zealand and they are restricted to the far north of the North Island. Unlike the *Powelliphanta* group, *Placostylus* is not carnivorous but mostly eats fallen leaves.

Powelliphanta hochstetteri, a native snail.

WETAS

To many people these are fearsome creatures. They could be regarded as large wingless grasshoppers and probably had flying ancestors. Their exoskeletons are in the form of overlapping armour-like plates and their legs are beset by sharp-pointed spines so they have the look of fearsome predators. In fact, most are gentle leaf-eaters, so their armoury is purely defensive. However, all weta will eat live or recently dead prey, and a group called **ground weta** are all carnivorous. Although unable to fly, weta can run and jump. They hide away during the day and emerge at night to feed.

A group of 6 species known as **tree wetas** (*Hemideina*), common from North Cape to Otago, live in holes in old trees. The body is up to 5 cm long with antennae up to 10 cm long, and the males have strangely elongated heads. One species of *Hemideina* lives under rocks in alpine vegetation.

The **giant weta**, also known as wetapunga (*Deinacrida heteracantha*), is even more impressive with a body up to 10 cm long and legs and antennae to match. It is now extinct on the mainland but is still found on Little Barrier Island. Related species are found on islands in Cook Strait and the subalpine regions of the South Island.

The group that is known as **cave wetas** (*Gymnoplectron*), although most readily observed on the walls of caves, can also be found under loose bark and similar places in the forest. They have small bodies only a few centimetres in length, but extremely long and slender legs and antennae up to 8 cm long.

A tree weta, *Hemideina crassidens*; note the very large head.

A tree weta, *Hemideina thoracica*.

A female cave weta.

STICK INSECTS

Stick insects are widespread in the tropics but most of them can fly, unlike the New Zealand species, which are flightless. Some of them are spiny on their bodies and legs, but with their soft texture and long slender shape, they don't seem as fearsome as the weta.

Stick insects eat leaves of a variety of trees and shrubs, and they are remarkable, because of their colouring and appearance, for being very difficult to see against their plant backgrounds.

Argosarchus horridus, one of the **spiny stick insects**, is found throughout the country and feeds on the leaves of rimu, totara, rata, pohutukawa and other native plants, as well as some introduced trees. The members of this group are generally brown with spines on the thorax and on the long thin legs. *A. horridus* is up to 13 cm in length. When disturbed it aligns its legs along its body and freezes against a twig, from which it cannot easily be distinguished. Most populations of spiny stick insects are entirely female as the eggs develop without fertilisation.

The **green stick insects**, including the common *Clitarchus laeviusculus* and the green form of *C. hookeri*, do not have spines and in most cases populations include males, which are smaller than the females. It is thought that fertilised eggs develop into males and unfertilised eggs into females. The green stick insects mostly feed on kanuka and manuka, where they are well camouflaged against the leaves.

A large female and a small male stick insect, *Micrarchus*.

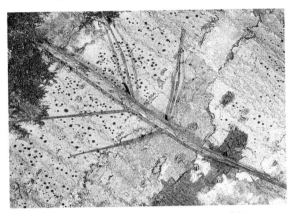

Clitarchis hookeri, well camouflaged against crustose lichens.

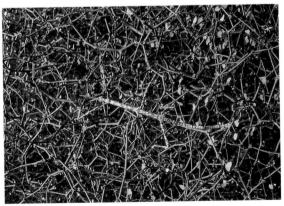

A stick insect on a twiggy shrub.

CICADAS

For **cicadas**, being large colourful singing insects, placement among sap-sucking bugs doesn't seem appropriate, but that group is where they belong. On warm summer days the air vibrates with the high-pitched endlessly repeated songs of cicadas. Some people dislike this chorus, regarding it as a headache-inducing racket. Others welcome it as the sound of summer. Only the males are able to sing and each of our many species has its own pattern of high-pitched longer and shorter notes, sometimes interspersed with clicks from the wings. The notes are produced by the vibrating of a pair of drum-like membranes on the abdomen.

The adults live for only a short time, sometimes only a few weeks. The silent females are attracted by the singing males, and when a female is ready to lay her eggs she makes a herring-bone series of cuts to receive them. When young cicadas (nymphs) hatch, they drop to the ground, burrow into the soil and spend many years sucking sap from plant roots. After a succession of moults the stage known as the final nymph burrows out of the soil, climbs and attaches to a tree trunk or other suitable surface and becomes immobile as the adult stage develops within it. Eventually the adult cicada emerges through a split in the back of the nymph and the singing begins.

Our largest and noisiest cicada is **Amphisalta zelandica**, which is found in forests throughout the country. Its body is about 3 cm long and dark green and black in colour. On sunny days cicadas of this species gather in large numbers on tree trunks and their chorus can be deafening. **A. cingulata** is almost as large but is restricted to the North Island.

Two bronze-green species are found in North Island forests, where they are unusual in that they

Amphisalta cingulata.

A subalpine cicada, *Kikihia subalpina*.

sing in the shade rather than the sun. The greater bronze, **Kikihia cauta**, has a body up to 2.1 cm long and is found on a variety of trees. The lesser bronze, **K. scutellaris**, is about 1.6 cm long and usually lives in mahoe trees.

A group of attractive bright green cicadas are well camouflaged against the foliage of shrubs and trees. They are all species of *Kikihia* ranging in length from 1.7 to 2.5 cm. Two species are restricted to the North Island; a third species, *K. subalpina*, ranges up into the subalpine shrub zone in the North Island but is confined to forests in the South Island.

Cicadas are widespread in warmer parts of the world, but New Zealand has the only alpine cicadas (*Maoricicada*).

BEETLES

Beetles are by far the largest insect group.

They are charcterised by their forewings being modified into hard covers overlying the softer body parts.

With such a large group, lifestyles are very diverse. Some beetles are carnivores at both the larval and adult stages; some eat living plant tissues including roots, leaves, nectar, pollen and fruits; and others eat dead plant material from rotting logs to leaf litter. Some, too, are fungus eaters, particularly of our wide range of bracket fungi. We can only consider a few examples from the many New Zealand forest beetles.

There are many species of **ground beetle** in New Zealand, some of which live in forests. They are large to very large, flightless, carnivorous, with prominent jaws, and are mostly dull to shiny black in colour. They hunt at night and hide away under stones and logs during the day. Some ground beetles emit a very strong and unpleasant odour.

Stag beetles, such as *Dorcus helmsii*, have even more strongly developed jaws, particularly in the males for fighting. They live under bark, particularly of rimu. The common stag beetle, *Lissotes reticulatus*, is very attractively patterned.

The larvae of some beetles eat the living roots of plants. The best-known example in New Zealand is the grass grub, which is very damaging to pastures and lawns. A forest example is the **large green chafer**, *Stethaspis suturalis* . This is a bright shining green beetle about 2.5 cm long. The larvae feed on the roots of trees and the adults are leaf-eaters in the forest canopy.

A chafer beetle.

A stag beetle, *Dorcus helmsii*, against crustose lichens.

A carabid beetle.

Metallic green rove beetle.

Huhu beetle, *Prionoplus reticularis*.

The giraffe weevil, *Lasiorhynchus barbicornis*.

Rove beetles are characterised by very short wing covers. There are many native species, mostly brown to black in colour. They are often found in leaf litter; some of them are carnivorous and others feed on decaying plant and animal matter.

Longhorn beetles have very long antennae, often longer than their bodies. There are many forest species in New Zealand, of which the best known is the **huhu beetle**, *Prionoplus reticularis*. The larvae of this group bore into trunks and branches of trees and of rotting wood. The huhu larva or 'grub', found in rotting wood, mostly of conifers, is large and white and was a sought-after food item by the Maori. The adult is our largest beetle at up to 5 cm long with attractively patterned wing cases. It can be a nuisance in summer when it is attracted into houses by lights at night and flies clumsily about.

Beetles known as weevils are the most abundant of all beetles. Their heads are strangely elongated with the often bent antennae towards the ends. Many of the larvae are wood-borers, in karaka or lacebarks, but the adults mostly feed on foliage. The extreme for head elongation is exhibited by the males of the **giraffe weevil**, *Lasiorrynchus barbicornus*, which can be as long as 10 cm with the elongated head making up almost half of that.

A native **ladybird beetle**, *Scymnus acceptus*, is abundant and widespread, and is very useful to some of our native trees because it eats aphids and scale insects. It is only about 3 mm long with a large pale yellow spot on the shoulder of each wing cover.

MOTHS AND BUTTERFLIES

These are the insects that are most often noticed, particularly the more brightly coloured species of butterfly. A characteristic of moths and butterflies is that their wings are covered with thousands of small overlapping scales, giving them their soft texture and varied colours and patterns.

Most of the adults have coiled sucking tubes that are used to feed on liquids such as the nectar of flowers, so moths and butterflies have an important role as pollinators. The larvae, or caterpillars, have chewing mouth parts and mostly feed on plants.

Moths and butterflies differ in several ways. Moths are mostly active at night or at dusk; at rest they spread their wings flat against the surface they are on or close against their bodies; and their antennae taper to a point. Butterflies are about during the day; at rest they fold their wings upwards so that they are pressed closely together; and their antennae are distinctly knobbed at the tip. The last is the most reliable distinction as a minority of moths are active during the day and fold their wings upwards.

Flowers pollinated by butterflies are usually brightly coloured, although not red, and pleasantly perfumed. Those pollinated by moths are white or at least pale in colour, so they can be more easily seen in dim light. They are also often heavily perfumed and so can be detected for some distance before they are seen.

MOTHS

Many New Zealand moths live in the forests and the adults are notable for being able to camouflage themselves against their backgrounds of leaf litter, tree trunks, twigs and leaves. Their wings are often attractively coloured in shades of green, brown and grey, and they can be almost impossible to detect against moss- and lichen-covered bark, dead and even green leaves.

The **puriri moth**, *Aenetus virescens*, with its 15 cm wingspan, is by far our largest native moth. Its apple green coloration makes it perhaps the most attractive. For a description and life history, see page 83.

Puriri moth (*Aenetus virescens*).

The **bag moth**, *Liothula omnivorus*, has a curious and often-noticed caterpillar stage. The latter forms and lives in an elongated case of silk with bits of leaves and twigs added for camouflage. The caterpillar partly emerges from the front of the case and moves around in and eats the foliage of a wide range of native and introduced trees. The adult male is dark coloured, inconspicuous and rapid in flight, but the female is flightless and never emerges from the case.

The caterpillars of most forest moths live above the ground in trees and shrubs, but New Zealand and Australia are unusual in having many species of moths whose caterpillars live in and eat forest litter. The adults of these species are mostly small and have a steeply roof-like arrangement of their wings when at rest.

The **cabbage tree moth**, *Epiphryne verriculata*, is a remarkable example of camouflage. This moth rests on the dead

A bag moth on totara.

leaves that hang below the living leaves of young cabbage trees. With its wings widely spread, it presses close to the leaf. It is brown coloured and has parallel darker lines running lengthwise to the wings; when these lines are aligned with the parallel veins of the leaf it is virtually invisible. The caterpillars of the moth feed at night on the young green leaves of the cabbage tree.

Cabbage tree moth on a dead cabbage tree leaf.

Kowhai moth caterpillar feeding on kowhai leaves.

BUTTERFLIES

By contrast with moths, we have few native species of butterfly. Only 20 have been recorded in New Zealand, 4 of which are associated with forests but mostly at the margins.

The **red admiral**, *Bassaris gonerilla*, is our largest and most colourful butterfly and is found throughout the country. The adults appear from January to April. The wing span is up to 6.5 cm and the wings are black with bars of red. The bars of the hind wings each have four black rings with blue centres. The caterpillars feed only on tree nettles and smaller nettles at forest margins and fold leaves over themselves to keep out of sight of predators.

The **forest ringlet butterfly**, *Dodonidia helmsii*, (see page 287 for photograph) can be found at beech forest margins throughout the country but is rarely seen. The wing span is a little less than that of the red admiral and the wings are yellowish with dark brown bars and pale brown rings with black centres. The adults appear in January.

Two similar copper butterflies, the **common copper**, *Lycaena salustius*, and the **glade copper**, *L. feredayi*, are both widespread. Their caterpillars feed on species of *Muehlenbeckia* at forest margins and the adults appear during the summer. The wing span is 3–4 cm and the wings are coppery brown with bars or spots of black or blue.

Red admiral butterfly, *Bassaris gonerilla*.

The common copper butterfly, *Lycaena salustius*.

NATIVE BEES

Our **native bees** are known as solitary bees as they do not form colonies. They are mostly small, often very hairy and gather pollen and nectar for food from manuka, rata and pohutukawa and also mistletoes (see page 194). These bees live in small burrows in dry banks and sand dunes.

Native bee arriving at its burrow with pollen.

LEAF MINERS

The larvae of a number of insect groups burrow into leaves when they emerge from the eggs and then eat their way through the leaf tissue to form straight or, more often, tortuous tunnels, visible on the leaf surface. In some cases the change to the adult state takes place within a tunnel but mostly the larva emerges at this stage.

Several groups of moths have leaf-mining larvae too, but in this case each species parasitises one particular plant. Thus in New Zealand we have silver beech, kowhai, kakabeak, ribbonwood, kauri, hinau and several other leaf miners, including some on the epiphytes *Astelia* and *Collospermum*. Mines are also made in mahoe leaves but in this case fly larvae are to blame.

Mahoe leaves with leaf-miner tunnels.

GALL FORMERS

The larvae of some chewing insects burrow into twigs and cause their tissues to proliferate into sometimes unsightly galls. The larva is situated in a cavity at the centre of the gall and happily feeds completely safe from any predators.

A frequently noticed gall, caused by a midge, is that on *Olearia paniculata*. Leaves and stems of many other native plants (hebes, olearias, putaputaweta) are commonly galled by insects.

A rather different but also conspicuous gall is often observed on silver beech. Here the tips of twigs become profusely and abnormally branched with malformed leaves, forming a structure called 'witches broom'. The perpetrator in this case is a mite.

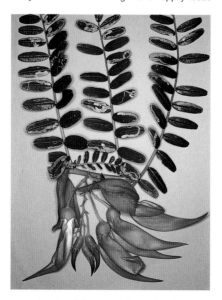

Kakabeak foliage with leaf-miner tunnels

Silver beech with 'witches brooms'.

SPIDERS

Unlike the insect groups, where only some of the species are carnivorous, no spiders are gentle vegetarians. Mostly they suck the juices of insects, but one group, the pirate spiders, specialise in attacking other spiders.

Apart from the 4 pairs of legs, lack of antennae and the distinctive body shape, spiders also differ from insects in having 8 or sometimes 6 eyes and pairs of poisonous fangs near their mouths, which they use to kill or immobilise their prey. Spiders also make more extensive use of silk, both to protect their eggs and young and, in some cases, to make insect-trapping webs. The box-like webs of the **nursery web spider**, which first contain eggs then many young spiders, are frequently seen on the twigs of a wide range of shrubs. There is no great contrast between juvenile and adult spiders; the young are miniature versions of the adults.

Web-forming spiders are perhaps the most specialised and certainly the best known of this group. Webs have a variety of forms and often species can be identified by the pattern of the web alone. The most familiar are the orb webs which are circular and vertical. Sheet webs are also common, particularly in the tropics. Here the webs are more irregular in overall shape and horizontal to the ground. There are anchoring threads below the web and irregularly arranged threads above. Insects blunder into these and fall onto the web where they are trapped by sticky threads. The resulting vibrations of the web bring out the spider to attack its prey.

Trapdoor or **tunnelweb** spiders are sometimes large, hairy and somewhat fearsome, especially when they wander into houses. In fact they are harmless to humans. The tunnels are often formed more or less vertically in the soil, lined with silk and each is furnished with a silken hinged lid at the opening at the surface. The spider watches from under the partly opened lid, catches and immobilises a passing victim and hauls it back into the tunnel. Spiders live in the same tunnel for their lifetimes of several years and the eggs are laid and hatch there.

In our forests there are a number of tunnelweb spiders. The bush tunnelweb spiders burrow through leaf litter into the ground and line the burrow with silk but do not construct lids. The small tree trunk trapdoor spiders build flat nests with incorporated moss and debris for camouflage, complete with lids.

Crab spiders, which are rather flattened and crab-like in appearance, depend on camouflage.

The nursery web spider, *Dolomedes minor*.

Crab spider with its prey, a black wasp.

A jumping spider with prey.

Those that live on the forest floor or tree trunks are dark brown with rough-textured bodies and legs; those inhabiting foliage are yellow to green. They depend on insects not detecting them and bumping into them, usually with a fatal result for the insect.

The **pirate spiders** are the renegades of the spider world. They creep stealthily into the webs of other spiders and when the owner of the web comes to investigate, it is swiftly despatched.

While most groups of spiders wait for their prey to come to them, the **hunting spiders** actively search them out. In some cases they detect their victims by movements and sounds, creep up on them and grasp them with their legs or entangle them with silk threads.

The **jumping spiders** have keen eyesight, as attested by their 2 large central eyes, and stalk their prey visually. When they get close they suddenly jump on their prey. For obvious reasons and unusually for spiders, jumping spiders are active during the day.

FURTHER READING

Allison, K. & Child, J., *The Liverworts of New Zealand*, University of Otago Press, Dunedin, 1975.

Beever, J., Allison, K. & Child, J., *The Mosses of New Zealand*, 2nd ed., University of Otago Press, Dunedin, 1992.

Brockie, R., *A Living New Zealand Forest*, Bateman, Auckland, 1992.

Brownsey, P. & Smith-Dodsworth, J.C., *New Zealand Ferns and Allied Plants*, 2nd ed., Bateman, Auckland, 2000.

Crowe, A., *A Field Guide to Native Edible Plants of New Zealand*, Godwit, Auckland, 1997.

Dawson, J., *The Ancient Forests of New Zealand* (Video), Learning Media, Wellington, 1991.

————— *Forest Vines to Snow Tussocks: The Story of New Zealand Plants*, Victoria University Press, Wellington, 1993.

————— & Lucas, R., *Lifestyles of New Zealand Forest Plants*, Victoria University Press, Wellington, 1993.

Eagle, A., *Eagle's Trees and Shrubs of New Zealand*, Collins, Auckland, 1975.

————— *Eagle's Trees and Shrubs of New Zealand*, 2nd series, Collins, Auckland, 1982.

Enting, B, & Dawson, J., *Seasons in the Forest: A New Zealand Photographer's Year,* Random Century, Auckland, 1990.

Gibbs, G., *New Zealand Butterflies*, Collins, Auckland, 1980.

————— *New Zealand Weta*, Reed, Auckland, 1998.

Heather, B. & Robertson, H., *Field Guide to the Birds of New Zealand*, Viking, Auckland, 1996.

Malcolm, W. & Malcolm, N., *The Forest Carpet*, Craig Potton Publishing, Nelson, 1988.

Malcolm, W. & Galloway, D., *New Zealand Lichens: Checklist, key and glossary*, Museum of New Zealand, Wellington, 1997.

Martin, W. & Child, J., *Lichens of New Zealand*, Reed, Wellington, 1972.

Metcalf, L., *The Cultivation of New Zealand Native Grasses*, Godwit, Auckland, 1998.

Miller, D., *Common Insects in New Zealand*, rev. ed., Reed, Wellington, 1984.

Poole, L. & Adams N., *Trees and Shrubs of New Zealand*, rev. ed., DSIR Publishing, Wellington, 1990.

Powell, A., *Native Animals of New Zealand*, 4th ed., ed. B. J. Gill, David Bateman, Auckland, 1998.

Salmon, J.T, *The Native Trees of New Zealand*, Reed, Wellington, 1981.

St George, I., *The Nature Guide to New Zealand Native Orchids,* Godwit, Auckland, 1999.

Sharell, R., *New Zealand Insects and their Story*, Collins, Auckland, 1971.

————— *The Tuatara, Lizards and Frogs of New Zealand*, Collins, London, 1966.

Stevens, Graeme, et al, *Prehistoric New Zealand*, Reed, Auckland, 1995.

Taylor, M., *Mushrooms and Toadstools*, Reed, Auckland, 1991.

INDEX